US WAR BIRDS
FROM WORLD WAR 1
TO VIETNAM

US WAR BIRDS FROM WORLD WAR 1 TO VIETNAM

Kenneth Munson
Associate RAes ARHistS

NEW ORCHARD EDITIONS
Poole · Dorset

First published in the UK 1985 by New Orchard
Editions, Robert Rogers House, New Orchard, Poole,
Dorset BH15 1LU

Distributed in the United States by Sterling Publishing
Company Inc, Two Park Avenue, New York 10016

Copyright © 1985 New Orchard Editions Ltd

ISBN 185079 029 9

Typeset by Poole Typesetting (Wessex) Ltd, England

Printed in Italy by
New Interlitho SpA, Milan

CONTENTS

PREFACE AND
ACKNOWLEDGEMENTS

This book brings together the best US military material from the fourteen volume *Pocket Encyclopaedia of World Aircraft in Color* published by Blandford Press between 1966 and 1977. This series enjoyed immense popularity and success – well over 1,000,000 copies were sold in nine languages. The selection in this book starts with the primitive and ends with the sophisticated, missile armed, radar guided, nuclear weapon carrying aircraft of today.

Any selection for a volume of this size must necessarily be an arbitrary one. It is hoped however that this book will provide a 'ready reckoner' for the aviation enthusiast, and that the marking and camouflage schemes, many infrequently illustrated in color, will provide inspiration for the aircraft modeller. Several aircraft are presented in periods of service or in the markings of services which may appear unfamiliar, but it is hoped that this will lend depth to the perspective.

The **color plates** are arranged in approximate chronological order of the aircraft's first entry into service. The 'split' plan view depicts the markings appearing above and below either the port side or the starboard side of the aircraft, according to the aspect shown in the side elevation. It should not be assumed however that the unseen portion of the plan view is necessarily a 'mirror image' of the half portrayed: for example, on post 1941 aircraft, national insignia normally appear only on the port upper and starboard lower wing surfaces. Neither should it be assumed that all color plates necessarily show either a standard color scheme or a pristine, ex-works finish; indeed, the intention has been to illustrate a wide variety of finishes, from ex-works to much-weathered aircraft.

The **specifications** relate to the specific machine illustrated, and may not necessarily apply in all details to the type or sub-type in general.

Preparation of the color plates owes a tremendous amount to Ian Huntley, whose comprehensive knowledge of aircraft colors and markings, based upon extensive researches, and whose general advice, formed the foundation upon which the plates were based. The plates were executed, under art editor and director John W. Wood, by Michael Barber, Norman Dinnage, Frank Friend, Brian Hiley, Bill Hobson, Alan ('Doc') Holliday, James Jessop, Tony Mitchell, Jack Pelling and Allen Randall.

The Publishers

Benoist

Benoist flying boat used for Tampa-St Petersburg service early 1914

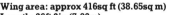

Wing area: approx 416sq ft (38.65sq m)
Length: 26ft 0in (7.92m)
Weight: 1,190lb (540kg)
Engine: 1 × 75hp Roberts 6-cyl in-line
Max speed: 64mph (103kmh)

Among the earliest American aeroplane manufacturing companies, the Benoist Aircraft Company also ran a flying school at its headquarters at St Louis, Missouri. One of its first pilots and instructors was Antony Jannus, joined there by his elder brother Rodger in 1913. In March of the previous year Tony Jannus was the pilot of a Benoist aircraft from which one Albert Berry, baling out at about 1,500ft (500m), attempted the firs parachute descent from an aeroplane in the United States. (Berry failed on this occasion, but made a successful attempt nine days later.) Tony Jannus, however, was to achieve a more permanent place in aviation history, for on 1 January 1914 he was pilot of the Benoist Type XIV flying-boat which inaugurated the first daily scheduled commercial service by aeroplane anywhere in the world. Known as the St Petersburg and Tampa Airboat Line, it was the inspiration of a St Petersburg businessman, P E Fansler, and linked the two Florida townships which lay 22 miles (35km) apart across Tampa Bay. At 10am on New Year's Day 1914, Jannus took off with Mayor Pheil of St Petersburg as his first passenger – and his only one, for the Type XIV was only a 2-seater. They landed at Tampa 23 minutes later. The service ran for nearly four months, making two (occasionally more) round trips per day, at a fare of $5 per passenger – provided that the passenger weighed no more than 200lb (91kg): fat people were charged more! During its brief life the Airboat Line covered some 11,000 miles (17,700km); only 18 flights were cancelled due to bad weather and four from other causes, and a total of 1,205 passengers was carried. The operating economics were, however, not good enough to justify the line's continued existence. The Benoist XIV was a three-bay, equal-span biplane with a single-step hull having two side-by-side seats ahead of the lower wing; the pilot occupied the left-hand seat. Aft of the cockpit, the engine was mounted low down inside the hull (giving a low centre of gravity for good stability on the water), flanked by the fuel tanks and with a chain drive to the pusher propeller. A small portion of the rudder projected downwards to serve as a water rudder during take-off, landing and taxying. A larger flying-boat, the Model C, appeared during 1915. This was powered by two 100hp Roberts in-line engines and could carry up to five passengers. The Jannus brothers also built a flying-boat of their own design, based largely on the Benoist XIV, and this was test-flown in late 1914/early 1915. By then both had left the Benoist company; Tony was killed in Europe in 1916, and Rodger in 1918, both in flying accidents, and by the end of World War I the Benoist company had eased to exist.

Burgess-Dunne

Burgess-Dunne No 3 delivered to the US Army Signal Corps in December 1914

Span: 45ft 0in (13.72m)
Length: 26ft 0in (7.92m)
Weight: 2,140lb (971kg)
Engine: 135hp Salmson M9 9-cyl radial
Max speed: 75mph (121 kmh)

The Burgess Company of Marblehead, Massachusetts, headed by W. Starling Burgess, was already well known for its boat-building activities when it entered the aviation arena in 1910 by building landplanes based on the Wright formula. It was, however, notable chiefly for the range of floatplanes and flyingboats which it produced between 1912 and 1917. The first of these, known variously as the I-Scout, Model I or Coast Defense Hydro, was built to an Army Signal Corps specification and flew for the first time on 1 January 1913. It was a 2-seat biplane, mounted on twin floats and powered by a 60hp Sturtevant engine with chain drive, Wright-fashion, to a pair of pusher propellers. After delivery the Model I served with the US Army in the Philippines, where it eventually crashed in January 1915. Three flying-boat designs which appeared in 1913 were the Models H, I and K. The Model K, which first flew on 16 April, was accepted in the following month by the US Navy, which gave it the designation D-1 (later changed to AB-6). A 2-seater, powered by a 70hp Renault engine, it crashed in February 1914. Also in May 1913 the USN took delivery of the Model H, as the D-2 (later AB-7). The Model I (some early Burgess types used the same Model letter for quite different floatplane and flying-boat designs) was a civil machine, built to the order of Robert J. Collier, doner of the Collier Trophy. Seating two persons in tandem, with the pilot in the rear cockpit, the flying-boat was powered by a 220hp Anzani engine and was completed in July 1913. During 1913, following a dispute with the Wright brothers, Burgess severed his business connections with them and sought the

basis of new designs with which to continue the company's activities. This he found in the swept-wing, tail-less biplanes designed in England by Captain John W. Dunne (see *Pioneer Aircraft* 1903-14). At about this time it was becoming clear to Dunne that he could expect little or no further backing for his work from the British government, and he agreed to allow Burgess to undertake further development of his designs in the United States. The first Burgess-Dunne 'hydro-aeroplane' – basically a Dunne biplane fitted with a large central float – underwent water trials in January 1914, during the course of which it was damaged. After being modified as an open 2-seater (originally a nacelle with a single seat had been fitted), it made a successful first flight in March 1914. The American services both expressed a close interest, and in the autumn two were ordered by the Navy and one by the Signal Corps. Two other machines were already under construction by that time, and the first delivery of a Burgess-Dunne floatplane was made in the early autumn to the Canadian government. The US Navy's first example (designated AH-7) was delivered in October, and that for the Signal Corps in December. The Navy had meanwhile ordered three more machines, with 140hp Sturtevant engines, shorter-span wings and a torpedo-shaped crew nacelle. Only one of these (A-54) was completed; it proved unstable in a dive, was returned to Burgess for redesign and the other two were apparently not delivered. The second of the Navy's original pair (AH-10), with a 100hp Curtiss engine and side-by-side seating, was accepted in April 1915.

Curtiss F-Boat

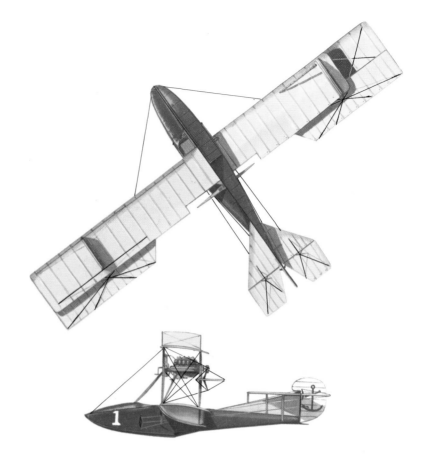

Curtiss F-Boat of the US Navy, circa late 1916

Wing area: 387sq ft (35.95sq m)
Length: 27ft 9¾in (8.48m)
Weight: 2,460lb (1,116kg)
Engine: 100hp Curtiss OXX 9-cyl vee type
Max speed: 69mph (111kmh) at sea level
Operational ceiling: 4,500ft (1372m)
Endurance: 5hr 30min

Second only to the Wrights in his work to pioneer powered flight in the United States, Glenn Hammond Curtiss was until 1910 associated with the design, construction and piloting of land-based aeroplanes, first with the Aerial Experiment Association and later in partnership with Augustus M. Herring. On 14 November 1910 Eugene Ely, piloting a modified Curtiss Golden Flyer landplane, took off from USS *Birmingham* in Hampton Roads, Virginia. On 18 January 1911 Ely completed the sequence by making a landing on the USS *Pennsylvania* in San Francisco Bay, and thus began the association of Curtiss with the early development of waterborne aircraft. His first seaplane, flown at San Diego on 26 January 1911, was little more than a modified Golden Flyer type, mounted on a single central float, with small stabilising skid-floats under the lower wing-tips. A later version had twin parallel main floats. By the end of February 1911, Curtiss had flown one of his seaplanes with a passenger on board, had developed an amphibious wheel-and-float seaplane, and had demonstrated (again on the *Pennsylvania*) how a seaplane could be lowered to the water from a warship, take off for a mission, land alongside and be winched back on board. Curtiss's demonstrations convinced the US Navy, which in July 1911 gave him an order for an amphibious seaplane; it was eventually designated A.1 (US Navy Airplane No.1), and was later named Triad after the addition of retractable wheels to the main float. On 21 June 1912 it set up a seaplane altitude record of 900ft (274m). About a dozen single-float seaplanes, later given AH (Airplane, Hydro) designations, were acquired

by the US Navy. In 1911 Curtiss also delivered to the US Army Signal Corps, and one of these also was fitted with floats. The next major advance in marine aircraft design came with the first Curtiss hull-type flying-boat, which made its maiden flight on 10 January 1912. It still bore the outdated frontal elevator of Curtiss's earlier aeroplanes, but this feature quickly disappeared and the standard 100hp Curtiss-engined 'pusher' flying-boat of 1912-13 was a first-class aeroplane. The Model F was adopted by the US Navy, originally with C-for-Curtiss designation numbers and in 1912 a similar aircraft was the first to fly with the newly invented Sperry gyroscopic automatic pilot. A British licence to build the Curtiss flying-boat was acquired by White and Thompson Ltd, the hulls of which were built by S E Saunders at Cowes. The original five US Navy aircraft were redesigned in March 1914 with AB prefix letters, and played an important part in the evolution of catapult launching before being relegated to a training role. One hundred and forty-four additional Curtiss Model F's, perhaps more, were ordered from Curtiss specifically for trianing purposes, and one Curtiss F-boat was built by the Burgess Company. In 1918 there appeared the Model MF (Modified F), a replacement for the ageing Model F that was, in fact, an almost complete redesign. Twenty-two were built by Curtiss during World War I, and a further eighty post-war by the Naval Aircraft Factory; one of the latter was converted experimentally as an amphibian. Curtiss also built a few flying-boat and amphibious examples of a civil equivalent known as the Seagull.

Navy-Curtiss NC-4

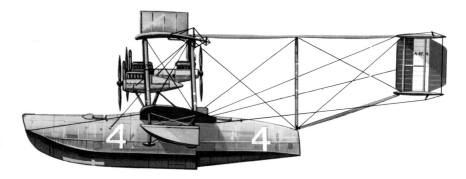

Navy-Curtiss NC-4 (NC-TA), 1919

Span: 126ft 0in (38.40m)
Length: 68ft 3in (20.80m)
Weight: 27,386lb (12,422kg)
Engines: 4 × 400hp Liberty 12 12-cyl
    Vee-type
Max speed: 91mph (146kmh)
Operational ceiling: 4,500ft (1372m)
Range: 1,470 miles (2,366km)

Once the accomplishment of powered flight became a reality, the urge was inevitable to improve upon the speeds, altitudes and distances of which aeroplanes were capable. From the earliest days a crossing of the North Atlantic by air had been a cherished ambition, and only the outbreak of war in 1914 prevented competition during that year for the *Daily Mail* prize of £10,000 offered in 1913 to the first aviators to accomplish a direct (i.e. non-stop) crossing. As recorded elsewhere in the series, the prize was ultimately won in June by Alcock and Brown for their flight in a modified Vickers Vimy, but in the month preceeding this another Atlantic crossing, with stops en route, had been made by an American flying-boat, the NC-4. That this aircraft should have been of Curtiss manufacture was particularly appropriate, for Glenn Curtiss was a pioneer of seaplane design (see *Pioneer Aircraft* 1903-14) and his company's flying-boat *America* was designed originally as a 1914 contestant in the trans-Atlantic competition. The NC-4 was one of four NC (Navy-Curtiss) flying-boats, built during World War 1 originally to provide patrol cover for American shipping in the Atlantic against the attentions of German U-boats. The requirement was drawn up, and the aircraft designed, by the Navy in September 1917. It featured a short hull (45ft = 13.72m in length) of advanced hydrodynamic design, and was intended to be powered by three engines. The first four aircraft were numbered separately NC-1 to NC-4, but the war was ending even as flight testing began. The NC-1 (three 400hp Liberty engines) flew for the first time on 4 October 1918, and on 25 November gave

striking proof of its load-lifting abilities by carrying 51 people on a single flight – a world record. Nevertheless, the three-engined installation was considered inadequate for trans-Atlantic flying, and completion of the second, third and fourth aircraft was delayed while a fourth engine was included in the design. First flights were made on 12 April (NC-2), 23 April (NC-3) and 30 April (NC-4), NC-2 having its four engines mounted back-to-back in tandem pairs while the other two aircraft retained the between-wings separate tractor layout of three engines and had the fourth mounted, as a pusher, at the rear of the hull. It was decided to enter the Navy-Curtiss machines for the trans-Atlantic attempt, for which they were redesignated NC-TA. Before the attempt NC-1, whose wings had sustained storm damage, was given the wings from NC-2, whose engine layout had proved unsatisfactory. The three 'boats took off from Trepassy Bay, Newfoundland, on 16 May 1919, their first intended stop being Horta in the Azores, some 1,400 miles (2,253km) away. The NC-4, captained by Lt Cdr Albert C. Read, arrived safely on the following day, but NC-1 came down in the water 100 miles (160km) west of Flores and sank after being damaged by heavy seas. The crew was rescued by one of the ships stationed along the route. The flagship of this trio, NC-3 commanded by Cdr John H. Towers, leader of the trans-Atlantic team, was also forced down, some 45 miles (72km) south-east of Fayal. It taxied the next 200 miles (362km), finally limping into Horta harbour 52 hours after leaving Newfoundland, but was unable to continue. Read in the NC-4 therefore continued alone, leaving on 20 May for

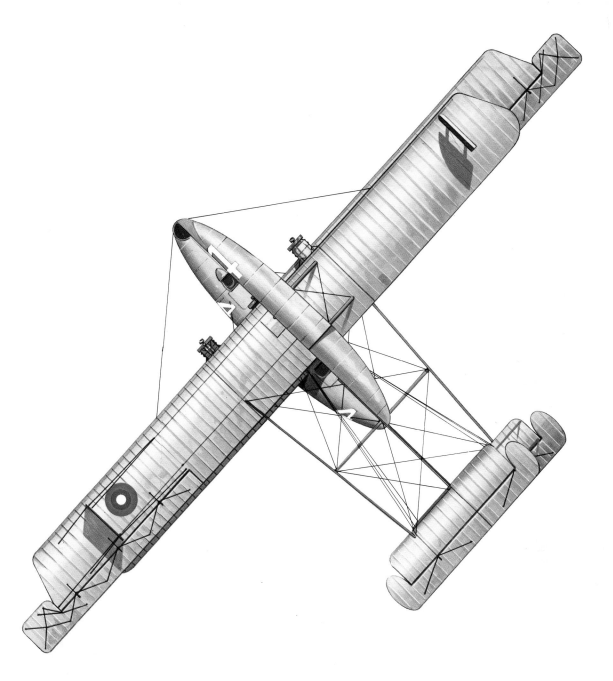

Ponta Delgada, where weather delayed him until 27 May when he flew on to Lisbon to complete the crossing of the North Atlantic. He subsequently continued his journey to arrive at Plymouth on 31 May, and was escorted into the harbour there by three Felixstowe F.2A flying-boats of the Royal Air Force. The NC-4 made a triumphal return to the USA later, ending a celebratory tour of the eastern and southern seaboard by flying up the Mississippi to St Louis. Here it was handed over to the Smithsonian Institution, in whose possession it remains today. After the Armistice the Naval Aircraft Factory at Philadelphia built six more NC-type flying-boats. These were built initially as tri-motors, but four were later converted to an NC-4-type four-engined layout, the other two meanwhile having been lost. The converted aircraft served during 1920-22 with the US Navy's East Coast Squadron before being retired.

Curtiss F-5L

Curtiss F-5L of the US Navy, *circa* 1921

Span: 103ft 9¼in (31.63m)
Length: 49ft 3¾in (15.03m)
Weight: 13,600lb (6,169kg)
Engines: 2 × 400hp Liberty 12A 12-cyl
    Vee-type
Max speed: 90mph (145kmh)
Operational ceiling: 5,500ft (1,676m)
Range: 830 miles (1,335km)

With the production of the F-5L the cycle of Curtiss/ Porte/Felixstowe flying-boat development completed its full circle, returning to the USA via Canada for good measure. In 1913 the London *Daily Mail* had offered a £10,000 prize for the first direct crossing of the North Atlantic by air, and a number of widely different aeroplanes was sponsored to make the attempt during 1914. Among these were two Curtiss *America* flying-boats, in one of which a former British Naval pilot, John C. Porte, hoped to compete for the prize. Prevented from doing so by the outbreak of World War 1, Porte returned to Britain to rejoin the Royal Navy, and persuaded the Admiralty to buy the two *America* machines. In the USA, the *America* design gave rise to the later Curtiss H.4, H.12 and H.16 series of flying-boats, while in Britain the Royal Navy, disappointed with the seaworthiness of its H.4's, appointed Sqn Cdr Porte (as he then was) to conduct a thorough investigation at Felixstowe Naval Air Station into both the strength and the hydrodynamic shape of the Curtiss-designed hull. The immediate result was the Felixstowe F.1, a converted H.4, with Hispano-Suiza engines and an entirely new and fully-seaworthy hull designed by Porte. Extending the same approach to the Curtiss H.12, Porte evolved the Felixstowe F.2A (*q.v.*), which became one of the most successful maritime aircraft of World War 1. It survived its supposed replacement, the F.3, and was in due course followed by the F.5, whose prototype (N90) underwent acceptance trials in May 1918. Plans had been made to place the latter type in production as the F.5L, powered by two 400hp Liberty

engines, but the advent of peace caused these to be abandoned and the aircraft in fact entered service powered, like the F.2A before it, with Rolls-Royce Eagle engines. Meanwhile, however, the US Navy had also decided to adopt a Liberty-engined version of the F.5, ordering four hundred and eighty from the Naval Aircraft Factory at Philadelphia, fifty from Canadian Aeroplanes Ltd of Toronto and sixty from Curtiss. Construction of these began in April 1918, and the first (a Canadian-built machine) was delivered in the following July. After the Armistice the Canadian order was reduced to thirty, and the NAF completed only one hundred and thirty-seven. The typical Curtiss/Felixstowe triangular-pattern fin and rudder were replaced during the early post-war period by larger-area surfaces comprising a quadrant-shaped fin and balanced rudder. These surfaces had first appeared on two NAF-built F-6Ls, ordered originally as part of the F-5L contract. In 1922, when a new designation system for USN aircraft was introduced, the flying-boats were allocated PN (Patrol-Navy) designations PN-5 and PN-6 respectively, though in practice they continued to be known by their original designations until their withdrawal from service in 1928. Development was, however, continued by the Navy Aircraft Factory, still using the Porte-developed hull as a basis. This produced two PN-7s (525hp Wright engines and new wing design), one PN-8 (475hp Packard engines and all-metal structure), one PN-9 (as PN-8 but with redesigned nacelles and tail surfaces), two PN-10s (V-12 engines), one Hornet-engined prototype and three Cyclone-engined PN-11s (new, wider hull), and two

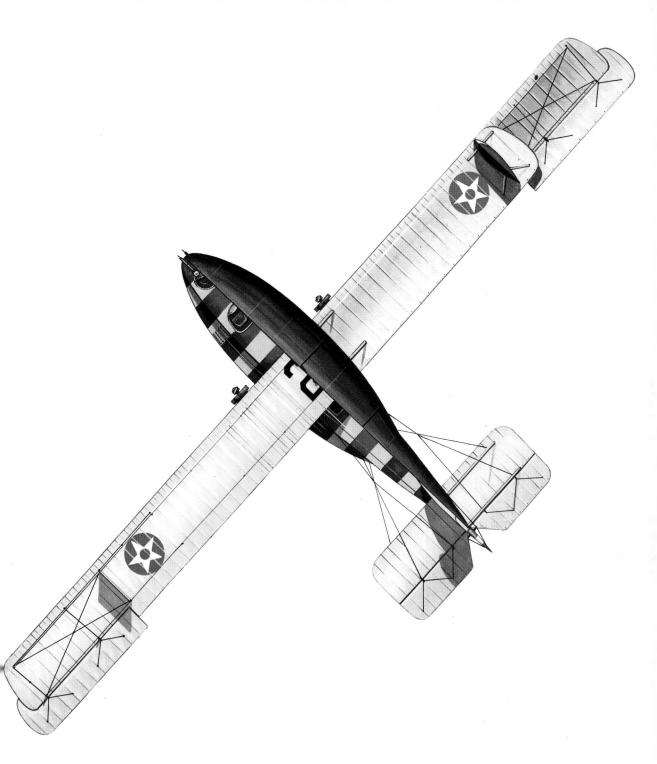

PN-12s (as PN-10 but one with Cyclone and one with Hornet engines). Production of PN-12 variants was undertaken by Douglas (twenty-five PD-1), Keystone (eighteen PK-1) and Martin (thirty PM-1 and twenty-five PM-2). The PK-1 and PM-2 versions were fitted with twin fins and rudders.

Curtiss Navy Racers

Curtiss CR-3 (A6081), winner of the 1923
Schneider Trophy race at Cowes UK

Span: 22ft 8in (6.91m)
Length: 25ft 0¾in (7.63m)
Weight: 2,746lb (1246kg)
Engine: 450hp Curtiss D-12 12-cyl
   Vee-type
Max speed: 194mph (312kmh)
Operational ceiling: 19,200ft (5852m)
Range: 522 miles (840km)

In 1918 Curtiss built for the US Navy two examples of the Model 18-T Wasp, a 2-seat triplane fighter powered by a 400hp Curtiss K-12, forerunner of the D-12 series of engines. The Model 18-T, a landplane, was remarkable for its extremely clean fuselage, the exterior of which exhibited an extremely smooth finish due to its outer skin of cross-laminated veneer strips and helped it to set a world speed record of 163 mph (262km/hr) on 19 August 1918. In modified form the two aircraft were entered for several post-war races, and much of the experience gained with them was built into two new racing biplanes which were completed in 1921. These were ordered as official Navy competitors in the Pulitzer Trophy race of September 1921, but were flown instead by company pilots when the USN withdrew from participation. Known initially as Curtiss Navy racers, the aircraft were each powered by a 405hp Curtiss CD-12 direct-drive engine, a development of the geared C-12 installed in two earlier Curtiss-financed competitors built for the 1920 Gordon Bennett Trophy race. The second Navy racer won the 1921 Pulitzer, at Omaha, Nebraska, at a speed of 176.7mph (284.4km/hr), and on 3 November that year the same aircraft set a new world speed record of 197.8mph (318.3km/hr). In 1922 the two aircraft were repurchased by the Navy, which in that year also introduced a new system of aircraft designation. Under this system the Curtiss biplanes were known initially as CF-1's and then, separately, as the CR-1 and CR-2. Both were refitted with new CD-12 engines and enlarged fin and rudder surfaces; the CR-2 was in addition given new wings, with surface radiators instead of the external Lamblin type fitted previously. Curtiss aeroplanes swept the board in the 1922 Pulitzer race, held near Detroit, for the first two places were taken by a pair of Army R-6 racers, developed from the Navy design, while the third and fourth places went, respectively, to the CR-2 and CR-1. Up to this point the two Navy racers had been flown as landplanes, but when the USN decided to enter them for the 1923 Schneider Trophy race at Cowes, Isle of Wight, both were converted to twin-float landing gear and redesignated CR-3. Both aircraft were provided with wing surface radiators, and the vertical tail surfaces were further enlarged. They captured the first two places in the race, though at speeds lower than their Pulitzer-winning performances of the year before. The 1924 Schneider competition was postponed by the US after all European entries had withdrawn, and the two racers were considered unlikely to win in 1925. Nevertheless, during those two years the second CR-3 (fitted with a later D-12 engine and redesignated CR-4) established a new closed-circuit speed record for seaplanes of 188.078mph (302.681km/hr), and was later used in the training programme for the 1925 US Schneider Trophy team. Meanwhile, the CR-1/R-6 design had been developed a stage further to produce a new Navy biplane racer, the R2C-1, to compete in the 1923 Pulitzer race. Again, two examples were built, both at first having a wheeled landing gear. They were powered by 488hp D-12A engines, with surface radiators on both sets of wings, and took first and second places, the winner having a speed of 243.68 mph

Curtiss CR-4 (A6081) in later colour scheme, October 1924. Details as opposite, except for later version of D.12 engine. On 25 October 1924 this aircraft set a closed-circuit speed record for seaplanes of 188.078mph (302.682kmh)

Curtiss R3C.2 (A6979) flown by Lt. 'Jimmy' Doolittle, US Army to win the 1925 Schneider Trophy race at Baltimore, Ma., USA

Span: 22ft 0in (6.71m)
Length: 19ft 18½in (6m)
Weight: 2,150lb (975kg)
Engine: 610hp Curtiss V-1400 12-cyl
 Vee-type
Max speed: 265mph (426kmh)
Operational Ceiling: 26,400ft (8,047m)
Range: 250 miles (402km)

(452.16km/hr). This machine, the second of the pair, was also converted to float gear (as R2C-2) in preparation for the 1924 Schneider race, while the other was sold to the US Army as the R-8. Both were lost in crashes, the R-8 in 1924 and the R2C-2 in 1926. For the 1925 National Air Races, the US Army and Navy combined their efforts and ordered three R3C-1 racers from Curtiss. Although externally similar to the R2C design, these had wings of improved aerofoil section and 610hp V-1400 engines, a development of the D-12. In October 1925 the Army-piloted R3C-1 set up the best Pulitzer performance, with a speed of 248.99mph (400.71km/hr). The three aircraft became R3C-2s when fitted with floats for the Schneider Trophy race later that month, and this event too was won by

the Army R3C-2, flown on this occasion by Lt 'Jimmy' Doolittle at 232.57mph (374.29km/hr). In the following year two of the trio, both flown by Navy pilots, were entered for the Schneider Trophy. These were by then known as R3C-3 and R3C-4, having been re-engined respectively with a 700hp Packard 2A-1500 and a 700hp Curtiss V-1550. Unfortunately, the R3C-3 sank after an accident during a practice flight, and its place in the competition was taken by the reserve aircraft, the modified R3C-2, which was placed second after the R3C-4 had to withdraw. The R3C-2 is preserved today by the Smithsonian Institution in the National Air Museum in Washington, DC.

Boeing/De Havilland DH-4

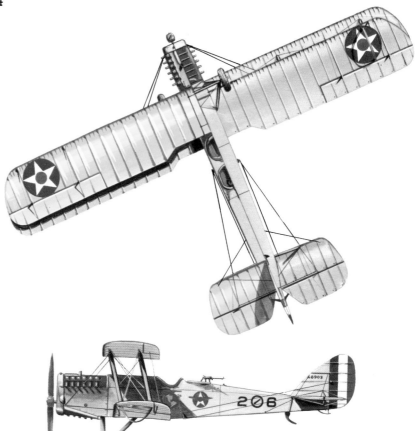

Boeing 02B-1 (DH-4M-1) of the US Marine Corps, *circa* 1927

Span: 42ft 5in (12.93m)
Length: 29ft 11in (9.12m)
Weight: 4,510lb (2,046kg)
Engine: 416hp V-1650 Liberty 12A 12-cyl Vee-type
Max Speed: 118mph (190kmh)
Operational ceiling: 12,800ft (3,902m)
Range: 330 miles (531km)
Armament: 0.30in machine-gun in rear cockpit

The D.H.4 was a high-speed, 2-seat day bomber, designed in Britain by Geoffrey de Havilland's Aircraft Manufacturing Co and flown for the first time in August 1916. Its wartime production and career with the RAF and its predecessors are detailed in the *Bombers 1914-39* volume in this series. By wartime standards the output of British-built DH4s was substantial enough, but plans were laid for American production of the aircraft on a scale that was then unprecedented, involving the manufacture of well over twelve thousand examples. The Armistice of November 1918 brought an extensive curtailment of these plans, but even so the number of American-built examples (known as DH-4As) actually built by 1919 reached four thousand eight hundred and forty-six. Two hundred and eighty-three were transferred to the US Navy and Marine Corps after World War 1. The Americans were never happy with the DH-4A: it was semi-obsolete by the time it entered US service, and had to be considerably redesigned and renovated to suit it to American production methods. The improved DH-4B was ready too late (October 1918) to replace it in France, but during the 1920s a considerable building and conversion programme (of DH-4As) kept the DH-4B, DH-4M and other variants in service until 1932. The major improvement introduced by the DH-4B was to transpose the main fuel tank and the front cockpit, thus bringing the crew members close together for easier communication and, at the same time, reducing the vulnerability of the fuel system itself. The Aeromarine, Gallaudet, LWF and Thomas-Morse factories carried out one thousand five hundred and thirty-eight conversions into DH-4Bs by 1926, and others were effected by various USAAS depots. There were many variants and sub-types of the DH-4B, for a multitude of duties that included ambulance, communications, dual-control training and photographic reconnaissance. Many others were utilised as test-beds for a variety of Liberty, Packard and other engines and miscellaneous equipment. In 1923 the next major version appeared as the DH-4M, the suffix letter signifying 'Modernised'. The principal innovation was the use of a steel-tube fuselage structure, increasing the empty and loaded weights, and the DH-4M was powered by a Liberty 12A engine. With this model, production was resumed, one hundred and fifty DH-4Ms and DH-4M-1s being ordered from Boeing for the Army and thirty with an O2B-1 designation for the US Marine Corps. Six others were completed for Cuba. In the following year an additional one hundred and thirty-five, designated DH-4M-2, were ordered from Atlantic Aircraft Corporation, the American factory of Anthony Fokker. The various DH-4B and DH-4M models continued to serve with observation and bombing squadrons until 1928, and with training and communications units for another four years after this.

Boeing PW-9

Boeing PW-9C of the 1st Pursuit Group
USAAC, *circa* late 1927

Span: 32ft 0in (9.75m)
Length: 23ft 1in (7.04m)
Weight: 3,170lb (1,438kg)
Engine: 435hp Curtiss D-12D 12-cyl Vee-
type
Max speed: 158mph (254kmh)
Operational ceiling: 18,230 (5,556m)
Endurance: 2hr 50min
Armament: 1×0.50in and 1×0.30in
machine-gun in upper front fuselage

The PW-9 (the designation indicating Pursuit, Water-cooled engine) originated as the Boeing Model 15, the prototype of which flew for the first time on 29 April 1923, powered by a 435hp Curtiss D-12 Vee-type engine. During the next few months it was evaluated both by Boeing and by the Army Air Service, the latter then placing a contract to cover this and two other prototype machines with the designation XPW-9. Production orders followed, in September and December 1924, for twelve and eighteen PW-9s respectively, and delivery of the first production aircraft to USAAS units in Hawaii and the Philippines began in October 1925. The PW-9 differed from the prototypes in having a divided-axle landing gear, and was armed with two fixed machine-guns in front of the pilot, firing through the propeller arc. At about the same time as the PW-9 began to enter service, an additional twenty-five fighters were ordered, incorporating minor modifications which earned them the new designation PW-9A. With other small changes the aircraft became the PW-9C; forty of these were completed, including fifteen originally ordered as PW-9Bs. The last Army order was for the PW-9D, sixteen of which were procured; these had wheel brakes, increased rudder area and other small refinements. The D-12 remained the standard engine throughout. Corresponding to the initial

PW-9, the FB-1 was the first US Navy model, ten of which were delivered in December 1925 and later served with the US Marine Corps in China. The designation was changed to FB-2 when deck arrester gear was installed on two aircraft prior to operating from the carrier USS *Langley*. The next production version for the Navy was the FB-5, twenty-seven of which were completed with 525hp Packard 2A-1500 engines and delivered in January 1927. There were several experimental models, flown with various types of powerplant. These included the XP-7 (a PW-9D with 600hp Curtiss V-1570), FB-3 (two built, with Packard 1A-1500), FB-4 (Wright P-1) and FB-6 (400hp R-1340 Wasp). The Wasp installation in the FB-6 was retained almost unchanged in Boeing's later XF2B-1 design, first flown on 3 November 1926 and subsequently evaluated by the US Navy. This led to thirty-two production F2B-1 fighter-bombers for the US Navy, delivered early in 1928, and two similar aircraft for Brazil and Japan. Further development of the basic design, with a more powerful engine and, ultimately, with longer-span wings, led to the F3B-1, one prototype and seventy-three production examples of which were built for the US Navy and served until arrival of the F4B in 1929-30.

Curtiss P-6

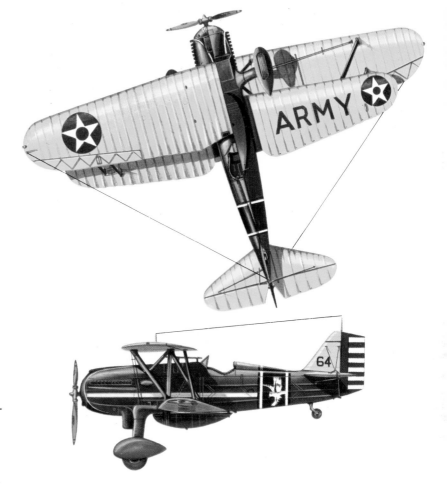

Curtiss P-6E Hawk of the 17th Pursuit Squadron, 1st Pursuit Group USAAC, *circa* 1932-34

Span: 31ft 6in (9.60m)
Length: 23ft 2in (7.06m)
Weight: 2,760lb (1,252kg)
Engine: 1 × 600hp Curtiss V-1570-23 Conqueror 12-cyl Vee-type
Max speed: 198mph (319kmh)
Operational ceiling: 24,700ft (7,529m)
Range: 570 miles (917km)
Armament: 1 × 0.30in Browning machine-gun on each side of front fuselage, or 1 × 0.30in and 1 × 0.50in

Origins of the famous line of Curtiss Hawk fighters go back to the PW-8 single-seater, in one of which, on 23 June 1924, Lt Russell Maughan of the USAAS made a dawn-to-dusk transcontinental flight across the USA. Twenty-five production PW-8s were built for the US Army, and from them stemmed the service's first fighter in the Pursuit category introduced in 1924. Fifteen P-1s were ordered initially, their design being based upon the XPW-8B with its tapered upper and lower wings. At the same time nine F6Cs were ordered by the US Navy, with 400hp Curtiss D-12 engines (instead of 435hp in the Army version) and provision for alternative wheel or float landing gear. Only minor improvements distinguished subsequent Army and Navy models, which included twenty-five P-1As, twenty-five P-1Bs, thirty-three P-1Cs and thirty-five F6C-3s. From 1929, forty-one lower-powered training models were re-engined with 435hp engines to become the P-1D, P-1E and P-1F; while the Navy acquired thirty-one F6C-4s with R-1340 Wasp radial engines. Meanwhile, in 1927 two much-modified Hawks had been refitted with examples of the new Curtiss Conqueror Vee-type engine, and when these two aircraft took first and second places in the National Air Races of 1928, the winner registering 201mph (323km/hr), such a performance could not be ignored. The two Hawk racers had been designated XP-6 and XP-6A, and in October 1928 the US Army ordered nine YP-6s – similarly powered, but with further aerodynamic refinements – for service trials, plus another nine as P-6As. All eighteen were fitted with engine turbo-superchargers in 1932 and in this form were redesignated P-6D. Final P-6 Hawk variant for the US Army was the P-6E, forty-six of which were delivered during the 1932 fiscal year. This represented a marked advance in both appearance and performance over the earlier models and was 20mph (32km/hr) faster than the P-6A. It followed from improvements on two other prototypes, the YP-20 and XP-22, which included faired cantilever main-wheel legs, wheel spats, a tail wheel instead of a skid, and a 700hp Conqueror engine in a new-style lower cowling which eliminated the deep-fronted appearance of the earlier P-6 models. Eight Curtiss P-6s were built for the Netherlands Indies Army Air Service, in addition to those for the US Army.

Boeing F4B

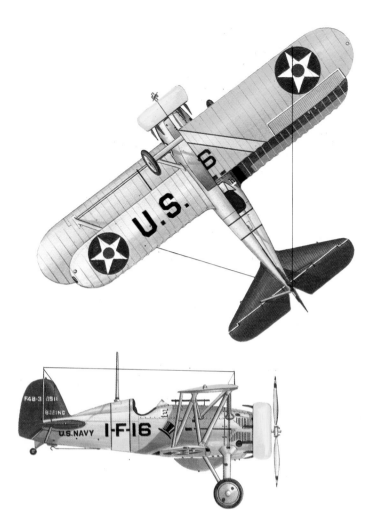

Boeing F4B-3 of VF-1B, US Navy, USS Saratoga, circa November 1932

Span: 30ft 0in (9.14m)
Length: 20ft 4¾in (6.22m)
Weight: 2,918lb (1,324kg)
Engine: Pratt & Whitney R-1340D Wasp
   9-cyl radial
Max speed: 187mph (301kmh) at 6,000ft
   (1,809m)
Operational ceiling: 27,500ft (8,380m)
Range: 585 miles (941km)
Armament: 2 × 0.30in (or 1 × 0.30in and
   1 × 0.50in) machine-guns
Max bomb load: 232lb (106kg)

The Boeing F4B and P-12 single-seat fighters were, respectively, US Navy and Army variants of the same basic design, the former being the first to be ordered into production. The fighter originated with the private-venture Boeing Model 83 and Model 89, of which the former flew for the first time on 25 June 1928, powered by a 400hp Pratt & Whitney Wasp radial engine. This aircraft, and the Model 89, were delivered to the US Navy some two months later for evaluation, and were given the designation XF4B-1. Successful trials were followed by an initial contract for 27 production aircraft, given the Boeing Model number 99 and the service designation F4B-1. The first F4B-1 was flown on 6 May 1929, and deliveries to the US Navy began in the following month. The US Army Air Corps was so impressed by the Navy's opinion of the Boeing fighter that it took the rare course of placing an order of its own, albeit a small one, without conducting an independent evaluation of the aircraft. Nine were ordered as P-12s (Boeing Model 102), plus a tenth machine designated XP-12A with Frise-type ailerons, modified landing gear and improved long-chord engine

cowling. Subsequent Navy models were the F4B-2 (Frise ailerons, Townend cowling ring and divided-axle landing gear: forty-two built); F4B-3 (similar, but with an all-metal fuselage: twenty-one built); and F4B-4 (enlarged headrest and broader fin and rudder: seventy-four built). Those ordered by the USAAC continued with the P-12B (ninety built, with Frise ailerons and shortened landing gear); P-12C (ninety-six with Townend rings and further undercarriage modifications); thirty-five P-12Ds and one hundred and ten metal-fuselage P-12Es with uprated R-1340-17 Wasp engines; and twenty-five P-12Fs with R-1340-19 radials. The Brazilian government purchased twenty-three of these fighters, fourteen of which were standard Navy-type F4B-4s. The remaining nine, designated Boeing Model 267, were of hybrid type combining various features of the F4B-3 and P-12E. Two other examples (Model 100E) were sold to the Spanish government. Altogether, including test aircraft, a total of 586 fighters in this basic design series were completed by Boeing, a production total that was not exceeded by any other US warplane until the eve of America's entry into World War 2.

Grumman FF-1

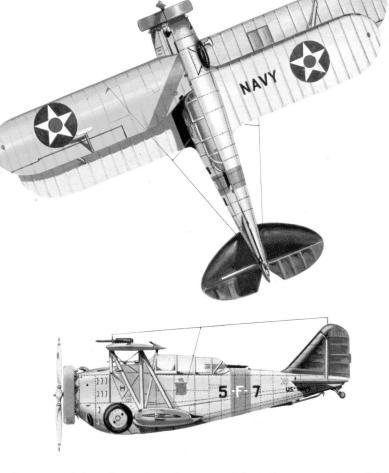

Grumman FF-1 of US Navy Squadron VF-5B, USS *Lexington, circa* winter 1933-34

Span: 34ft 6in (10.52m)
Length: 24ft 6in (7.47m)
Weight: 4,655lb (2,111kg)
Engines: 1 × 700hp Wright R-1820-78
  Cyclone 9-cyl radial
Max speed: 207mph (333kmh)
Operational ceiling: 22,400ft (6,828m)
Range: 920 miles (1,481km)
Armament: 2 × 0.30in Browning machine-
  guns
Max bomb load: 1 × 100 (45kg) bomb

For forty of aviation's first seventy years the name of the Grumman Aircraft Engineering Corporation has been almost synonymous with US naval aviation, and in the early part of that period, particularly, with naval fighters. Moreover, the FF-1, which was Grumman's first aircraft design for the US Navy, was a trend-setter in itself, for it was the first US Navy fighter to have a retractable landing gear. The prototype XFF-1 (A8878) was built to a contract placed on 2 April 1931, and made its first flight towards the end of that year. A 2-seater, it was powered initially by a 575hp Wright Cyclone radial engine, and when this was exchanged for a 750hp Cyclone the XFF-1 reached a speed during test of 201mph (323km/hr), faster than any US Navy fighter then serving. A production order ensued for twenty-seven FF-1s, delivery of which began to Fighter Squadron VF-5B (USS *Lexington*) in June 1933. In service the FF-1 became familiarly known, almost inevitably, as the 'Fifi'. Meanwhile Grumman had completed a second prototype (A8940) to 2-seat scout configuration as the XSF-1, from which thirty-three production SF-1s were subsequently ordered. They differed from the FF-1 principally in having revised internal equipment and in being powered by R-1820-84 Cyclones instead of the R-1820-78 model installed in the fighter version. Delivery of SF-1s started in March 1934, and they served (also aboard the *Lexington*) with Scout Squadron VS-3B. One XSF-2 was also completed, this having a Pratt & Whitney Wasp engine in place of the Cyclone. Both the FF-1 and SF-1 were withdrawn from first-line US Navy squadrons by the end of 1936 and reallocated to reserve units, most of the FF-1s still being in service late in 1940. Later, when fitted with dual controls, the FF-1 was redesignated FF-2 and was used for instructional duties. The Canadian Car & Foundry Co acquired a manufacturing licence for the FF-1, of which it completed a total of fifty-seven, some of them assembled from US-built components. Fifteen entered service with No 118 Squadron of the Royal Canadian Air Force in 1940, with the name Goblin I. Prior to this a single example was delivered to Nicaragua, and (allegedly) one to Japan; the remaining forty were ostensibly purchased by the Turkish government but were in fact received by the Spanish Republican Air Force in 1937.

Curtiss F9C

Curtiss F9C-2 Sparrowhawk of the airship USS
Macon, *circa* 1934

Span: 25ft 6in (7.77m)
Length: 20ft 1in (6.12m)
Weight: 2.888lb (1.310kg)
Engine: 1 × 420hp Wright R-975-22
Whirlwind 9-cyl radial
Max speed: 176.5mph (284kmh)
Operational ceiling: 19,200ft (5,852m)
Range: 366 miles (589km)
Armament: 2 × 0.30in machine-guns

A concept which exercised the attention of a number of air forces during the 1920s and 1930s was that of the 'parasite' fighter, carried into the air as a 'passenger' beneath a military airship and launched in the air to serve as defensive cover to the airship, much in the way that naval aircraft carriers carry their own fights to defend them while at sea. The concept has never achieved general acceptance, and most experiments of this kind have been conducted with existing types of fighter. One aircraft produced specifically for this 'parasite' role, however, was the Curtiss Sparrowhawk, eight of which were built in 1931-32 to serve with the US Navy's early-warning airships *Akron* and *Macon*. The primary purpose of the airships was reconnaissance, and it was envisaged that the Sparrowhawks, in addition to their protective duties, might also be used to extend the reconnaissance potential of their parent carrier. An XF9C-1 Sparrowhawk prototype (A8731) was ordered in June 1930, one of three designs to be evaluated, originally for a shipboard fighter role; it made its first flight on 12 February 1931. There followed one XF9C-2,

embodying modifications suggested after tests with the first Sparrowhawk, and six production F9C-2s. These six, and the original XF9C-1, were assigned to USS *Akron* for operational trials, and between 16 June and 11 July 1932 they made a total of one hundred and four successful 'hook-ons' to prove the feasibility of the concept. Each airship had a hangar in the rear that could accommodate five fighters, and below it was a trapeze of lattice-work girders which was lowered for the fighter to hook on to in flight by engaging it with the hooked superstructure mounted above the upper wing centre-section. Once engaged, the trapeze lifted the aeroplane into the hanger. On 4 April 1933, *Akron* was lost in a crash, whereupon the Sparrowhawks were transferred to her sister ship *Macon,* with whom they gave a further two years of satisfactory service. But on 12 February 1935, while carrying four of the Sparrowhawks, *Macon* also crashed and was destroyed, and further 'parasite' experiments were discontinued.

Corsair

Vought SU-1 Special Corsair, staff officer's aircraft of the US Navy, *circa* 1934

Span: 36ft 0in (10.97m)
Length: 26ft 2¼in (7.98m)
Weight: 4,765lb (2,161kg)
Engine: 1 × 600hp Pratt & Whitney
  R-1690-42 Hornet 9-cyl radial
Max speed: 170mph (274kmh)
Operational ceiling: 20,500ft (6,248m)
Range: 680 miles (1094km)
Armament: 3 × 0.30in machine-guns

The name Corsair achieved world-wide renown through the exploits of Chance Vought's famous gull-winged World War 2 fighter, but more than a dozen years before its appearance other Vought Corsairs had formed an entire family of naval observation and scouting biplanes produced in a veritable profusion of variants, not only for the US Navy and Marine Corps but for export to nearly a dozen other countries. The design, based upon the Pratt & Whitney Wasp radial engine and featuring an all-metal fuselage structure, originated in 1926, when two O2U-1 prototypes were ordered for evaluation. Delivery of a hundred and thirty production O2U-1 Corsairs to the USN and USMC began in the following year. These were open-cockpit 2-seaters, carrying two guns and (optionally) a small bomb load, and served in landplane, floatplane and amphibian forms at shore stations or on board carriers such as the *Langley*. They were followed in 1928-29 by successive batches of thirty-seven O2U-2, eighty O2U-3 and forty-two O2U-4 Corsairs, differing chiefly in tail design and lesser details. One O2U-3 was evaluated by the US Army (designation O-28), but no orders resulted. Chance Vought's next development was the O3U-1 amphibian, basically an improved O2U-4 with increased wing sweepback, of which eighty-seven were delivered from 1930 for shipboard service. Twenty-nine examples followed of the O3U-2 (600hp Hornet cowled engine, redesigned fin and landing gear); this model, for the Marine Corps, was redesignated SU-1 in service to denote its primary function of scout biplane. The Wasp-engined O3U-3 (seventy-six built) introduced an enlarged and more rounded rudder, and was followed by sixty-four Hornet-powered O3U-4 (SU-2 and SU-3) aircraft. The XSU-4 represented a much-modernised version, featuring a long-chord NACA-type engine cowling, further enlargement of the tail surfaces and fully-enclosed crew accommodation; the old-style narrow cowling was, however, retained on the forty series-built SU-4s. The XO3U-5 did not go into production, but a prototype and thirty-two production O3U-6s for the Marine Corps were built in 1935. When America entered World War 2 there were a hundred and forty-one Corsairs of different types on Navy strength, although by this time they were no longer in first-line service. The Corsair design also yielded a number of export variants, most of them with one or another variant of the Hornet engine. Model V-65s, corresponding broadly to the O2U-1, were built for the Argentine Naval Air Service, Brazil Army Air Service, and the air forces of China, Mexico and Peru. Mexican factories built Corsairs under licence after purchasing ten from the USA, and licence production of the V-935 model was undertaken in Thailand, where seventy-two were built. A lower-powered version was the V-100 Corsair Junior, suitable for primary or specialised advanced training or general-purpose duties. Variants with Twin Wasp engines included the V-99 and V-135, the latter being a single-seat fighter model.

Curtiss O2C-1 Helldiver

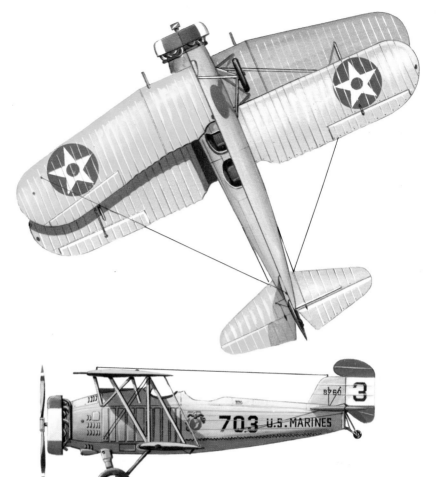

Curtiss O2C-1 Helldiver of the US Marine Corps, *circa* 1934

Span: 32ft 0in (9.75m)
Length: 25ft 7⅜in (7.82m)
Weight: 4,020lb (1,823kg)
Engine: 1 × 450hp Pratt & Whitney
  R-1340-4 Wasp 9-cyl radial
Max speed: 146mph (235kmh)
Operational ceiling: 16,250ft (4,953m)
Range: 720 miles (1159km)
Armament: 3 × 0.30in machine-guns
Max bomb load: 1 × 500lb (227kg) or
  2 × 116lb (53kg) bombs

To replace the American-built version of the war-vintage de Havilland DH-4 light bomber and reconnaissance aircraft in the middle and late 1920s, Curtiss evolved for the US Army in 1924 a prototype aircraft known as the XO-1, powered by a Liberty engine. This was unsuccessful at first, but in 1925, after being re-engined with a Packard 1A-1500, it was rewarded with a production contract. Curtiss subsequently built one hundred and four, with Curtiss D-12 engines, under O-1 series designations, and sixty-six similar but Liberty-engined O-11s, these aircraft having the name Falcon in Army service. Between 1927 and 1930 a further one hundred and fifty-four examples of a ground attack version, designated A-3 and A-3B, were also completed for the Army. With these Army models already in production and service it was therefore logical when, in 1927, the US Marine Corps also sought a DH-4 replacement, to consider adaptation of the Falcon for the purpose. The Marine Corps requirement was originally for a

2-seat fighter, with secondary capability as a light bomber and reconnaissance type, and two XF8C-1 prototypes were ordered in mid-1927. Their completion early in 1928 was followed by four F8C-1 and twenty-one F8C-3 aircraft, all of them differing from the Army Falcons principally in having a Pratt & Whitney Wasp radial engine as their powerplant. In USMC service they were later redesignated OC-1 and OC-2. Two other prototypes, the XF8C-2 and XF8C-4, appeared in 1929 and represented development of the aircraft to fulfil the role of dive-bomber. No production of the former was undertaken, but twenty-seven F8C-4s were built for Navy and Marine Corps service. They were given the name Helldiver, a name which stuck to later and quite separate Curtiss designs for naval dive-bombers. The final two F8SC-4s were converted to F8C-5s by substituting a different model Wasp engine, and a further sixty-one F8C-5 (later O2C-1) Helldivers were delivered from 1931.

Curtiss F11C

Curtiss BFC-2 (F11C-2) of US Navy Squadron
UB-2, USS *Saratoga, circa* mid-1934.

Span: 31ft 6in (9.60m)
Length: 25ft 0in (7.62m)
Weight: 4,638lb (2,104kg)
Engine: 1 × 700hp Wright R-1820-78
    Cyclone 9-cyl radial
Max speed: 198 mph (319kmh)
Operational ceiling: 24,300ft (7,407km)
Range: 560 miles (901km)
Armament: 2 × 0.30in machine-guns

Although allocated (initially) an F-for-fighter designation, the Curtiss Goshawk was one of several dual-purpose aircraft employed by the US Navy in the 1930s, as acknowledged by the allocation of a BF (Bomber-Fighter) designation later in its career. It was, in essentials, a radial-engined development from the P-6/F6C Hawk series built for the US Army and Navy. Two prototypes were ordered, an XF11C-1 powered by a Wright Whirlwind two-row radial engine and an XF11C-2 with a single-row Wright Cyclone. The latter aircraft (9213) was the first to fly, on 25 March 1932, and it was the Cyclone-engined model that was selected for production. Twenty-eight F11C-2s were ordered in October 1932, and delivery of the first aircraft began in the following April to US Navy Squadron VF-1B aboard the USS *Saratoga*. The F11C-2s were recategorised as BFC-2 in March 1934, undergoing modifications which included a semi-enclosed cockpit canopy and built-up rear fuselage; they remained in service until February 1938. The twenty-eighth F11C-2 was retained for conversion into a new prototype, the XF11C-3 (XBF2C-1 later) with a later-model Cyclone engine and retractable main

landing gear. Although less elegant than its contemporary, the Grumman FF-1, the F11C-3 also secured a production order, for twenty-seven aircraft, which were delivered as BF2C-1s to Squadron VB-5 aboard the USS *Ranger*. Production of Goshawks for the US Navy (fifty-seven, including prototypes) was thus on a fairly modest level, but Curtiss achieved considerable success with exports of the aircraft, known simply as Hawks. The Hawk I and II corresponded to the BFC-2, with 710hp Cyclones and differing only in internal fuel capacity, while the Hawk III and IV both had retractable landing gear and 750hp Cyclone engines. Altogether, two hundred and fifty-one Hawks were sold abroad, to Argentina (Hawk IV), Bolivia, China (over one hundred Hawk II and III), Colombia, Cuba, Germany (two Hawk II), Siam (Hawk III), Spain and Turkey (twenty-four Hawk II). In addition, licence production of the Hawk was undertaken in China. It was a group of Chinese Hawk IIIs whose bombs dropped in the international zone during a raid on a Japanese ship in the Yangtse River, that provoked the so-called 'Yangtse Incident' in August 1937.

Grumman F2F

Grumman F2F-1 of US Navy Squadron VF-2B,
USS *Lexington, circa* 1935-36

Span: 28ft 6in (8.69m)
Length: 21ft 4¾in (6.52m)
Weight: 3,847lb (1,745kg)
Engine: 1 × 700hp Pratt & Whitney
R-1535-72 Twin Wasp Junior 14-cyl
radial
Max speed: 231mph (372kmh)
Operational ceiling: 27,100ft (8,260m)
Range: 985 miles (1.585km)
Armament: 2 × 0.30in machine guns

The high performance of the Grumman XFF-1 2-seat fighter, which exceeded that of any current type of US Navy fighter, made it almost inevitable that a single-seat development should be evolved. This took the form of an XF2F-1 prototype (serial number 9342), ordered in November 1932 and flown for the first time on 18 October 1933. In the tubby shape of this little prototype can be seen the first real signs of the outlines later to become famous on such well-known wartime Grumman types as the Wildcat, Hellcat and Avenger. The XF2F-1 showed, during trials, a top speed 280mph (450km/hr) greater than the already-impressive XFF-1 had done, and this performance was very quickly rewarded with an order from the US Navy in May 1934 for fifty-four production F2F-1s,

delivery of which started in early 1935. The recipients were Squadrons VF-2B (USS *Lexington*) and VF-3B (USS *Ranger*), which continued to operate these fighters until 1940 and 1939 respectively. Following their subsequent withdrawal from first-line service with the US Fleet they were reallocated for duty as gunner training aircraft. In June 1934 one additional F2F-1 was ordered and this aircraft was delivered two months later. It had increased wing span and a longer fuselage, and was intended to serve as a prototype for the next Grumman fighter development, the F3F-1. It first flew on 20 March 1935, but was destroyed in a crash only two days later, and a new XF3F-1 was ordered to replace it.

Martin T3M

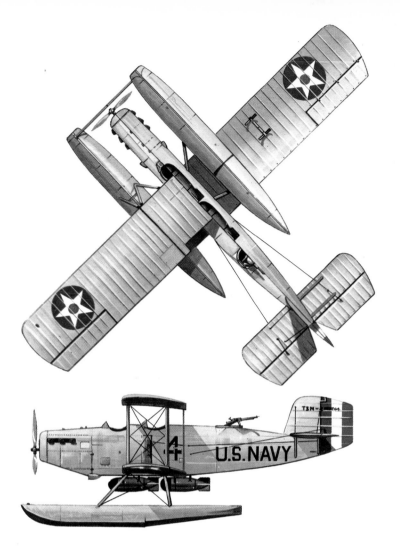

Martin T3M-2 of the US Navy, *circa* 1927-28

Span: 56ft 7in (17.25m)
Length: 41ft 4in (12.60m)
Weight: 9,503lb (4,310kg)
Engine: 1 × 770hp Packard 3A-2500 6-cyl
in-line
Max speed: 109mph (175kmh)
Operational ceiling: 7,900ft (2.408m)
Range: (With torpedo), 634 miles
(1,020km)
Armament: 1 × 0.30in machine gun
Max bomb load: 1 × 18in torpedo or
equivalent bomb load

The design of these torpedo-bomber-scout biplanes was based upon a Curtiss torpedo-bomber, the CS-1, which first appeared in 1923. The Curtiss Aeroplane and Motor Co itself built only six CS-1's and two examples of the similar CS-2. Major production of the aircraft was undertaken by the Glenn L. Martin Company, which built thirty-five and forty respectively under designations SC-1 and SC-2. Martin then put to good use the experience gained in manufacturing these aeroplanes by offering an improved version to follow them into service in the second half of the 1920s. The major improvements included the introduction of a steel-tube fuselage, in which the front cockpit was sited further forward, and the use of the uprated T-3B version of the Wright Vee-type engine fitted in the SC-2. As before, a wheeled or twin-float landing gear could be utilised at the operator's option. No separate prototype was built of the T3M-1, as the new model was known. A Navy contract for twenty-four production aircraft was placed in October 1925, and delivery of these began in September of the following year. Like the SC-2, the T3M-1 had unequal-span wings, with the upper mainplane of shorter span than the lower. A change to equal span, by extending the upper wing, was made in the next model, the T3M-2, which had individual cockpits in tandem for the three

crew members and a change of powerplant to the 770hp Vee-type Packard 3A-2500. One hundred T3M-2s were built, the first recipients of which were US Navy Squadrons VT-1S and VT-2B, embarked in USS *Lexington* and *Langley,* in 1927. The first machine off the T3M-2 contract was retained by Martin for conversion as the XT3M-3 prototype (Hornet radial engine) and later the XT3M-4 (Wright Cyclone radial), but these did not go into production as such. The Navy did, however, order a new Hornet-engined prototype, the XT4M-1, which flew for the first time in April 1927 and featured reduced-span wings and redesigned, horn-balanced rudder. Two production orders, totalling one hundred and two aircraft, were placed for the T4M-1, which began to enter service in August 1928 with VT-1B (*Lexington*) and VT-2B (*Saratoga*). In October of the same year Martin's Cleveland, Ohio, factory where the T4Ms were manufactured was acquired by the Great Lakes Aircraft Corporation, and the latter company continued production of the type under TG-1 and TG-2 designations. These remained essentially similar to the T4M series except for the change from Hornet engines to Cyclones; the TG-1 (eighteen built) was powered by the R-1820-26 Cyclone and the TG-2 (thirty-two built) by the R-1820-86. These aircraft remained in US Navy service until 1937.

Douglas DT-2

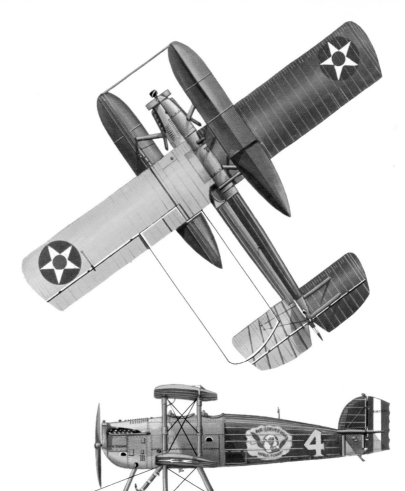

Douglas DWC World Cruiser (modified DT-2) of the US Army Air Service, flown by Lts Nelson and Harding, spring/summer 1924

Span: 50ft 0in (15.24m)
Length: 37ft 8in (11.48m)
Weight: 7,715lb (3,499kg)
Engine: 1 × 420hp V-1650 Liberty 12A
    12-cyl Vee-type
Max speed: 100mph (161kmh)
Operational ceiling: 7,000ft (2,134m)
Range: 1,650 miles (2,655km)

The first product of the Douglas Aircraft Co after its formation in 1920 was a single Liberty-engined civil biplane known as the Cloudster, and in some measure this contributed to the evolution of the first Douglas military aircraft, designed in 1921. This was the DT-1, a single-seat unstaggered biplane powered by a 400 hp Liberty engine, having an interchangeable landing gear of wheels or twin floats, and intended for the torpedo-bomber role. The US Navy ordered three DT-1s for trials in 1921, but only one was actually delivered as a DT-1, distinguishable by having twin radiators mounted on the sides of the fuselage. The other two machines were completed as DT-2s, built as 2-seaters with single nose-mounted radiators but otherwise similar to the DT-1. A further sixty-four DT-2s were built, thirty-eight by Douglas, twenty by the LWF Engineering Co and six by the Naval Aircraft Factory. Delivery of these was made between 1922-24, initially to the San Diego Naval Air Station and subsequently to other USN torpedo-bomber squadrons. The DT-2 could carry a single 1,835lb (832kg) torpedo beneath the forward fuselage, and had foldable wings to facilitate stowage on board ship. Some DT-2s were later redesignated following conversion to different powerplants. These included four of the NAF machines, which became DT-4s when fitted with Wright T-2 engines; two of them later had a geared T-2, with which they became DT-5s. The sole DT-6 was one of the Douglas-built DT-2s with a 450hp Wright P-1 radial engine. Later in their career, which ended in 1926, some of the DT-2s were utilised as scout, observation of armament training aircraft; these

included three of the LWF-built machines specially converted as SDW-1 long-range scouts with increased fuel tankage in an enlarged fuselage. By far the best-known aircraft of the DT type, however, were not Navy machines at all: they were four specially-modified aircraft ordered by the US Army to participate in a six-nation competition to make a complete round-the-world flight in 1924. They were ordered after trials in the preceding year with a prototype aircraft (23-1210), and were basically similar to the Navy DT-2. They were stripped of non-essential military equipment, fitted with dual controls and RDF (Radio Direction Finding) and provided with increased fuel tankage for the global flight. Designated DWC (Douglas World Cruiser), the four aircraft were delivered in March 1924. They were numbered 1 to 4 and named, respectively, *Seattle, Chicago, Boston* and *New Orleans.* Three of them left Clover Field, California, for Seattle on 17 March 1924, on the first leg of their journey, being joined there the following day by the fourth machine. All four left Seattle on 6 April, but soon lost *Seattle,* which crashed near Port Moller, Alaska, on 30 April. The remaining three had almost completed their global tour (during which no less than twenty-nine engines were used in the four aircraft) before *Boston* was forced to ditch in the North Atlantic on 3 August during the homeward flight. The two survivors were joined at Nova Scotia by the original prototype (now named *Boston II*), arriving safely back at Seattle on 28 September 1924 after a 175-day flight covering some 28,000 miles (45,062km).

Martin 130

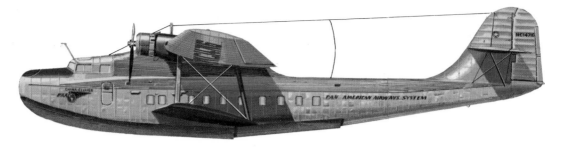

Martin 130 *China Clipper* of Pan American
Airways, *circa* 1936

Span: 130ft 0in (39.62m)
Length: 90ft 7½in (27.62m)
Weight: 52,000lb (23,587kg)
Engines: 4×830hp Pratt & Whitney
R-1830-SIA4G Twin Wasp 14-cyl radials
Max speed: 163mph (262kmh)
Operational ceiling: 17,000ft (5,182m)
Range: 3,200 miles (5,150km)

Second of the huge trans-oceanic flying-boats used by Pan American Airways System between the wars, the Martin Model 130 resulted from the same specification to which Sikorsky had evolved the S-42. Unlike the Sikorsky design, however, the Martin 'China Clipper', as it was to become known, truly possessed the long overwater capability that the airline required. PanAm's planned trans-Pacific route to the Philippines was San Francisco-Honolulu-Midway Island-Wake Island-Guam-Manila, the five stage lengths being, respectively, 2,410, 1,380, 1,260, 1,450 and 1,550 miles (3,880, 2,220, 2,030, 2,335 and 3,220km). To accomplish this it required an aircraft with a non-stop range of 2,500 miles (4,025km) carrying 12 passengers, which even by mid-1930s standards was hardly an economic payload/weight ratio. While the routes were being surveyed in 1935 by S-42B, Martin was building three M-130s, which in service were named *China Clipper* (NC14716), *Philippine Clipper* and *Hawaii Clipper*. Of all-metal construction, the M-130 had a two-step hull, the upper portions of which were clad in corrugated duralumin sheet, and sponsons (sometimes called 'sea wings') were fitted to the hull sides at cabin floor level. These aerofoil-shaped surfaces fulfilled a dual function: they helped to stabilise the aeroplane while resting or manoeuvring on the water, and served also as storage areas for nearly half of the flying boat's 3,800 US gallon (14,383 litre) fuel load. Retractable platforms were built into the leading-edge of each wing on either side of the engine nacelle, to provide access for servicing the engines, two of which were completely

changed every three trips. The flight crew of five comprised captain, first officer, radio officer, flight engineer and steward. Aft of the flight deck, in order, were the forward passenger compartment, lounge and two rear passenger compartments. Each passenger compartment could accommodate 8 seats or 6 sleeping berths, and the lounge seated 12. Since the long-distance payload was only 12 passengers altogether, one can appreciate the declaration by one American observer that passengers 'rattled around in the vast expanse of hull in a degree of comfort never known before'. Proving flights were made in the late 1935 and early 1936, *China Clipper* making the first-ever commercial double crossing of the Pacific between 22 November and 6 December 1935. The full, regular trans-Pacific M-130 service opened on 21 October 1936, the flight spanning five days and occupying a total of 60 hours actual flying. By 1940 (*Hawaii Clipper* having been lost at sea) the surviving pair of M-130s had accumulated some 10,000 flying hours each – equal to an average daily utilisation of 5½ hours – and had flown 12,718,200 passenger miles (20,467,930 passenger-km) in addition to express and mail flights. In 1942 they were impressed for war service as US Navy transports, though not given a Naval designation. *China Clipper* was wrecked early in 1945, shortly after the tenth anniversary of its first flight, when it struck an unlit boat during a night landing. An even larger flying-boat than the M-130 was built by Martin in 1937. This was the Model 156, whose design followed closely that of its predecessor except for the provision of twin fins and rudders. Powered by four 1,000hp Wright Cyclone

engines, it could accommodate 33-53 passengers (compared with a maximum of 52 in the M-130) and had a gross weight of 63,000lb (28,576kg).

Boeing P-26

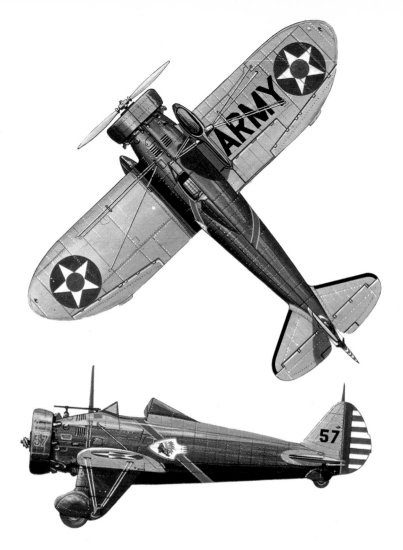

Boeing P-26A of the 94th Pursuit Squadron, 1st Pursuit Group USAAC, *circa* 1935

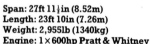

Span: 27ft 11½in (8.52m)
Length: 23ft 10in (7.26m)
Weight: 2,955lb (1340kg)
Engine: 1 × 600hp Pratt & Whitney
  R-1340-27 Wasp 9-cyl radial
Max speed: 234mph (377kmh)
Operational ceiling: 27,400ft (8,352m)
Range: 635 miles (1,022km)
Armament: 2 × 0.30in machine-guns
Max bomb load: 2 × 100lb, (45kg) or 5 × 30lb
  (14kg) bombs

Known affectionately as the 'pea-shooter', the Boeing P-26 single-seat fighter was one of the more distinctive monoplane designs of the 1930s, combining several forward-looking features with others that, in retrospect, seem outmoded by comparison. It retained a well-streamlined but none the less drag-creating fixed landing gear, yet at the time of its design (in 1931) Boeing was installing retractable gear in its B-9 bomber. At the same time, its low-wing monoplane layout and all-metal construction were truly modern features, even though the wings were somewhat extensively braced. The P-26 originated with three private-venture prototypes, known as the Boeing Model 248, designed and equipped with assistance from the USAAC. These three aircraft were in due course evaluated by the Army, which in January 1933 ordered one hundred and eleven examples of an improved version

under the designation P-26A. As originally built, ailerons were the P-26As only wing control surfaces, but all aircraft in service later had flaps fitted. The first P-26As began to be delivered at the end of the year, and they soon became standard pursuit squadron equipment in Hawaii and the Panama Canal area. A subsequent contract was placed for a further twenty-five fighters, two of these (designated P-26B) having fuel injection engines. The remainder were delivered initially as P-26Cs, having the same powerplant as the A model and minor control system changes, but later were converted to B standard. Boeing also exported a small quantity, eleven going to the Chinese Air Force (which used them in operations against attacking Japanese raiders in 1937) and one to Spain. A number of USAAC P-26As were transferred in 1941 to the Philippine Army.

Shrike

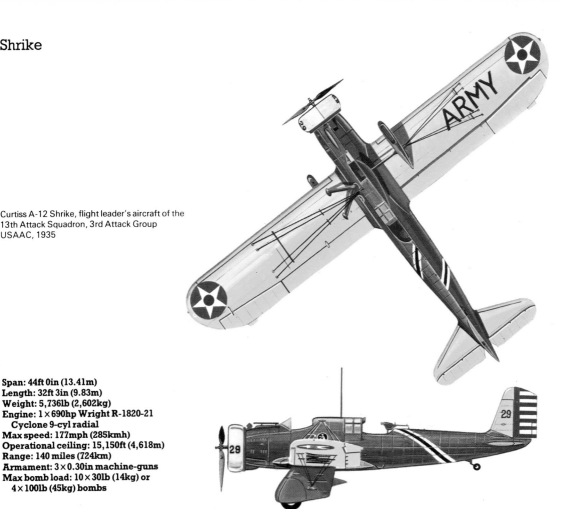

Curtiss A-12 Shrike, flight leader's aircraft of the
13th Attack Squadron, 3rd Attack Group
USAAC, 1935

Span: 44ft 0in (13.41m)
Length: 32ft 3in (9.83m)
Weight: 5,736lb (2,602kg)
Engine: 1 × 690hp Wright R-1820-21
    Cyclone 9-cyl radial
Max speed: 177mph (285kmh)
Operational ceiling: 15,150ft (4,618m)
Range: 140 miles (724km)
Armament: 3 × 0.30in machine-guns
Max bomb load: 10 × 30lb (14kg) or
    4 × 100lb (45kg) bombs

Late in 1927 Curtiss began to deliver to the US Army Air Corps the first of one hundred and fifty-four examples of the A-3 and A-3B, armed versions of the Curtiss Falcon 2-seat observation biplane produced to serve in a ground-attack role. By the end of the decade the USAAC had indicated a need for a more modern warplane to fulfil this task, to which end it ordered two prototype aircraft, the Fokker XA-7 and the Curtiss XA-8, each powered by a 600hp Curtiss Conqueror Vee-type engine. Flight trials of the two prototypes took place during the summer and autumn of 1931, from which a contract followed in September 1931 for thirteen YA-8 and Y1A-8 pre-production Shrikes for service trials. Most of these were operated from 1932-34 by the Air Corps' 3rd Attack Group. The first of the five YA-8s was modified in 1932 for the installation of a 630hp Pratt & Whitney R-1690D Hornet radial engine, in which form it was redesignated YA-10 and assigned, after service testing, to the 13th Attack Squadron. With this and other units it had completed over two thousand hours of flying before finally being scrapped in February 1939. A prototype similar to the YA-10 was the Whirlwind-engined XS2C-1; it was evaluated by the US Navy in 1933, but no production order was placed. The Army Air Corps, however, viewed the radial-engined model with more favour

than the version with the Conqueror engines, on the grounds that it was less vulnerable as well as more economical to operate. This, plus the better all-round performance of the Hornet-engined YA-10, led it to order, in 1933, forty-six examples of a generally similar model with the slightly more powerful Wright Cyclone radial. The designation A-8B given originally to these Shrikes was altered to A-12 before the start of deliveries. All but three of the production A-12s were delivered to the 3rd Attack Group between December 1933 and February 1934, and from February to May 1934 their primary function was the carriage of air mail, pending the issue of new contracts to civilian mail carriers. The Shrikes began to be replaced in first-line service by Northrop A-17s in 1936, after which several served with the AAC Tactical School at Maxwell Field, Alabama; others were allocated to units in Hawaii, where there were still nine in service when Pearl Harbor was attacked on 7 December 1941. They survived the attack, eight of them being returned to the US in 1942 to end their days as instructional airframes. Twenty Shrikes, generally similar to the A-12 except for an uprated Cyclone engine, were supplied to China in 1936-37, but most of these were destroyed during the first year of the Pacific war.

Martin MB-1 and MB-2

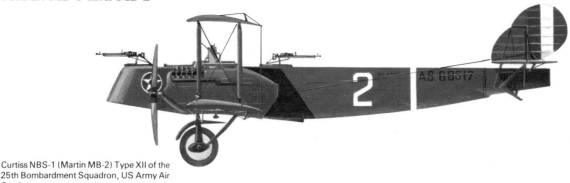

Curtiss NBS-1 (Martin MB-2) Type XII of the
25th Bombardment Squadron, US Army Air
Service

Span: 74ft 2in (22.61m)
Length: 42ft 8in (13.00m)
Weight: 12,064lb (5,472kg)
Engines: 2 × 420hp V-1650 Liberty 12A
   12-cyl Vee-type
Max speed: 99mph (159kmh)
Operational ceiling: 8,500ft (2,591m)
Range: 550 miles (898km)
Armament: 5 × 0.30in machine-guns
Max bomb load: 2,000lb (907kg)

During the year and a half of its involvement in World War I, the United States relied almost entirely upon European aircraft industries for the provision of its combat aircraft. One of these types was the Handley Page O/400 bomber, which was also built under licence in the US, and it was to find a successor to the British type that Glenn Martin was asked by the US government in 1917 to design a new bomber, with a performance superior to the Handley Page machine and a secondary capability as an aeroplane for both visual and photographic reconnaissance missions. Martin's answer was a twin-engined, twin-tailed biplane, powered by 400hp Liberty engines and bearing the company designation MB-1. In January 1918 Martin was awarded a contract for ten of these new aircraft, and the first of them made its maiden flight on 17 August of the same year. This and the next three machines were equipped for the observation role, while the fifth, sixth and seventh MB-1s were completed to bomber configuration, carrying a crew of four, a five-gun armament and a maximum bomb load of 1,040lb (472kg). The three final MB-1s on the initial contract were completed as experimental aircraft. The eighth had augmented fuel capacity, increasing the range from the normal 390 miles (628km) to 1,500 miles (2,414km); the ninth, a bomber, had a final installation of a 37mm cannon on the nose; and the tenth was completed as a transport, seating ten passengers in a much-modified fuselage stripped of its military equipment. None of these modifications went into production, although a second MB-1 was later converted to the transport configuration. This aircraft was one of four

additional MB-1s built for the US Army; two others were built for evaluation as torpedo-bombers by the US Navy (which then ordered ten as TM-1s), and six 'civilianised' MB-1s were completed for use by the Government Postal Service. In 1919-20 Martin evolved a developed version, known as the MB-2, for night bomber duties. Dimensionally, this was not much different from the MB-1, although it weighed about a ton more and was powered by uprated Liberty 12 engines of 420hp in nacelles of modified shape, mounted directly on the lower wings and with overhead radiators instead of the frontal radiators of the MB-1 installation. In addition, whereas on the MB-1 all except the outermost bays of interplane struts were canted outward at an angle of about 60 degrees, those of the MB-2 were all of an upright nature. As on the MB-1, the wing panels of the MB-2 outboard of the engine nacelles could be folded back alongside the fuselage – a feature inherited from the Handley Page O/400. In 1920 Martin received an Army contract for five MB-2s and fifteen identical aircraft given the Army designation NBS-1 (Night Bomber, Short Range). A further fifty NBS-1s were ordered from Curtiss, thirty-five from the LWF Engineering Co, and twenty-five from Aeromarine. The MB-2/NBS-1 remained in service until 1927-28, when it was replaced by the Keystone LB types. It was an aircraft of this type which sank the former German battleship *Ostfriesland* during the demonstration of bombing techniques given to US officials in July 1921 by Colonel 'Billy' Mitchell.

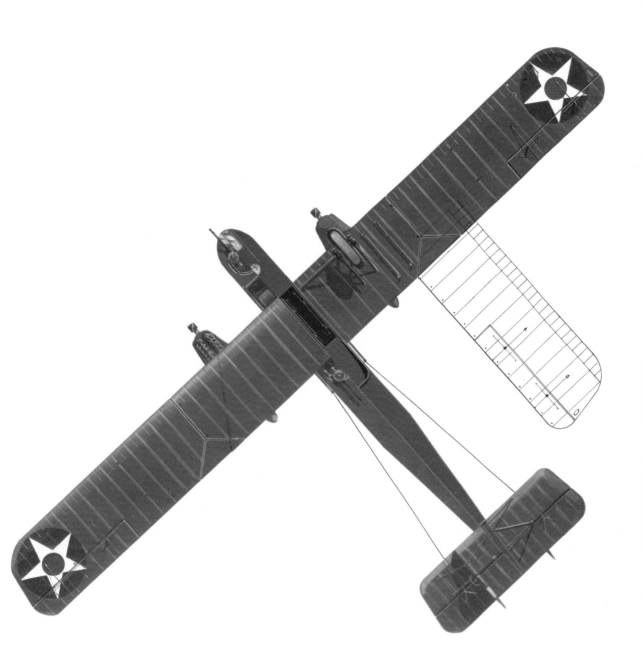

Keystone B-4A

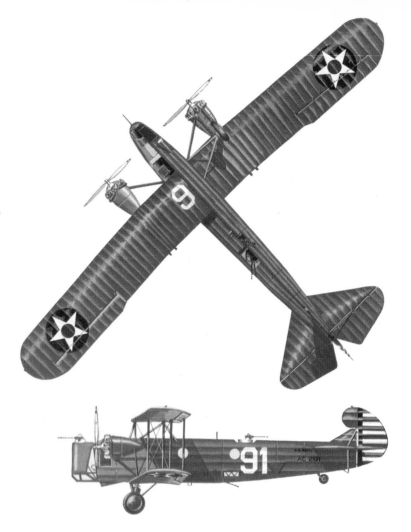

Keystone B-4A of the US Army Air Corps, *circa* 1933

Span: 74ft 9in
Length: 48ft 10in
Weight: 13,209lb (5,992kg)
Engines: 2×575hp Pratt & Whitney R-1860-7 Hornet 9-cyl radials
Max speed: 121mph (195kmh)
Operational ceiling: 14,000ft (4,267m)
Range: 855 miles (1,376km)
Armament: 3×0.30in machine guns
Max bomb load: 2,500lb (1,134kg)

The rather complicated assortment of twin-engined LB (Light Bomber) types produced by the Keystone Aircraft Corporation in the middle 1920s actually derived from a single-engined biplane bomber. This was the LB-1, one prototype and nine service trials specimens of which were produced in 1923-26 by the Keystone Company under its former title of Huff-Daland and Co Inc. It was the basic airframe of the 3-seat LB-1 that was adapted to become the Keystone prototype XLB-3A. The single nose-mounted Packard engine was replaced by two 410hp Pratt & Whitney Wasp radials, mounted midway between the upper and lower wings; accommodation was increased to five crew members, and the bombardier's station was located in the more traditional nose position instead of amidships as on the LB-1. First production bomber was the LB-5, ten of which were completed with 420hp Liberty engines mounted on the lower wings and vertical tail surfaces consisting of a single central main rudder and two smaller rudders outboard. The later configuration was replaced, in the twenty-five LB-5As which followed, by a more conventional arrangement of twin fins and rudders of equal size. The tapered wing planform, inherited from the LB-1, disappeared in the prototype and seventeen production LB-6s which followed, in favour of wings of constant chord throughout; and the Liberty engines were replaced by 525hp Wright Cyclones mounted in the mid-gap position. Thus modified, this airframe became the

standard configuration for the remainder of the LB series. Major production models were the LB-7 and LB-10A. Eighteen of the former and sixty-three of the latter were built, all with 525hp Pratt & Whitney Hornet engines; the LB-10A was distinguished by having a single instead of a twin tail assembly. Single examples were completed, with various-model Cyclone or Hornet engines, of the LB-8, LB-9, LB-10, LB-11/11A and LB-12; and the Keystone LB range was completed by orders for seven LB-13s and three LB-14s. However, in 1930 it was decided to discontinue the differentation by designation of the US Army's light and heavy bomber categories, and a new series of bomber designations was introduced using the single prefix letter B. Under this arrangement the LB-10As became known (before they had actually been delivered) as B-3As. The LB-13s became single-tailed Y1B-4s or Y1B-6s; the LB-14s were redesignated Y1B-5, though their completion or delivery has not been confirmed. The final twenty-seven LB-10A/B-3A machines later had Cyclone engines installed in place of their original Hornets, and in this form received yet another designation, B-5A. The final production models, built in 1932 after the designation confusion had settled down, were the B-4A (twenty-five built) and B-6A (thirty-nine built). These were both single-tailed models, powered respectively by Hornet and Cyclone engines, all of 575hp.

Loening OL9

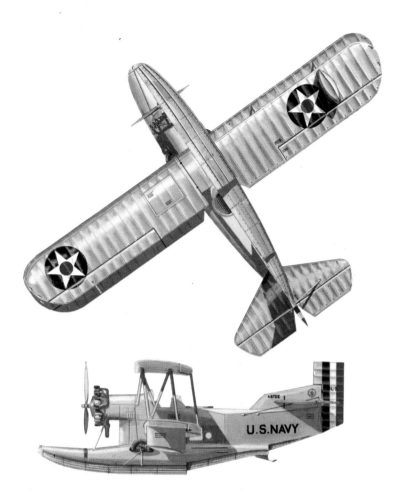

Loening OL-9 of he Naval Academy, US Navy, *circa* 1927-28

Span: 45ft 0in (13.72m)
Length: 34ft 9in (10.59m)
Weight: 5,404lb (2,451kg)
Engine: 1 × 450hp Pratt & Whitney
R-1340-4 Wasp 9-cyl radial
Max speed: 122mph (196kmh)
Operational ceiling: 14,300ft (4,359m)
Range: 625 miles (1,006km)

The Loening Aeronautical Engineering Co of New York was founded by Grover C. Loening, an inventive pioneer who had graduated as an aeronautical engineer in 1911 and had in his early days worked with Orville and Wilbur Wright. In the early 1920s he was responsible for a series of amphibious aircraft for the US Army and Navy, beginning with the COA-1 (Corps Observation Amphibian) in 1924. The main feature of these aircraft was that, instead of having a separate fuselage and central float united by struts, the area between these two structures was completely faired in, enabling the internal space thus provided to accommodate working equipment and, at the same time, providing an aerodynamically better shape. This feature was facilitated by use of the inverted-Vee Liberty engine, whose high thrust line permitted the distance from fuselage to float to be kept to a minimum. The first of two XCOA-1s was flown in July 1924, after which nine COA-1s were built for service trials, fifteen OA-1As (with modified fins and rudders), nine basically similar OA-1Bs, and ten OA-1Cs in which the vertical tail was again redesigned. The main landing wheels retracted into the sides of the central float, at the rear of which was a small tail skid, and small stabilising floats were fitted beneath the outer panels of the lower wings.

Final Army version was the OA-2, eight of which were built in 1929 and which had more up-to-date Wright V-1460 Tornado engines of 480hp in place of the 400hp Libertys. The Navy amphibians began with the OL-1, a 3-seat version powered by a 440hp Packard 1A-1500 engine; two of these were built. The OL-2 was the Naval counterpart to the COA-1, and five were completed. One of the OL-1s was used to incorporate a number of design improvements, leading to a contract for four more similar aircraft as OL-3s, and six with Liberty engines as OL-4s. There was no OL-5, but twenty-eight examples were ordered of the OL-6. This introduced the tall, angular vertical tail of the OA-1C and was powered by the Packard engine. The XOL-7, with redesigned wings of thicker section, remained only a prototype, but the XOL-8 led to orders for twenty OL-8s and twenty OL-8As, which introduced, for the first time, a radial engine to the series – the 450hp Pratt & Whitney Wasp. The OL-8As had deck arrester gear fitted, but were otherwise similar to the OL-8. Final version was the OL-9, twenty-six of which were built after the amalgamation of Loening with the Keystone Aircraft Corporation; these were preceded by two other machines, designated XHL-1, which were intended for use as 6-passenger ambulance aircraft.

Sikorsky S-42

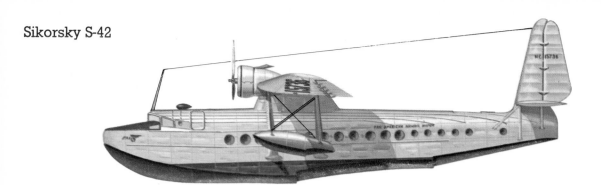

Sikorsky S-42B of Pan American Airways, *circa* 1937

Span: 118ft 2in (36.02m)
Length: 68ft 0in (20.73m)
Weigth: 42,000lb (19,051kg)
Engines: 4 × 750hp Pratt & Whitney R-1860
   Hornet 9-cyl radials
Max speed: 188mph (303kmh)
Operational ceiling: 15,000ft (4,572m)
Range: 1,200 miles (1,931km)

Seemingly unaffected by the prevailing economic depression, the air transport business continued to grow during the closing years of the 1920s. One of the most thriving airlines at that time was Pan American Airways, which at the end of 1929 boasted a total fleet of forty-four aircraft. A large proportion of its route network was spread over water, and to meet the growing need for greater size, speed and range PAA contracted with Sikorsky Aircraft for an amphibious aircraft with a range of 950 miles (1,530km) or a maximum capacity for 40 passengers and a ton of baggage or freight over shorter distances. This resulted in the S-40, three of which were built for Pan American. The first of these was flown in August 1931, christened *American Clipper* two months later, and the S-40 went into regular operation the following year on the airline's Caribbean routes. The era of luxurious trans-oceanic air travel had begun. At the time of its construction the S-40 was the largest aeroplane to be built in the USA, and was powered by four 575hp Pratt & Whitney Hornet radial engines mounted on the wing-bearing struts. A wheel landing gear was fitted to provide against possible forced landings over land areas, such as Cuba, en route. The S-40 had not been in service for long before Pan American announced a further requirement, for an even larger, faster and longer-range seaplane – one with a 2,500 mile (4,025km) non-stop range carrying 12 passengers. Both Sikorsky and Martin submitted designs to meet this requirement, the S-42 and M-130 respectively. The S-42 was the first to be completed, and the prototype was flown on 29 March 1934. The PanAm specification had

necessitated the evolution of a much more modern design than the S-40, and the S-42 represented a considerable advance over its predecessor. Apart from small areas of the wings and tail it was of all-metal construction, with a flush-riveted skin, two-step hull, wing-mounted Hornet engines with three-blade variable-pitch propellers, and split trailing-edge wing flaps. The wings were carried above the hull on a faired superstructure and braced by two struts on each side; stabilising floats beneath the outer wings were preferred to the more fashionable hull-mounted 'sea wings' or sponsons. During its development programme the S-42 set up ten payload-to-height records, and ten were ordered (three S-42s, four S-42As and three S-42Bs. From April 1935 the S-42s went into service with Pan American, initially between San Francisco and Hawaii and subsequently on the New York-Bermuda, Miami-South America and Manila-Hong Kong routes of the PAA system. Normal seating accommodation was for 32 day-time passengers and a crew of five, the former divided equally between four cabins. A 14-passenger 'sleeper' configuration was evolved, but seldom if ever used. On short stages the S-42A could carry up to 40 passengers by adapting the forward baggage/freight compartment as an additional cabin. But, even with the payload reduced to 12 passengers, the S-42As range was still well below that required, and in due course the Martin M-130 operated over the longer stages, the Sikorsky serving on the Manila-Hong Kong sector of the China route. The designation S-42B was applied to three aircraft equipped with additional fuel tanks

(total load 2,414 US gallons = 9,137 litres) to carry out survey flights over both the Atlantic and Pacific. One S-42B was used during 1935 to survey the trans-Pacific routes to Manila to be flown later by the airline's M-130 'China Clipper' flying-boats. Another, NC16736 *Pan American Clipper III,* made three out-and-back survey flights across the North Atlantic in the summer of 1937. (The generic name 'Clipper' was applied by PAA to all types of flying-boat – and there were several – in service on its world-wide network. At one time it had no fewer than fourteen types of water-borne aircraft in its fleet, with pasenger seating capacities ranging from 6 to 40, and several of these were flying-boats or amphibians of Sikorsky design.) Pan American began regular trans-Atlantic services, with Boeing 314 flying-boats, on 23 May 1939.

Martin B-10

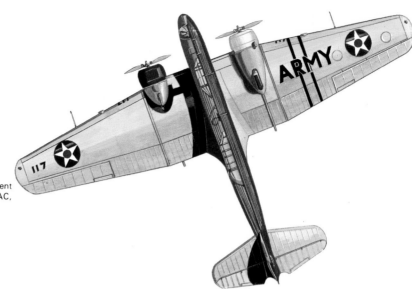

Martin B-10B of the 31st Bombardment Squadron, 3rd Bombing Group of the USAAC, *circa* 1935

Span: 70ft 6in (21.49m)
Length: 44ft 8¾in (13.63m)
Weight: 14,600lb (6.622kg)
Engines: 2×775hp Wright R-1820-33
  Cyclone 9-cyl radials
Max speed: 213mph (343kmh)
Operational ceiling: 24,200ft (7,376m)
Range: 590 miles (950km)
Armament: 3×0.30in machine-guns
Max bomb load: 2,200lb (998kg)

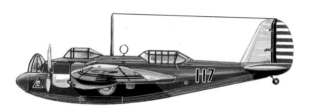

A smooth, sleek monoplane with fully-enclosed bomb load and a retractable main undercarriage, the Martin B-10 was yet another classic example of what a good aircraft designer can do when not subservient to the limitations of an official specification. As the Martin Model 123, this twin-engined bomber design appeared in the early months of 1932, and the prototype was handed over to the U.S. Army in March of that year for evaluation with the designation XB-907. In its original form it had a top speed of 197mph (317km/hr), and when later modified as the XB-907A, with increased wing span, higher-powered Cyclone engines in long-chord cowlings and a rotatable gun turret in the nose, it added another 10mph (16km/hr) to this already-impressive figure. Such a performance clearly could not be ignored, and the award to Martin of the 1933 Collier Trophy was backed at the start of that year by a USAAC contract for forty-eight production examples of the new bomber. The first fourteen of these were completed as Cyclone-engined YB-10s for service trials, followed by one YB-10A with turbo-supercharged Cyclones, seven YB-12s with 775hp Pratt & Whitney Hornet radials, one XB-14 with 950hp Twin Wasp engines and twenty-five B-12As, similar to the YB-12 but with increased fuel capacity. The manufacturer's designation for the production version was Model 139. First deliveries to the Army Air Corps were made in mid-1934, for the commencement of service trials, and in 1935

the aircraft began to reach operational units, among them the 2nd, 7th, 9th and 19th Bombardment Groups in the U.S. and other units in Panama and Hawaii. Some Martins were converted to a twin-float landing gear and employed as coastal defence aircraft. Production and deliveries continued during 1935-36 with a further one hundred and three B-10Bs, these reverting to the 775hp Cyclone powerplant and incorporating detail improvements. Advanced though the Martin bomber was at the time of its first appearance, its first-line service in its intended role was relatively short, for it was overtaken in the late 1930s by the twin-engined Douglas B-18 and the four-engined long-range Boeing B-17. Consequently, in 1936 the U.S. government authorised the release of the Martin 139 design for export, and in this sphere the bomber achieved a commercial success equivalent to its production for the U.S. Army. The basic export version was known as the Model 139W, and was sold to Argentina (twenty-five), China (nine), the Netherlands Indies (one hundred and seventeen), Siam (six), Turkey (twenty) and the U.S.S.R. (one). Only the first thirty-nine of the Dutch East Indies Martins were Model 139Ws, corresponding broadly to the B-10B; the remainder, designated Model 166, differed in having one long 'greenhouse' canopy embracing both the forward and rear cockpits.

Grumman F3F

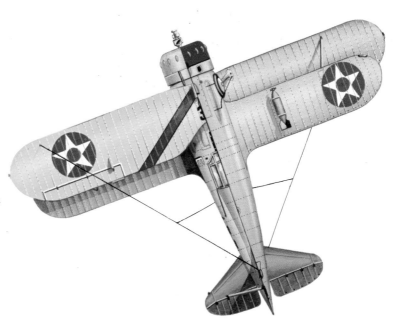

Grumman F3F-1 of US Navy Squadron VF-4
USS *Ranger,* March 1938

Span: 32ft 0in (9.75m)
Length: 23ft 3¼in (7.10m)
Weight: 4,116lb (1,867kg)
Engine: 1 × 700hp Pratt & Whitney
  R-1535-84 Twin Wasp Junior 14-cyl
  radial
Max speed: 231mph (372kmh)
Operational ceiling: 28,500ft (8,687m)
Range: 530 miles (853km)
Armament: 2 × machine-guns
Max bomb load: 1 × 110lb (50kg)

As explained on page 25, the first aircraft intended to serve as prototype for Grumman's F3F-1 fighter design crashed before completing its acceptance trials. A replacement aircraft was therefore built, but this too was short-lived: it made its first flight on 9 May 1935 and crashed on 17 May. Some undamaged components of this machine were used in the construction of a third XF3-F-1 (serial number 9727), and this completed the remaining Navy trials satisfactorily. In August 1935 an order was placed for fifty-four production F3F-1s; the first of these began to be delivered in 1936 to Squadrons VF-5B (USS *Ranger)* and VF-6B (USS *Saratoga),* with whom they continued to serve until 1940. The F3F-1 was powered by a Pratt & Whitney Twin Wasp engine, but this powerplant was exchanged for a single-row Wright Cyclone radial in the next production model, the F3F-2, resulting in an increase in the diameter of the nose cowling. One XF3F-2 prototype (0452) was followed by eighty-one production aircraft, the first of which was delivered to a squadron in December 1937. Official

flight test reports on the F3F-2 declared it 'the most satisfactory single-place fighter developed for the Navy to date', and this model served with VF-6 (USS *Enterprise)* and with Marine Corps Squadrons VMF-1 and VMF-2. Trials took place in 1938 with the XF3F-3 prototype (1031), a converted F3F-2 fitted with various different propellers, split landing-flaps, modified cowling and other devices intended to improve overall performance. They resulted in what was to be the final production order for Grumman fighter biplanes, for twenty-seven F3F-3s which were delivered in 1938-39 and which brought the overall production of F3F series fighters to one hundred and sixty-four aircraft. Most of the F3F-3s went either to VF-5 (USS *Yorktown)* or VF-7 (USS *Wasp).* By September 1939 all U.S. Navy and Marine Corps fighter squadrons were equipped with either F2F or F3F series single-seaters, which were not finally withdrawn from first-line service until 1941, when they were reallocated to training duties.

Consolidated PBY and Catalina

Consolidated PBY-1 of US Navy Squadron
VP-12, Patrol Wing 1, *circa* 1937

Span: 104ft 0in (31.70m)
Length: 65ft 1¾in (19.86m)
Weight: 28,447lb (12,904kg)
Engines: 2×900hp Pratt & Whitney
  R-1830-64 Twin Wasp 14-cyl radials
Max speed: 178mph (286kmh)
Operational ceiling: 20,800ft (6,340m)
Range: 2,115 miles (3,404km)

The Consolidated XP3Y-1, or Model 28, was one of two prototypes (the other being the Douglas XP3D-1) commissioned by the US Navy in October 1933 for comparative evaluation as patrol flying-boats. Isaac M. Laddon's design for the Consolidated Aircraft Corporation showed extremely clean lines, particularly in its near-cantilever wings, which were mounted on a pylon above the hull and had stabilising floats which retracted to form the wing-tips when in flight. The XP3Y-1 (serial number 9459) flew for the first time on 21 March 1935, powered by two 825hp R-1830-54 Wasp engines, and later that year (after a change to the 'Patrol Bomber' designation XPBY-1) sixty production PBY-1s were ordered. These could carry up to 2,000lb (907kg) of bombs, and were armed with four 0.30 in machine-guns. Delivery of the XPBY-1 was made to Squadron VP-11F in October 1936, and was followed shortly afterwards by the first production aircraft. Fifty PBY-2s followed in 1937-38, and in the latter year three PBY-3s and a manufacturing licence were sold to the USSR. The Soviet version, designated GST, was powered by M-62 engines. Orders for the US Navy continued with sixty-six PBY-3s (R-1830-66 engines) and thirty-three PBY-4s (1,050hp R-1830-72s), the latter introducing the prominent waist blisters that characterised most subsequent versions. The RAF received on Model 28-5 for evaluation in July 1939, resulting in an order for fifty aircraft similar to the US Navy's PBY-5, which had 1,200hp R-1830-82 or -92 engines and a redesigned rudder. The RAF name Catalina was subsequently adopted for the PBYs in USN service. During

1940 the RAF doubled its original order, and other Catalinas were ordered by Australia (eighteen), Canada (fifty), France (thirty) and the Netherlands East Indies (thirty-six). Of the US Navy's original order for two hundred PBY-5s the final thirty-three were completed as PBY-5A amphibians, and an additional one hundred and thirty-four were ordered to PBY-5A standard. Twelve later became RAF Catalina IIIs, and twelve more were included in the Dutch contract. Seven hundred and fifty-three PBY-5s were built and seven hundred and ninety-four PBY-5As, fifty-six of the latter being completed as OA-10s for the USAAF. Lend-Lease supplies to Britain included two hundred and twenty-five PBY-5Bs (Catalina IA) and ninety-seven Catalina IVAs with ASV radar. Production continued with the tall-finned Naval Aircraft Factory PBN-1 Nomad (one hundred and fifty-six, most of which went to the USSR) and the similar PBY-6A amphibian (two hundred and thirty-five, including seventy-five USAAF OA-10Bs and forty-eight for the USSR). Canadian Vickers-built amphibians went to the USAAF (two hundred and thirty OA-10As) and Royal Canadian Air Force (one hundred and forty-nine, named Canso). Boeing-Canada production included two hundred and forty PB2B-1s (mostly as RAF Catalina IBVs), seventeen RCAF Catalinas, fifty tall-finned PB2B-2s (RAF Catalina VI) and fifty-five RCAF Cansos. Total US/Canadian production of PBY models was three thousand two hundred and ninety, to which must be added several hundred GSTs built in the Soviet Union. A prominent ocean-going patrol and reconnaissance type during World War 2,

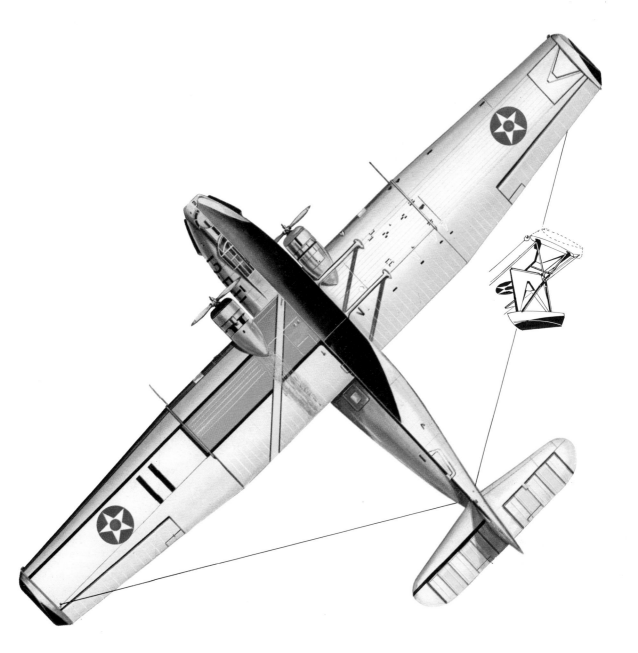

the Catalina possessed a performance that enabled it to maintain its viability with the military and naval air arms of many countries, as well as in a commercial transport role, for many years after the war, particularly in South America. Among those still operating Catalinas for maritime reconnaissance up to the mid-1960s were Argentina, Brazil, Chile, Ecuador and Mexico, at which time Nationalist China, Dominica, Indonesia and Peru still used the type for search and rescue, and France and Israel retained a few for

miscellaneous duties. Although the Catalina was clearly not an especially economic type for commercial services, its other advantages led to its use in such areas as the Amazon basin and among the island groups of south-east Asia and Australasia. As an example, the six owned by Panair do Brasil until its dissolution in February 1965 were operated very successfully as 22-passenger transports along the Amazon river. By 1970, however, very few military or civil Catalinas remained in service.

Boeing B-17

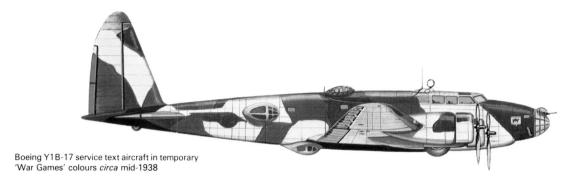

Boeing Y1B-17 service text aircraft in temporary
'War Games' colours *circa* mid-1938

Span: 103ft 9in (31.62m)
Length: 67ft 11in (20.70m)
Weight: 37,997lb (17,235kg)
Engines: 4×1,200hp Wright R-1820-51
   Cyclone 9-cyl radials
Max speed: 292mph (470kmh)
Operational ceiling: 36,000ft (10,973m)
Range: 2,400 miles (3,862km)
Armament: 5×0.30in machine-guns
Max bomb load: 8,000lb (3,629kg)

Later to become one of the most famous (and most prolific) bombers ever built, the Boeing Fortress was the outcome of a 1934 USAAC requirement for an offshore anti-shipping bomber. Boeing had already undertaken preliminary design work for a Model 299 bomber project and a transport counterpart, the Model 300; and in August 1934 it began in earnest to develop the former design to meet the Army requirement. The Boeing 299 prototype (X13372), powered by four 750hp Pratt & Whitney Hornet radial engines, made its first flight on 28 July 1935. Just over three weeks later it made an impressive 2,100 mile (3,380km) non-stop flight from Seattle to Wright Field to begin its evaluation trials with the USAAC, but it was destroyed in a take-off accident on 30 October 1935. Already, however, the new aircraft had given sufficient promise of its potential worth, and in the following January Boeing received a contract for thirteen Y1B-17 and one Y1B-17A aircraft for more exhaustive service trials. These differed from the prototype in having 930hp Wright Cyclone engines, those of the Y1B-17A being fitted with turbo-superchargers. Twelve of the Y1B-17s were placed in service with the Army's 2nd Bombardment Group, with whom they remained (simply as B-17s) after the successful completion of their service trials. Due to a conflict of opinion between Army and Navy staffs over the responsibility for protecting the American coastline, it was not until 1938 that the first Fortress production contract was placed – and this was for the comparatively modest quantity of thirty-nine aircraft. These incorporated a number of improvements, notably a modified nose and a larger rudder, and were designated B-17B. Successive production batches included thirty-eight B-17Cs (increased armament and a different mark of Cyclone engine), twenty of which were supplied to the Royal Air Force in 1941 as the Fortress Mk I; and forty-two B-17Ds, which had a tenth crew member, self-sealing fuel tanks and no external bomb racks. Most of the USAAF's remaining B-17Cs were eventually converted to D standard. The last Fortress variant to appear before America's entry into World War 2 was the B-17E, which first flew in September 1941. This involved a more extensive redesign to bring the bomber into line with current requirements. It was the first model to introduce the huge, sail-like fin and rudder that characterised all subsequent Fortresses, and firepower was considerably increased by the installation of power turrets above and below the fuselage, the provision for the first time of a tail gun position and of a multi-gun nose, bringing total defensive armament to thirteen guns. Five hundred and twelve B-17Es were built by Boeing, including forty-five supplied to the RAF as the Fortress IIA. Other wartime variants are described elsewhere in this volume. The early service life of the B-17 series was punctuated by a number of impressive long-distance flights. These included the flights of six aircraft from Miami to Buenos Aires (5,260 miles = 8,465km) in 1938, with only one refuelling stop en route, many non-stop coast-to-coast flights across the USA and another formation flight to Rio de Janeiro in November 1939. In August 1939 the Y1B-17A, carrying an 11,000lb (4,990kg) payload, set an altitude record

of 34,000ft (10,363m) and a 621 miles (1,000km) closed-circuit
speed record of 259.4mph (417.5km/hr).

Douglas B-18

Douglas B-18A of the USAAC, *circa* 1939

Span: 89ft 6in (27.28m)
Length: 57ft 10in (17.63m)
Weight: 27,673lb (12,552kg)
Engines: 2×1,000hp Wright R-1820-53
Cyclone 9-cyl radials
Max speed: 215mph (346kmh)
Operational ceiling: 23,900ft (7,285m)
Range: 1,200 miles (1,931km)
Armament: 3×0.30in machine-guns
Max bomb load: 6,500lb (2,948kg)

As the contours of its wing and tail surfaces so plainly indicate, the Douglas B-18 medium bomber was a military derivative of the DC-2 commercial airliner. These features, together with the twin-Cyclone powerplant, were combined with a new-design fuselage accommodating a 6-man crew and a substantial internal bomb load, in a private-venture prototype given the manufacturer's designation DB-1 (Douglas Bomber 1). The DB-1 was one of three designs (another being the four-engined Boeing 299, forerunner of the B-17) submitted in response to a 1934 USAAC requirement for a successor to the Martin B-10. Army trials began in August 1935, resulting in the adoption of both the Boeing and the Douglas designs, the latter receiving a contract for one hundred and thirty-three B-18 bombers in January 1936. The DB-1 prototype was accepted as the first aircraft of this batch, the subsequent machines being essentially similar except for an increased gross weight resulting from the installation of military equipment. The final aircraft on this first contract, completed late in 1937, differed in having a power-operated nose turret installed experimentally, and was designated DB-2. In June 1937 the US Army Air Corps placed a further contract for one hundred and seventy-seven Douglas bombers. These aircraft, and forty of an additional seventy-eight on option, were completed as B-18As, having uprated Cyclone engines of 1,000hp (compared with 930hp in the original B-18), a modified dorsel turret and a redesigned nose section. The former snub-nosed contours of the B-18 were replaced by a longer and extensively-glazed section, of which the upper portion, housing the bomb-aimer, protruded well forward of the lower. Production continued through 1937-38, and the Douglas type was well established as a standard US Army bomber well before America's entry into World War 2, serving *inter alia* with the 5th and 11th Bombing Groups. Early in 1940 a further twenty B-18A bombers were built for the Royal Canadian Air Force. Given the manufacturer's designation DB-280, they were named Digby I by the RCAF, which employed them as convoy escorts or anti-submarine patrol aircraft. A similar maritime role was allotted to those in US service in 1942, when one hundred and twenty-two conversions were made to B-18B standard. Modifications included removing most or all of the nose glazing, in some cases installing a radome in the extreme nose and in others adding an extended tail-cone containing submarine detection gear. Two aircraft of this type were supplied to the Brazilian Air Force for duties over South American waters. The B-18 (sometimes referred to, unofficially, as the Bolo) ended its days as a paratroop training aircraft.

Duck

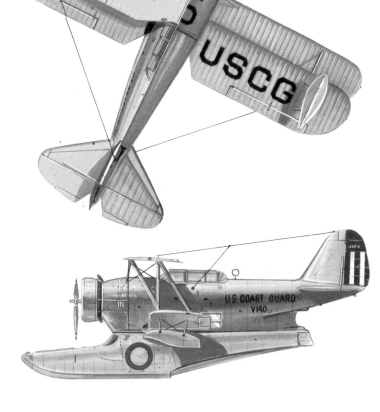

Grumman J2F-2 Duck of the US Coast Guard, *circa* 1938-39

Span: 39ft 0in (11.89m)
Length: 34ft 0in (10.36m)
Weight: 6,170lb (2,799kg)
Engine: 1×750hp Wright R-1820-20
  Cyclone 9-cyl radial
Max speed: 180mph (290kmh)
Operational ceiling: 21,000ft (6,401m)
Range: 780 miles (1,255km)

Much of the early work conducted by the Grumman Aircraft Engineering Corporation after its formation at the end of 1929 was directed towards the evolution of retractable landing gear for US Naval aircraft. In one direction this took practical form in the little FF-1 fighter (see page 20). Another aspect of the same approach led to the evolution of amphibious aircraft, through the development of an aircraft float which incorporated a fully-retractable wheel landing gear. Leroy Grumman had formerly been an associate of Grover Loening, and the OL types produced by the latter's company (see previous description) typified the earlier work in this field which Grumman had carried out. After forming his own company, Grumman began the development of a new observation/utility amphibian which materialised as the XJF-1 prototype, flown for the first time on 4 May 1933 and powered by a 700hp Pratt & Whitney Twin Wasp Junior radial engine. Twenty-seven production JF-1s were ordered shortly afterward, these having R-1830-62 Twin Wasp engines and an enclosed cockpit for the 2-man crew. The first deliveries of JF-1s were made in mid-1934 to US Navy Squadron VS-3 in the aircraft carrier USS *Lexington*. Intended originally for utility and communications duties, the JF-1s eventually found themselves employed on a range of tasks which included photographic reconnaissance, target towing, ambulance work and rescue. Fourteen aircraft, similar to the JF-1 except

for their internal equipment and 750hp Wright Cyclone engines, were built as JF-2s for the US Coast Guard. One of these aircraft, flown by Cmdr E. F. Stone, set up a new world speed record for amphibious aircraft of 191.796mph (308.665km/hr) on 21 December 1934. Five Cyclone-engined aircraft were acquired by the US Navy as JF-3s, one JF-2 was supplied to the US Marine Corps, and eight similar aircraft were sold to the Argentine Navy. An improved model of the JF design appeared in 1935. First flown on 25 June of that year, this was known as the J2F-1 and was later given the name Duck officially. Improvements were primarily directed towards specific use of the Duck from aircraft carriers of the US Fleet, and included the provision of catapult points and deck arrester gear. The US Navy purchased twenty J2F-1s, which were powered by Cyclone engines. Successive orders for later models, differing in minor detail only, included twenty-one J2F-2s, twenty J2F-3s and thirty-two J2F-4s. A major external change – the long chord NACA-type cowling for the 850hp Cyclone engine – was evident in the next model, the J2F-5, of which one hundred and forty-four were ordered early in 1941. Grumman factories were from then onward fully occupied in building the F4F fighter, but a further three hundred and thirty Ducks, with the Grumman-style designation J2F-6, were manufactured during 1939-45 by the Columbia Aircraft Corporation with 900hp Cyclone engines.

Curtiss SBC Helldiver

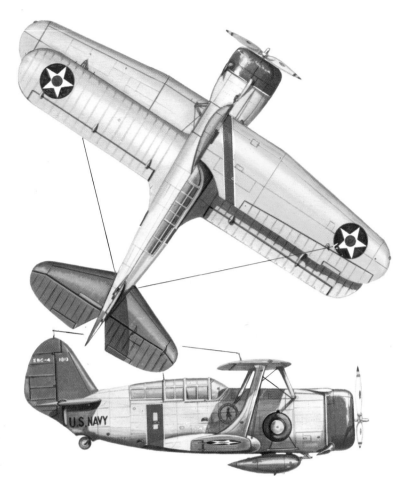

Curtiss SBC-4 Helldiver of the US Navy, USS
Enterprise autumn 1939

Span: 34ft 0in (10.36m)
Length: 27ft 6¾in (8.40m)
Weight: 7,141lb (3,239kg)
Engine: 1×950hp Wright R-1820-34
    Cyclone 9-cyl radial
Max speed: 237mph (381kmh)
Operational ceiling: 27,300ft (9,144m)
Range: 555 miles (893km)
Armament: 2×0.30in machine-guns
Max bomb load: 1,000lb (454kg)

Aviation history records very few examples indeed of a biplane developed from an original monoplane design, but one such was the Curtiss SBC carrier-based scout bomber, which had its origins in the parasol-winged XF12C-1 fighter prototype produced by Curtiss to a 1932 Navy contract. It was first flown in the autumn of 1933, becoming redesignated XS4C-1 in the scout category at the end of that year and XSBC-1 for the scout-bomber role in January 1934. Dive-bombing trials in the following September proved the parasol-wing layout to be unsatisfactory and a second prototype, a biplane, was ordered in April 1935. This machine (BuAer number 9225) was designated XSBC-2 and made its first flight on 9 December 1935, being almost completely redesigned from the original fighter prototype. Its experimental two-row Whirlwind engine was later replaced by an R-1535-82 Wasp, gaining it yet another change of designation to XSBC-3, and in virtually unchanged form this was ordered into production in August 1936. The first of eighty-three SBC-3s were delivered to US Navy Squadron VS-5 in July 1937; they later served also with VS-3 and VS-6, and sixty-nine were still on strength at the time of Pearl Harbor.

Meanwhile, Curtiss had fitted a single-row Cyclone in the final SBC-3, which thus became the XSBC-4 and prototype for the major production version of this Helldiver family. Delivery began in March 1939 of an initial order for fifty-eight SBC-4s, and in June 1940 fifty USN Helldivers were diverted in partial fulfilment of a French order for ninety Curtiss Model 77s (export equivalent of the SBC-4). Forty-four of these were embarked in the French aircraft *Béarn,* which had sailed for France just before news of France's surrender reached America. The carrier put in at Martinique, where the aircraft were put ashore and left to deteriorate in the open. Five other Model 77s found their way to the UK, where the RAF gave them the name Cleveland, but they were not used operationally. Production of SBC-4s continued for the US Navy, the overall total built of this version reaching one hundred and seventy-five by April 1940. In December 1941 the USN had a hundred and seventeen SBC-4s on strength; they equipped, *inter alia,* Marine Squadron VMO-151 and two USN squadrons in USS *Hornet* (VB-8 and VS-8), and were the last combat biplanes to be manufactured in the USA.

Curtiss P-36/Hawk 75

Curtiss P-36C of the 27th Pursuit Sqdn, USAAC, in colours adopted for 1936 'War Games'

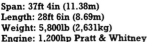

Span: 37ft 4in (11.38m)
Length: 28ft 6in (8.69m)
Weight: 5,800lb (2,631kg)
Engine: 1,200hp Pratt & Whitney
    R-1830-17 Twin Wasp 14-cyl radial
Max speed: 311mph (500kmh) at 10,000ft
    (3,050m)
Operational ceiling: 33,700ft (10,270m)
Range: 820 miles (1,320km)
Armament: 1×0.50in and 0.30in machine-
guns

The Curtiss Hawk monoplane fighter was one of four contenders for a 1935 USAAC design competition. Its design, as the Curtiss Model 75, had begun in 1934, the prototype aircraft (X17Y) first flying in May 1935, the month planned for holding the USAAC competition, but none of the other contenders was ready and it was deferred. Improvements in all candidates were recommended after initial evaluation, the Curtiss design re-emerging as the Model 75B with modified cockpit and tail surfaces and a Wright Cyclone in place of the R-1760 fitted originally. Although the Seversky SEV-1XP fighter was the competition winner, three variants of the Curtiss 75B, with Twin Wasp engines, were ordered for trials, designated Y1P-36. Evaluation of these after their delivery in February 1937 led to a substantial production order for one hundred and seventy-seven P-36As and thirty-one P-36Cs, the latter having two additional wing guns and different variant of Twin Wasp engine. Deliveries to the USAAC began in April 1938. P-36s remained in US operational service into World War 2; a few, indeed, were engaged against the Japanese force that attacked Pearl Harbor on 7 December 1941. A novel feature of the P-36 was its method of landing gear retraction whereby the main wheel legs pivoted to enable the wheels to lie flat in the wings. Curtiss produced a simplified model for export in 1937, having an 875hp Wright Cyclone engine and a faired, non-retractable landing gear. Presentation of the prototype to the Chinese Air Force was followed by an order for one hundred and twelve similar aircraft, designated Hawk 75M and delivered in 1938; twenty-five generally similar 75Ns were built for Thailand, and thirty 75Os for the Argentine Air Force; the FMA factory in Argentina built a further one hundred of this model. Exports were also made of retractable-undercarriage models. The first orders came from France, which from May 1938 placed orders totalling seven hundred for Hawk 75A series fighters with revised armament, some with Twin Wasp and some with Cyclone engines. Delivery was still incomplete when France surrendered in June 1940, and the remaining aircraft were diverted to serve the RAF, which named them Mohawk. Other 75A series Hawks were ordered by Iran (ten with Cyclone engines), Norway (twenty-four Twin Wasp Hawks and thirty-six with Cyclones) and the Netherlands (thirty-five Cyclone Hawks), and HAL in India built five under licence. The German invasion interrupted deliveries of the Norwegian Hawks, and twenty-four of the Dutch aircraft were diverted to the Netherlands East Indies, where they fought against the Japanese in the Pacific war.

Kellett KD-1

Kellett KD-1B of Eastern Air Lines Inc, July 1939

Rotor Diameter: 40ft 0in (12.19m)
Length: 28ft 10in (8.79m)
Weight: 2,250lb (1,020kg)
Engine: 1×225hp Jacobs L-4MA 7-cyl radial
Max speed: 127mph (204kmh)
Operational ceiling: 14,000ft (4,267m)
Range: 200 miles (322km)

The products of the Kellett Autogiro Corporation, formed in 1929, showed strongly the influence of the early Cierva Autogiros, for which the American company held a manufacturing licence. Kellett's first Autogiro was the 2-seat K-2 of 1931, but its best-known design was the KD-1 which first appeared in late 1934. This was a direct control Autogiro (hence the D in the designation) and was also a 2-seater, the cockpits in this case being open and placed in tandem. The pylon for the 3-blade main rotor was situated immediately in front of the forward cockpit, and the blades could be folded back over the fuselage. Standard powerplant for the KD-1A production version was the 225hp Jacobs L-4MA radial engine, the torque from which was corrected by giving the port and starboard tailplane halves opposing incidence. On 19 May 1939 a single-seat converted KD-1A, still with an open cockpit, carried out a demonstration flight from the centre of Washington to the city's Hoover Airport with a cargo of mail. Two months later, on 6 July, a similar aircraft in Eastern Air Lines colours and with an enclosed cockpit (see illustration) commenced the first-ever scheduled air mail service by a rotary-winged aeroplane, between the Philadelphia Post Office and Camden Airport, New Jersey. This version of the Autogiro was known as the KD-1B, and it continued to operate the service for about 12 months. In 1935 the US Army Air Corps acquired one KD-1A for trials, giving it the designation YG-1. Subsequently it received one YG-1A, seven YG-1Bs and seven XO-60s. One of the YG-1Bs was converted to YG-1C and

later to XR-2 with a 330hp Jacobs L-6 engine, and another to XR-3 with a new rotor mounting after the XR-2 had suffered destruction due to ground resonance troubles. The XO-60 (later YO-60) was a further development in which the chief differences were a 300hp Jacobs R-915-3 engine, a bulged Perspex cabin enclosure and observation windows in the fuselage floor. Because of the advent of successful helicopter designs, notably those of Sikorsky, further military development of the YO-60 was discontinued after 1943. The Japanese government, after acquiring and testing a KD-1A in 1939, turned the aircraft over to the Kayaba Industrial Co, which subsequently built a version of the aircraft powered by a 240hp Kobe-built version of the German Argus As 10C engine and known as the Ka-1; the first Ka-1 was flown on 26 May 1941 and eventually some two hundred and forty aircraft of this type were built. They were employed during World War 2 by the Imperial Japanese Army for 2-seat artillery observation and co-operation duties, and by the Navy for single-seat coastal or carrier-based anti-submarine patrol carrying two 60kg (132lb) bombs or depth charges. One Ka-1 was modified for trials with small auxiliary rockets at the tips of the rotor blades, and another was redesignated Ka-2 after refitting with a 240hp Jacobs L-4MA-7 engine. Some fifteen years after the end of World War 2 the KD-1A design was resurrected and offered as a production Autogiro, either in its original open-cockpit form or with a YO-60 type cabin hood and a fully-cowled Jacobs R-775-9 of 225hp.

Sikorsky VS-300

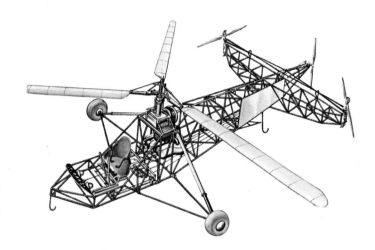

Sikorsky VS-300 in mid-1940 configuration *(top)* with 90hp Franklin horizontally-opposed engine and *(bottom)* in early 1942 configuration with 150hp Franklin. Data apply to latter version

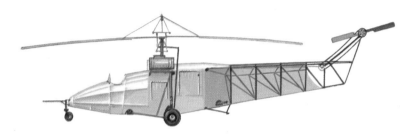

Rotor Diameter: 30ft 0in (9.14m)
Length: 28ft 0in (8.53m)
Weight: 1,150lb (522kg)
Max speed: 50mph (80kmh)
Range: 75 miles (121km)

Russian-born Igor Sikorsky built his first helicopter, powered by a 25hp Anzani engine, in 1909. It would not leave the ground, and a second machine, completed in 1910, was little better; it did rise a short distance, but was incapable of lifting a pilot, and Sikorsky turned his attention to fixed-wing aeroplanes. After the 1917 Revolution he left the country, settling in the United States some two years later, and soon entering the aircraft industry of his new country. In 1938, when he was Engineering Manager of the Vought-Sikorsky Division of United Aircraft Corporation, years of study and research into rotary-wing flight problems were rewarded when the directors of UAC agreed to let him try once again to build a practical helicopter. The VS-300, as the project was named, was designed during the spring and built during the summer of 1939, and on 14 September Sikorsky was at the controls when the aircraft made its first vertical take-off. At this stage the aircraft was still tethered to the ground and had weights suspended underneath it to help keep it stable. It was powered by a 4-cylinder Lycoming engine of 75hp, had full cyclic pitch control for the 28ft (8.53m) diameter main rotor and a single anti-torque tail rotor at the end of a narrow enclosed tailboom which also supported a large underfin. The cyclic control was not fully satisfactory, however, and was temporarily discarded. By the time the VS-300 made its first free flight on 13 May 1940 (then powered by a 90hp Franklin motor) the configuration had changed to an open-framework steel-tube fuselage with outriggers at the tail end. Each of these mounted a 6ft 8in (2.03m) diameter horizontally-

rotating airscrew to provide better lateral control; the vertical tail screw was retained. By mid-1940 the VS-300 was staying airborne for 15 min at a time, and on 6 May 1941 it beat the world endurance record held by the Fw 61 by staying aloft for 1 hr 32 min 26.1 sec. Various modifications were made during 1940-41, the most important being the restoration of a cyclic pitch control system and the replacement of the tail outriggers in June 1941 by a short vertical pylon carrying a single horizontal tail rotor, and the reinstatement in December of a now fully satisfactory cyclic pitch control for the main rotor. Other alterations concerned the arrangement of the main undercarriage and the fitting of nose and tail wheels in place of skids. In April 1941 Sikorsky made a successful take-off from water by fitting pneumatic flotation bags under the main undercarriage wheels. In its final form the VS-300 had a 150hp Franklin engine, a fabric-covered fuselage and a tricycle undercarriage. Testing continued throughout 1942 (by which time development of Sikorsky's first production helicopter, the R-4, was well advanced), and in 1943 the VS-300 was delivered to the Henry Ford Museum in Dearborn, Michigan, where it is still housed today. The first practical helicopters, in the sense that they accomplished satisfactorily manoeuvres that we now take for granted – vertical take-off and landing, hovering, and forward, backward and sideways flight – were the Breguet-Dorand and the Fw 61. The VS-300 accomplished more, by paving the way for production aircraft that could carry a useful load and perform a productive job of work.

Fairchild PT-19

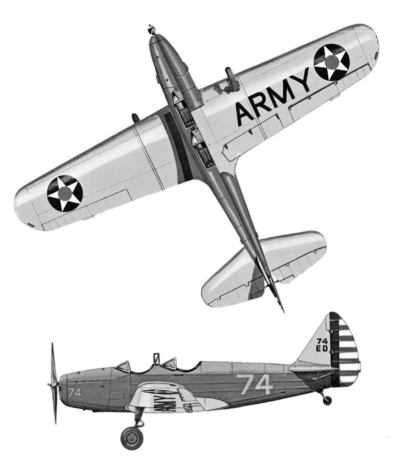

Fairchild PT-19A of the USAAF, *circa* 1941-42

Span: 35ft 11⅛in (10.97m)
Length: 28ft 0in (8.53m)
Weight: 2,545lb (1154kg)
Engine: 1×200hp Ranger L-440-3
　　inverted in-line
Max speed: 132mph (212kmh)
Operational ceiling: 15,300ft (4,663m)
Range: 430 miles (692km)

Originating as the Fairchild M-62, this monoplane primary trainer was a contemporary of the Boeing-Stearman Kaydet biplane, and was ultimately built in almost as a great a quantity. First purchases were made in 1940 as part of the US Army Air Corps expansion programme, the initial model having open tandem cockpits and a 175hp Ranger L-440-1 engine. Two hundred and seventy-five of this model, designated PT-19, were delivered during FY 1940. Mass production then began in 1941 of three thousand one hundred and eighty-one PT-19As, with 200hp L-440-3 engines, by Fairchild, with an additional four hundred and seventy-seven by Aeronca and forty-four by the St Louis Aircraft Corporation. Nine hundred and seventeen PT-19Bs, built by Fairchild and Aeronca, differed only in being equipped for blind-flying training and having a collapsible canvas hood for the front cockpit. The PT-23, introduced to avoid delays in the supply

of sufficient Ranger engines, was essentially the same airframe mounting an uncowled Continental R-670 engine of 220hp. Eight hundred and sixty-nine PT-23s were completed by Aeronca, Fairchild, Howard Aircraft Corporation and St Louis in the USA and by Fleet Aircraft Corporation in Canada. Howard and St Louis also produced two hundred and fifty-six PT-23As with blind-flying equipment. For use in Canada in the Empire Air Training Scheme, a variant of the PT-19A was evolved with a fully-enclosed canopy for the two occupants. Fairchild contributed six hundred and seventy, with L-440-3 engines, to the RCAF under Lend-Lease, and production of eight hundred and seven PT-26As and two hundred and fifty PT-26Bs by Fleet, with L-440-7 engines, was also financed by US funds. The Canadian-built PT-26 and PT-26A aircraft were designated Cornell I and II, and were used at RAF flying schools in Southern Rhodesia as well as in Canada.

Coronado

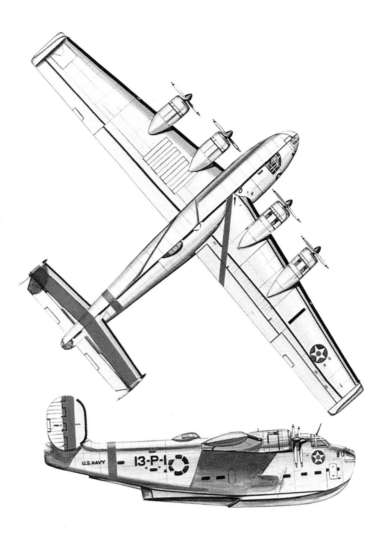

Consolidated PB2Y-2 Coronado of US Navy
Squadron UP-13, *circa* 1941

Span: 115ft 0in (35.05m)
Length: 79ft 0in (24.08m)
Weight: 60,441lb (27,416kg)
Engines: 4×1,200hp Pratt & Whitney
R-1830-78 Twin Wasp 14-cyl radials
Max speed: 255mph (410kmh)
Operational ceiling: 24,100ft (7,346m)
Range: 3705 miles (5,963km)

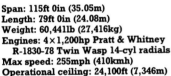

The Coronado resulted from a requirement drawn up by the US Navy in 1936 for a long-range maritime reconnaissance flying-boat, powered by four engines and having a performance and load-carrying capability even greater than that of the twin-engined PBY which was then in production. Two American manufacturers, Consolidated and Sikorsky, submitted prototype designs (XPB2Y-1 and XPBS-1 respectively) to meet this requirement, of which the former made its first flight on 17 December 1937. Powered by 1,050hp Pratt & Whitney XR-1830-72 Twin Wasp engines, the XPB2Y-1 incorporated a number of PBY design features, notably its all-metal construction and retractable wing-tip floats. The deep, capacious two-step hull could accommodate a 10-man crew, and a maximum bomb load of 12,000lb (5,443kg) could be carried. Defensive armament comprised single 0.50in guns in the bow turret and tail, and a pair of 0.30in guns firing laterally from hatches amidships. Development flying was somewhat prolonged, mainly due to the pronounced lateral instability of the original design. Attempts to rectify this resulted first in oval auxiliary fins to supplement the original single fin and rudder, then in the adoption of twin endplate fins and rudders of circular shape. Other modifications to the prototype included doubling the distance between the first and second steps of the hull. By the time that the US Navy orderd six PB2Y-2 production aircraft in March 1939 Consolidated had made further extensive redesigns. The circular fins and rudders were replaced by broad-oval units similar to those of

the B-24 Liberator, the hull had been made considerably deeper and the original step beneath the bow turret had been eliminated in a new, smoothly-contoured nose design incorporating a ball-type turret. The number of crew members was decreased by one, despite an increase in the armament to a total of six 0.50in guns. Deliveries of the PB2Y, to Squadron VP-13, began on 31 December 1940, these aircraft being used primarily for experimental work. In November 1940 an initial order was placed for the PB2Y-3 model, for which the sixth PB2Y-2 was modified to serve as prototype. Principal changes were the substitution of 1,200hp R-1830-38 engines, addition of two more 0.50in guns, and the provision of self-sealing fuel tanks and armour protection for the crew which raised the gross weight to 68,000lb (30,844kg). The PB2Y-3 remained in production until the autumn of 1943, by which time two hundred and ten of this model had been built. Ten of these, designated PB2Y-3B, were supplied under Lend-Lease to the RAF; intended originally for use by Coastal Command, they were actually employed as freighters by No 231 Squadron of Transport Command. The USN designation PB2Y-3R was applied to thirty-one other Coronados converted in the USA as 44-seat unarmed transports with 1,200hp R-1830-92 'low altitude' engines. Some PB2Y-3s in service as maritime reconnaissance-bombers were equipped with ASV radar in a fairing just behind the pilots' cabin, but during 1944 the Coronado began to be replaced in the patrol role by Navy Liberator landplanes.

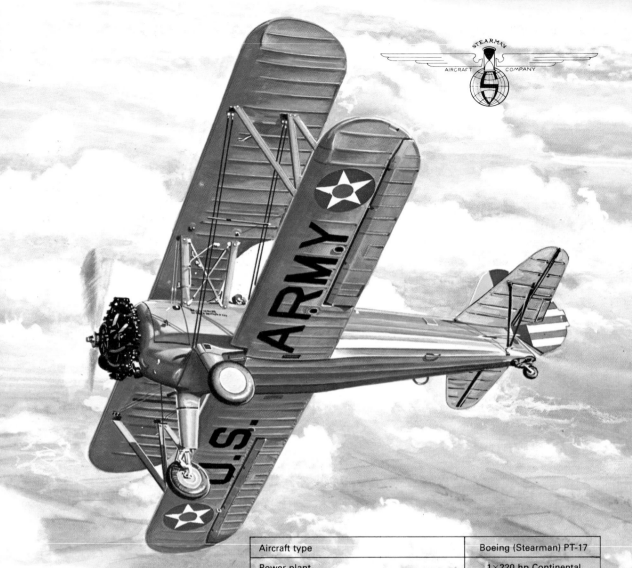

Boeing (Stearman) PT-13 Kaydet of the USAAC
in standard early-war trainer colours

Aircraft type		Boeing (Stearman) PT-17
Power plant		1×220 hp Continental R-670-5
Accommodation		2
Wing span	m : ft in	9·80 : 32 2
Length overall	m : ft in	7·54 : 24 9
Height overall	m : ft in	2·95 : 9 8
Wing area	m² : sq ft	27·68 : 298·0
Weight empty	kg : lb	876 : 1,931
Weight loaded	kg : lb	1,195 : 2,635
Max wing loading	kg/m² : lb/sq ft	43·15 : 8·84
Max power loading	kg/hp : lb/hp	5·43 : 11·98
Max level speed	km/h : mph	217 : 135
at (height)	m : ft	S/L
Cruising speed	km/h : mph	154 : 96
Time to 3,050 m (10,000 ft)		17·3 min
Service ceiling	m : ft	4,025 : 13,200
Endurance		approx 4 hr

15102	33538	37056
30109	37875	35044

Douglas XSB2D/BTD Destroyer

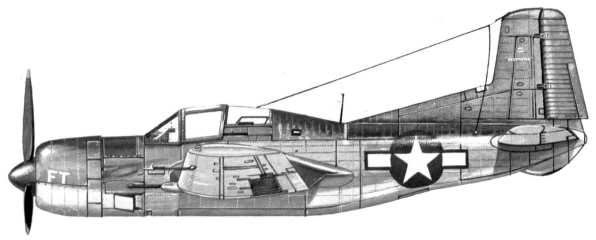

Pre-production Douglas BTD-1 Destroyer, 1944

Aircraft type		Douglas BTD-1
Power plant		1×2,300 hp Wright R-3350-14
Accommodation		1
Wing span	m : ft in	13·72 : 45 0
Length overall	m : ft in	11·76 : 38 7
Height overall	m : ft in	4·14 : 13 7
Wing area	m² : sq ft	34·65 : 373·0
Weight empty	kg : lb	5,851 : 12,900
Weight loaded (max)	kg : lb	8,618 : 19,000
Max wing loading	kg/m² : lb/sq ft	248·78 : 50·94
Max power loading	kg/hp : lb/hp	3·75 : 8·26
Max level speed	km/h : mph	554 : 344
at (height)	m : ft	4,910 : 16,100
Cruising speed	km/h : mph	303 : 188
S/L rate of climb	m/min : ft/min	503 : 1,650
Service ceiling	m : ft	7,195 : 23,600
Range (with torpedo)	km : miles	2,382 : 1,480

Two XSB2D-1 prototype two-seat carrier-borne attack bombers were ordered in June 1941, the first being flown on 8 April 1943. Modified as prototypes for the BTD-1 Destroyer single-seat torpedo-bomber, their dorsal and ventral remotely-controlled gun barbettes were removed, leaving only the two wing-mounted 20mm cannon. The internal weapons bay held two torpedos or up to 3,200lb (1,451kg) of bombs. Thirteen pre-production and fifteen production BTD-1s were built, being delivered from June 1944 to October 1945; a further three hundred and thirty were cancelled. Two became XBTD-2 prototypes for the BT2D, better known as the AD Skyraider.

Mitchell

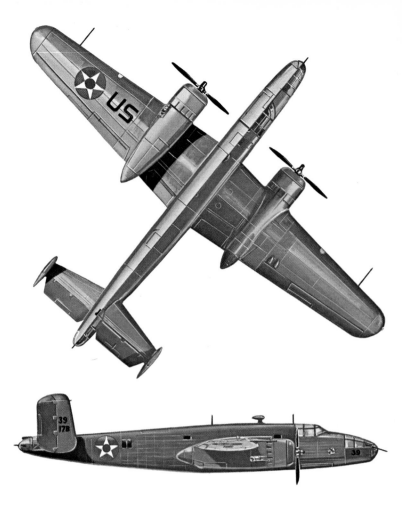

North American B-25A of the 34th Bomber Squadron, 17th Bombardment Group USAAC, summer 1941

Span: 67ft 7in (20.60m)
Length: 54ft 1in (16.48m)
Weight: 27,100lb (12,292kg)
Engines: 2×1,700hp Wright R-2600-9 Cyclone radials
Max speed: 315mph (507kmh)
Operational ceiling: 27,000ft (8,230m)
Range: 1,350 miles (2,173)
Armament: 1×0.50in and 3×0.30in machine-guns
Max bomb load: 3,000lb (1361kg)

North American Aviation was awarded an immediate production contract for its NA-62 design, without the usual preliminary protypes, and the first B-25 was flown on 19 August 1940. By the end of the year twenty-four had been delivered, all except the first nine having the gull-winged appearance that was a characteristic of the bomber. They were followed in 1941 by forty B-25As, then by one hundred and nineteen B-25s with dorsal and ventral gun turrets. First operational unit was the 17th Bombardment Group, which began to receive its B-25s in 1941. Production continued with one thousand six hundred and nineteen B-25Cs and two thousand two hundred and ninety B-25Ds from early 1942, and in April that year B-25Bs flying off the USS *Hornet* made their epic raid on Tokyo. The B-25E and F were experimental models, production continuing with the B-25G, which carried two 0.50in guns alongside a 75mm cannon in a new 'solid' nose. Four hundred and five B-25Gs were built, and a hundred and seventy-five earlier Mitchells were modified to carry a total of ten 0.50in guns. An even more heavily armed 'gunship'

was the B-25H, one thousand of which were produced with the 75mm nose cannon and fourteen 0.50in guns; this entered operational service in February 1944, joining the earlier multi gunned Mitchells on anti-shipping strikes in the Pacific battle areas. Final production model, the B-25J (four thousand three hundred and eighteen built), reverted to the standard bomber nose, but retained the forward placing of the dorsal turret introduced on the H model. Mitchells in US service operated predominantly in the Pacific war zone, but large numbers were supplied elsewhere during the war. Two hundred and forty-eight B-25Hs and four hundred and fifty-eight B-25Js were transferred to the US Navy from 1943 as PBJ-1Hs and -1Js, most being operated by Marine Corps squadrons. Eight hundred and seventy Mitchells of various models were supplied to the USSR under Lend-Lease; twenty-three Mitchell Is (B-26B) and five hundred and thirty-eight Mitchell IIs (B-25C and D) were received by the RAF; and others were supplied to Brazil (twenty-nine), China (one hundred and thirty-one) and the Netherlands (two hundred and forty-nine).

Grumman F4F Wildcat

Grumman F4F-3 Wildcat of VF-8, US Navy, USS *Hornet,* late 1941

Span: 38ft 0in (11.58m)
Length: 28ft 9in (8.76m)
Weight, normal take-off: 7,002lb
(3,176kg)
Engine: 1,200hp Pratt & Whitney
R-1830-76 Twin Wasp 14-cyl radial
Max speed: 330mph (531kmh)
Operational ceiling: 37,500ft (11,430m)
Range, normal: 845 miles (1,360km)
Armament: 4×0.50in M-Z Browning
machine-guns
Max bomb load: 200lb (96kg)

Originally, the Grumman proposals which won a 1936 USN development contract were for a biplane carrier fighter based on its earlier successful biplane types but this design, the XF4F-1, was shelved in favour of a monoplane fighter. The prototype, the XF4F-2, was flown on 2 September 1937 powered by a 1,050hp R-1830-66 Twin Wasp engine. The Navy decided to develop this still further, by ordering it to be rebuilt in a much-redesigned form as the XF4F-3, with an improved, supercharged XR-1830-76 engine. This aircraft flew on 12 February 1939, and was followed six months later by an initial production order for the F4F-3. Eventually, two hundred and eighty-five F4F-3s were built. Deliveries to the USN late in 1940 were preceded by an order from France for one hundred G-36A fighters, the export designation of the F4F-3 when fitted with a 1,200hp Wright R-1820-G205A engine. This order, later reduced to eighty-one, was diverted to Britain in mid-1940 after the fall of France, these aircraft and nine others being employed by the FAA under the title Martlet Mk I; thirty G-36As, ordered by Greece, were also diverted to Britain to become Martlet Mk IIIs. Neither the F4F-3 nor the Martlet Mk I

had wing-folding, but this feature was incorporated in all but the first ten of an order for one hundred Martlet Mk II (G-36B) fighters placed by Britain in 1940. (The other ten corresponded to the USNs sixty-five F4F-3As, having non-folding wings and R-1830-90 engines). The USNs first folding-wing Wildcat was the Twin Wasp-engined F4F-4, Grumman building 1,389, including two hundred and twenty F4F-4Bs with Cyclone engines as Martlet Mk IVs for the FAA. The Eastern Aircraft Division of General Motors delivered eight hundred and thirty-eight similar but four-gunned aircraft, designated FM-1, to the USN and two hundred and twenty-two to the FAA as Martlet Mk Vs. Eastern also built the FM-2, production version of Grumman's XF4F-8, with a 1,200hp Wright R-1820-56 Cyclone engine and taller fin and rudder. The USN received 4,407 and the FAA three hundred and seventy; the latter's were designated Wildcat Mk VI, the FAA having by now adopted the US name. Grumman's final production version (twenty-one built) was the F4F-7, a heavier and slower unarmed version, with fixed wings, extra fuel and photo-reconnaissance cameras.

Bell P-39 Airacobra

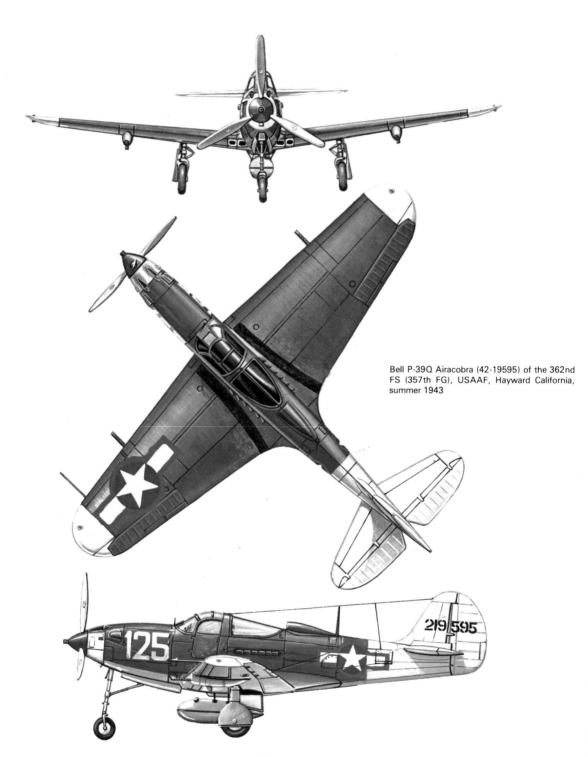

Bell P-39Q Airacobra (42-19595) of the 362nd
FS (357th FG), USAAF, Hayward California,
summer 1943

Aircraft type		Bell P-39D	Bell P-39N	Bell P-39Q
Power plant		1×1,150 hp* Allison V-1710-35	1×1,200 hp Allison V-1710-85	1×1,200 hp Allison V-1710-85
Accommodation		1	1	1
Wing span	m : ft in	10·36 : 34 0	10·36 : 34 0	10·36 : 34 0
Length overall	m : ft in	9·19 : 30 2	9·19 : 30 2	9·19 : 30 2
Height overall	m : ft in	3·61 : 11 10	3·78 : 12 5	3·78 : 12 5
Wing area	m² : sq ft	19·79 : 213·0	19·79 : 213·0	19·79 : 213·0
Weight empty	kg : lb	2,477 : 5,462	2,566 : 5,657	2,560 : 5,645
Weight loaded (max)	kg : lb	3,719 : 8,200	3,719 : 8,200	3,765 : 8,300
Max wing loading	kg/m² : lb/sq ft	187·88 : 38·50	187·88 : 38·50	190·17 : 38·97
Max power loading	kg/hp : lb/hp	3·23 : 7·13	3·10 : 6·83	3·14 : 6·92
Max level speed	km/h : mph	592 : 368	642 : 399	620 : 385
at (height)	m : ft	4,205 : 13,800	2,955 : 9,700	3,355 : 11,000
Time to 4,570 m (15,000 ft)		5·7 min	3·8 min	4·5 min
Service ceiling	m : ft	9,785 : 32,100	11,735 : 38,500	10,670 : 35,000
Range (with 500 lb bomb)	km : miles	1,287 : 800	1,207 : 750	1,046 : 650

*at 4,205 m (13,800 ft)

Demonstration of a 37mm cannon led Bell's design team to develop a fighter to utilise this weapon. The cannon, firing through the propeller hub, dictated its configuration: the power-plant in the mid-fuselage aft of the cockpit, the propeller driven via an extension shaft. Tricycle-type landing gear was used for the first time on a USAAC single-engine fighter. An XP-39 prototype, order on 7 October 1937, first flew on 6 April 1938. A low-wing monoplane, it was powered by a 1,150hp Allison V-1710-17 engine with turbocharger. Additional firepower was provided by two 0.50in synchronised guns in the nose. Orders followed for twelve YP-39s, and one YP-39A without turbocharger. NACA evaluated the XP-39, recommending deletion of the turbocharger, resiting of engine air intake and coolant radiators, and introduction of main landing gear doors and a lower-profile canopy. The modified prototype became the XP-39B, the thirteen trials aircraft conforming except for 1,090hp V-1710-37 engines and two 0.30in guns added in the nose. On 10 August 1939, eighty were ordered as P-45, later becoming P-39. Deliveries began in January 1941. The first twenty P-39Cs were similar to YP-39s; the remaining sixty were delivered as P-39Ds, with the two 0.30in nose guns deleted and replaced by four 0.30in wing guns, self-sealing fuel tanks introduced, plus under-fuselage provisions for a 500lb bomb or seventy-five US gallon (284 litre) drop-tank. Production of P-39Ds totalled eight hundred and sixty-three, some with armament variations. Production of two hundred and twenty-nine P-39Fs followed, these differing only by a change from Curtiss to Aeroproducts propellers; twenty-five similar aircraft with 1,100hp V-1710-59 engines were designated P-39J. P-39K production totalled two hundred and ten; they had a 1,325hp V-1710-63 engine with Aeroproducts propeller. The two hundred and fifty P-39Ls which followed substituted a Curtiss propeller; and P-39Ms (two hundred and forty built) had 1,200hp V-1710-83 engines with larger diameter propellers. Major production centred on the P-39N (2,095 built) and P-39Q (4,905), a large proportion of which were supplied to Russia under Lend-Lease. The former had 1,200hp V-1710-85 engines, and less fuel capacity and armour to provide better rate of climb and speed. The P-39Qs retained the same engine, but the standard wing guns were deleted and replaced by two 0.50in guns, one in a small fairing beneath each wing. Throughout the long production run of P-39Qs there were some variations in armament, armour, fuel capacity, and propellers. Under Lend-Lease Russia received some 4,900 P-39s of various versions. A British Purchasing Commission also order six hundred and seventy-five export Bell Model 14s, similar to P-39Ds, but only the RAF's No 601 Squadron used these aircraft: about eighty were received by the RAF; some two hundred and twelve diverted to Russia; and the balance was acquired by the USAAF (about two hundred in the USA and two hundred in Britain), designated P-400. Variants included three XP-39Es, with laminar flow square-tip wings, redesigned tail unit, and 1,325hp V-1710-47 engines, and a small number of two-seat trainer conversions as TP-39F and RP-39Q.

Boeing B-17 Flying Fortress

First of 512 B-17Es, in flight near Seattle

Chin turret of the B-17G

This B-17F got back to base after colliding with a BF109 over North Africa

During 1934-35 Boeing built as a private venture a prototype multi-engine bomber to meet a USAAC requirement. This was expected to carry a 2,000lb (907kg) bomb load over ranges of up to 2,200 miles (3,540km) at speeds of 200-250mph (322-402km/h). This was then a somewhat daunting requirement, and Boeing chose to interpret multi-engine as a four-engine powerplant. When the prototype was rolled out on 16 July 1935, its size and appearance excited the Press, one newsman introducing his article with the headline '15-ton Flying Fortress'. Boeing was to register this name for the new bomber, highlighting its procurement as a mobile flying fortress to defend America's coastline. This apparently inexplicable role for a strategic bomber resulted from Army versus Navy politics, which made it necessary for the USAAF to acquire the bomber it needed by such devious means. The Model 299 flew for the first time on 28 July 1935, and just over three weeks later was flown 2,100 miles (3,380km) non-stop to Wright Field, Ohio. Less than three months later came the news that it had crashed on take-off during its test programme, but the aircraft was exonerated from blame when it was discovered that take-off had been attempted with the controls locked. A cantilever low-wing monoplane with retractable tailwheel-type landing gear, the prototype was powered by four 750hp Pratt & Whitney R-1690-E radial engines. Its defensive armament of five machine-guns was far from that of a 'flying fortress', but the bomb bay could accommodate up to 4,800lb (2,177kg). Initial orders covered thirteen YB-17s (later Y1B-17s) and one example for static

testing. The first of these, powered by 930hp Wright GR-1820-39 radials, flew on 2 December 1936. It had accommodation for a crew of nine, and minor changes in detail. All thirteen were delivered between January and August 1937. One survived without damage the turbulence of a violent storm, which suggested that static testing was superfluous, and the airframe built for this purpose was completed instead as the Y1B-17A, with 1,000hp GR-1820-51 engines and Moss/General Electric turbochargers. When tested, following a first flight on 29 April 1938, it gave convincing proof of the superior performance of the turbocharged engines, and they were to become standard on future versions. First production contract was for thirty-nine B-17Bs, generally similar to the Y1B-17A, except for a redesigned nose, and all were delivered by March 1940. In 1939 thirty-eight B-17Cs had been ordered, having 1,200hp R-1820-65 engines, seven machine-guns (comprising one 0.30 in gun in the nose and six 0.50in guns, disposed two each in dorsal and ventral and one each in two waist positions), and maximum bomb load of 10,496lb (4,761kg). Twenty of this version were supplied to the RAF in 1941, designated Fortress Mk I, and first used operationally on 8 July 1941. The RAF found that they had some shortcomings, particularly their inadequate defensive armament when intercepted at altitude by Messerschmitt Bf 109s. B-17Ds, of which forty-two were built, differed little from the B-17C, being provided with self-sealing fuel tanks and accommodation for a tenth crew member. The first version built in large numbers (five

Boeing B-17G Flying Fortress (42-38091) in standard Olive Drab Finish

hundred and twelve) was the B-17E, which incorporated modifications based on RAF experience. These included a redesigned tail unit, to improve stability at altitude, and a complete revision of armament to provide a total of one 0.30in and twelve 0.50in machine-guns. B-17Ds and B-17Es were the first to be used operationally by the USAFF in the Pacific and European theatres respectively, the B-17Ds highlighting the need for greater range capability. This and the incorporation of other desirable features led to the B-17F, the first version built in massive quantity, totalling 3,405: Boeing building 2,300, Douglas 605 and Lockheed Vega 500. Initial changes included the introduction of 1,200hp R-1820-97 engines, a frameless transparent nose, and strengthened landing gear, but extra fuel capacity was later provided in the wings, plus external racks for an increased bomb load of 8,000lb (3,630kg) over short ranges. Extensive use of B-17Fs by the US Eighth Air Force in Europe during 1943 brought unacceptably high losses, highlighting the need for long-range fighter escort, and the lack of suitable defence against determined head-on attack. The latter weakness was tackled in the definitive B-17G built by Boeing (4,035), Douglas (2,395) and Lockheed Vega (2,250). This had a chin turret below the nose mounting two 0.50in machine-guns, and all thirteen guns were of this calibre. Later production models also had improved turbochargers which increased the service ceiling to 35,600ft (10,850m). B-17E/F/Gs also served with the RAF as Fortress Mks IIA, II and III respectively.

Aircraft type		Boeing B-17C	Boeing B-17E	Boeing B-17G
Power plant		4×1,200 hp* Wright R-1820-65	4×1,200 hp* Wright R-1820-65	4×1,200 hp* Wright R-1820-97
Accommodation		9	9	9
Wing span	m : ft in	31·62 : 103 9	31·62 : 103 9	31·62 : 103 9
Length overall	m : ft in	20·70 : 67 11	22·50 : 73 10	22·66 : 74 4
Height overall	m : ft in	4·70 : 15 5	5·84 : 19 2	5·82 : 19 1
Wing area	m² : sq ft	131·92 : 1,420·0	131·92 : 1,420·0	131·92 : 1,420·0
Weight empty	kg : lb	12,542 : 27,650	14,628 : 32,250	16,391 : 36,135
Weight loaded (max)	kg : lb	21,160 : 46,650	24,040 : 53,000	29,710 : 65,500
Max wing loading	kg/m² : lb/sq ft	160·32 : 32·85	182·14 : 37·32	225·10 : 46·13
Max power loading	kg/hp : lb/hp	4·41 : 9·72	5·01 : 11·04	6·19 : 13·65
Max level speed	km/h : mph	468 : 291	510 : 317	462 : 287
at (height)	m : ft	7,620 : 25,000	7,620 : 25,000	7,620 : 25,000
Cruising speed	km/h : mph	372 : 231	338 : 210	293 : 182
Time to height		7·1 min to 3,050 m (10,000 ft)	7·0 min to 1,525 m (5,000 ft)	37·0 min to 6,095 m (20,000 ft)
Service ceiling	m : ft	10,975 : 36,000	11,155 : 36,600	10,850 : 35,600
Range	km : miles	3,862 : 2,400**	3,219 : 2,000**	3,219 : 2,000**

*at 7,620 m (25,000 ft) **with 1,814 kg (4,000 lb) bomb load
*at 7,620 m (25,000 ft) **with 1,814 kg (4,000 lb) bomb load
*at 7,620 m (25,000 ft) **with 2,722 kg (6,000 lb) bomb load

Consolidated PB2Y Coronado

Consolidated PB2Y-5 Coronado (BUNO 7162)
of the US Navy, summer 1943

A larger development of the PBY, for long-range patrol, the single-finned prototype XPB2Y-1 first flew on 17 December 1937. The six initial PB2Y-2s had a twin tail unit, uprated R-1830-78 engines and a deeper hull with redesigned planning bottom. Armament comprised six 0.50in machine-guns, two each in nose, tail and beam positions; maximum bomb load was 12,000lb (5,443kg). These were followed by two hundred and ten PB2Y-3s, with self-sealing fuel tanks, two extra 0.50in guns in a dorsal turret and armour protection; ASV radar was installed in some aircraft. Ten became Lend-Lease

PB2Y-3B Coronado Mk Is for RAF Transport Command, serving as freight or passenger transports over the North and South Atlantic. USN Coronados operated mostly on reconnaissance or anti-submarine duties until 1944, but thirty-one unarmed PB2Y-3Rs were converted for low altitude cargo/passenger carrying. Some -3s, fitted with extra fuel tanks and other equipment, were redesignated as PB2Y-5 or -5R patrol bombers (8,000lb: 3,629kg bomb load) or -5H (25-stretcher) ambulances.

Aircraft type		Consolidated PB2Y-3
Power plant		4 × 1,200 hp Pratt & Whitney R-1830-88
Accommodation		10
Wing span	m : ft in	35·05 : 115 0
Length overall	m : ft in	24·16 : 79 3
Height overall	m : ft in	8·38 : 27 6
Wing area	m² : sq ft	165·37 : 1,780·0
Weight empty	kg : lb	18,611 : 41,031
Weight loaded	kg : lb	30,844 : 68,000
Max wing loading	kg/m² : lb/sq ft	186·52 : 38·20
Max power loading	kg/hp : lb/hp	6·43 : 14·17
Max level speed	km/h : mph	360 : 224
at (height)	m : ft	5,945 : 19,500
Cruising speed	km/h : mph	225 : 140
at (height)	m : ft	455 : 1,500
S/L rate of climb	m/min : ft/min	168 : 550
Service ceiling	m : ft	6,370 : 20,900
Range	km : miles	2,211 : 1,380

Vought OS2U Kingfisher

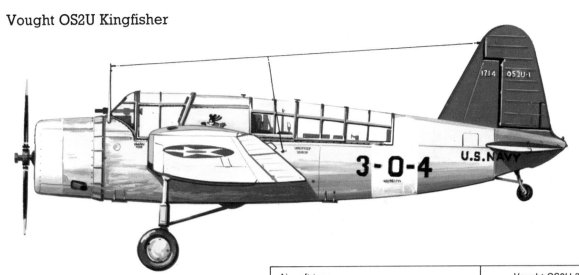

Vought OS2U-1 (BUNO 1714) of VO-3, US Navy, USS *Mississippi,* early 1941

Emblem on a VO-3 section leaders OS2U-1

Aircraft type		Vought OS2U-3*
Power plant		1×450 hp Pratt & Whitney R-985-AN-2 or -8
Accommodation		2
Wing span	m : ft in	10·94 : 35 10⅞
Length overall	m : ft in	10·31 : 33 10
Height overall	m : ft in	4·61 : 15 1½
Wing area	m² : sq ft	24·34 : 262·0
Weight empty	kg : lb	1,870 : 4,123
Weight loaded	kg : lb	2,722 : 6,000
Max wing loading	kg/m² : lb/sq ft	111·76 : 22·90
Max power·loading	kg/hp : lb/hp	6·05 : 13·33
Max level speed	km/h : mph	264 : 164
at (height)	m : ft	1,675 : 5,500
Cruising speed	km/h : mph	192 : 119
at (height)	m : ft	1,525 : 5,000
Time to 1,525 m (5,000 ft)		12·1 min
Service ceiling	m : ft	3,960 : 13,000
Range	km : miles	1,296 : 805

*floatplane version

A production total of more than 1,500 made the Kingfisher the most widely used Observation-Scout type used by the US Navy during World War 2, and it was operable as either a landplane or (more usually) a floatplane. The XOS2U-1 prototype was ordered by the US Navy in March 1937, and flew for the first time on 20 July 1938. With a different variant of R-985 engine and minor improvements to the float attachments, it entered production as the OS2U-1, joining USN service in the late summer of 1940. Fifty-four of this model were followed by one hundred and fifty-eight OS2U-2s, which were generally similar except for minor engine and equipment changes. The major version – 1,006 were built by

Vought – was the OS2U-3, with self-sealing fuel tanks, armour protection for the crew, another minor engine change, two 0.30in machine-guns (one in the nose, one in the rear cockpit), and provision for carrying a pair of 325lb depth charges or 100lb bombs underwing. Three hundred basically similar OS2N-1s were built by the Naval Aircraft Factory, which also assembled some OS2U-3s. One hundred OS2U-3s were supplied to the Royal Navy. Plans for an OS2U-4 version with a more powerful engine were abandoned, but two prototypes were produced by fitting high aspect ratio wings, full-span flaps, squared-off wingtips and a straight-tapered tailplane to two OS2U-2s.

Douglas SBD/A-24 Dauntless

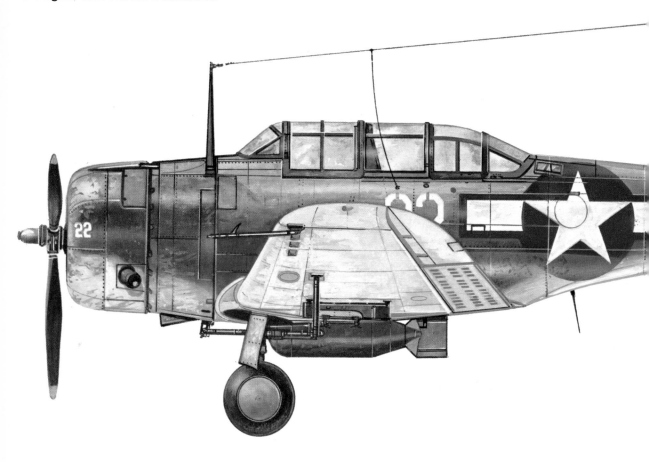

Aircraft type		Douglas SBD-3	Douglas SBD-5
Power plant		1×1,000 hp Wright R-1820-52	1×1,200 hp Wright R-1820-60
Accommodation		2	2
Wing span	m : ft in	12·65 : 41 6	12·65 : 41 6
Length overall	m : ft in	9·96 : 32 8	10·06 : 33 0
Height overall	m : ft in	4·14 : 13 7	3·94 : 12 11
Wing area	m² : sq ft	30·19 : 325·0	30·19 : 325·0
Weight empty	kg : lb	2,878 : 6,345	2,963 : 6,533
Weight loaded (max)	kg : lb	4,717 : 10,400	4,853 : 10,700
Max wing loading	kg/m² : lb/sq ft	156·16 : 32·00	160·65 : 32·92
Max power loading	kg/hp : lb/hp	4·72 : 10·40	4·05 : 8·92
Max level speed	km/h : mph	402 : 250	406 : 252
at (height)	m : ft	4,875 : 16,000	4,205 : 13,800
Cruising speed	km/h : mph	245 : 152	224 : 139
S/L rate of climb	m/min : ft/min	363 : 1,190	518 : 1,700
Service ceiling	m : ft	8,260 : 27,100	7,405 : 24,300
Range	km : miles	2,165 : 1,345*	1,794 : 1,115*

*with 1,000 lb bomb   *with 1,000 lb bomb

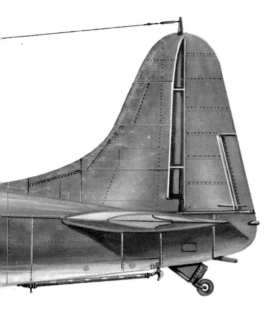

SBD-3 Dauntless of VS-41 (USS *Ranger,* Task Force 34) over the Mediterranean during the invasion of Morocco, October 1942

Development of this aircraft was started in 1934 by Northrop Corporation (a Douglas subsidiary), based on the Northrop A-17A, a derivative of the Gamma mailplane. First flown in July 1935 as the XBT-1, it was powered by an 825hp Pratt & Whitney R-1535-94 engine, and had semi-retractable landing gear. BT-1 production aircraft (fifty-four ordered) had perforated dive flaps, replacing the prototype's split trailing-edge flaps, a feature of the SBD series. The last BT-1, with inward-retracting main wheels and an 800hp Wright XR-1820-32 engine, was redesignated XBT-2. Testing resulted in several changes of ailerons and tail surfaces, the optimum arrangement being designated XSBD-1, as Northrop was by then a division of the Douglas company. Orders for fifty-seven SBD-1s and eighty-seven SBD-2s for the Marine Corps and Navy respectively were received in February 1939. Both had two 0.30in guns in the upper cowling, plus one (SBD-1) and two (SBD-2) in the rear cockpit. A 1,000lb bomb, carried on an under-fuselage cradle, could be augmented by a 100lb bomb under each wing. Both versions had additional armour and fuel. Deliveries of these aircraft, by then named Dauntless, started in late 1940, and the first of one hundred and seventy-four SBD-3s for the Navy began in March 1941. This improved version had 1,000hp R-1820-52 engines, reduced fuel, and 0.50in forward-firing guns. An additional four hundred and ten SBD-3s joined the Navy subsequently, and aircraft of the US carriers *Enterprise, Hornet* and *Yorktown* became renowned for sinking the Japanese carriers *Akagi, Kaga* and *Soryu* at Midway in June 1942. In 1940 the USAAC ordered seventy-eight SBD-3s without arrester gear, and with pneumatic instead of solid tailwheel tyres. Designated A-24, ninety more were acquired between June and October 1941 but, proving unsuitable for the island-hopping action in the Pacific, were used subsequently for training. Nevertheless, one hundred and seventy A-24As were ordered in 1942, and six hundred and fifteen A-24Bs in 1943. The former differed from the A-24/SBD-3 by having a 24V (instead of 12V) electrical system; seven hundred and eighty similar SBD-4s were produced for the Navy. The A-24B/SBD-5 was the major production version, the USAAF receiving six hundred and fifteen, and the USMC sixty (which had been built for the Army) as SBD-5As; Navy orders for this version, which had a 1,200hp Wright R-1820-60 engine and fuel capacity of 370 US gallons (1,400 litres), totalled 2,965. One Navy SBD-5 served as prototype for a final version, the SBD-6, with a 1,350hp Wright R-1820-66 engine. A total of four hundred and fifty were built for the Navy and the USMC before Dauntless production ended in 1944. Small numbers were supplied also to Allied air arms, including nine SBD-5s to Britain as Dauntless Mk I; eighteen SBD-3 and twenty-three SBD-5 to the RNZAF; thirty-two SBD-5 and forty/fifty A-24Bs to the French Navy and *Armée de l'Air* respectively. Conversions included eight SBD-1s and fourteen SBD-2S as photo-reconnaissance SBD-1Ps and SBD-2Ps respectively.

Boeing B-29 Superfortress

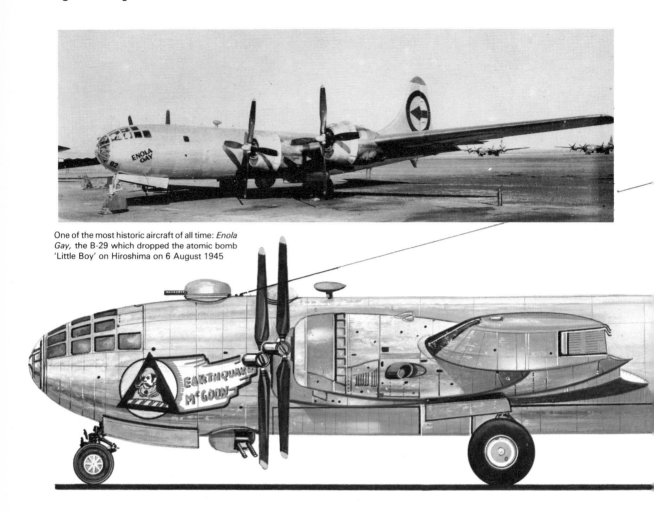

One of the most historic aircraft of all time: *Enola Gay,* the B-29 which dropped the atomic bomb 'Little Boy' on Hiroshima on 6 August 1945

Produced for the US Army Air Corps in March 1938, Boeing's Model 334 design study was for a pressurised, tricycle-gear development of the B-17. At that time the Army had no specific requirement for such an aircraft, but encouraged Boeing to keep the concept alive. In December 1939 the company built a mock-up of a modified Model 334A, but a month later revised the specification in the light of combat reports from the war in Europe. By late August it had obtained funding for two XB-29 (Model 345) prototypes, and a third was ordered at the end of 1940. In January 1942 the USAAF ordered fourteen service trials YB-29s and five hundred production B-29s. In February it announced a nationwide production programme involving Bell, North American and General Motors (Fisher). By the time the first XB-29 flew, on 21 September 1942, a total of 1,664 B-29s were on order. The Superfortress was the first military aeroplane ever to have pressurised accommodation for all crew members, including the tail gunner. The armament – ten 0.50in machine-guns and one 20mm cannon – was installed in five remotely controlled turrets, sighted and fired from within the pressurised areas; and division of the bomb load between two separate bays required gear to release weapons alternately from the front and rear bays, to maintain CG trim. Above all, the all-up weight posed a tremendous headache. The heaviest aircraft ever to enter production up to 1942, its narrow-chord wings of 11.5 aspect ratio produced terrifying wing-loading figures. Large-area Fowler flaps cut down the risks during take-off and landing; eventually, Boeing persuaded the Army that it could perform both safely and efficiently. Power plant comprised four of the new Wright R-3350 Cyclone eighteen radial engines, fitted with twin turbo-superchargers. R-3350-13s were installed in the XB-29, -21 models in the YB-29, and -23s in the initial production version. One YB-29 was later refitted, as the XB-39, with 2,100hp Allison V-3420 liquid-cooled engines. First mention of the Superfortress in action came after an attack on 5 June 1944 on railway marshalling yards at Bangkok. This was carried out by aircraft based in India, where they had been flown via the Atlantic and North Africa in the vain hope of concealing their presence in the Far East. In fact the Japanese already knew of the B-29s existence, and in any case Japan itself was on the receiving end of the B-29s bombs only nine days later on the night of 14/15 June. From then on an offensive was built up, reaching its peak after the recapture of the Marianas Islands; eventually twenty bomber groups were able to operate from the Marianas, formations of up to five hundred B-29s taking part in day and night raids against Japan. Their most effective weapon was the incendiary bomb, against which flimsy Japanese buildings were virtually defenceless. The main objective of this campaign was to destroy Japan's defences and production centres, as a preliminary to invasion.

This view emphasises the high aspect ratio (11.5) of the B-29s wing

Boeing B-29 Superfortress of the 6th BG, 313th Bombardment Wing, Tinian, summer 1945

Emblem carried by Bockscar, the B-29 of the 393rd BS (pilot Major Charles W. Sweeney) which dropped the second atomic bomb, on Nagasaki, on 9 August 1945

Aircraft type		Boeing B-29
Power plant		4×2,200 hp Wright R-3350-23/51/57/79/81
Accommodation		10
Wing span	m : ft in	43·07 : 141 3
Length overall	m : ft in	30·18 : 99 0
Height overall	m : ft in	9·02 : 29 7
Wing area	m² : sq ft	161·28 : 1,736·0
Weight empty	kg : lb	31,815 : 70,140
Weight loaded (max)	kg : lb	56,245 : 124,000
Max wing loading	kg/m² : lb/sq ft	348·57 : 71·43
Max power loading	kg/hp : lb/hp	6·39 : 14·09
Max level speed	km/h : mph	576 : 358
at (height)	m : ft	7,620 : 25,000
Cruising speed	km/h : mph	370 : 230
Time to 6,095 m (20,000 ft)		38·0 min
Service ceiling	m : ft	9,710 : 31,850
Range	km : miles	5,230 : 3,250*

*with 9,072 kg (20,000 lb) bomb load

Vought F4U Corsair

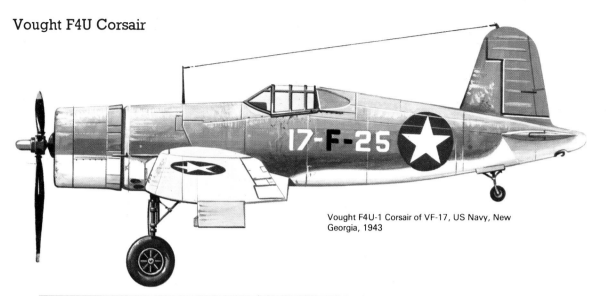

Vought F4U-1 Corsair of VF-17, US Navy, New Georgia, 1943

Aircraft type		Vought F4U-1	Goodyear F2G-2	Vought F4U-4
Power plant		1×2,000 hp Pratt & Whitney R-2800-8	1×3,000 hp Pratt & Whitney R-4360-4	1×2,100 hp Pratt & Whitney R-2800-18W
Accommodation		1	1	1
Wing span	m : ft in	12·50 : 41 0	12·50 : 41 0	12·50 : 41 0
Length overall	m : ft in	10·16 : 33 4	10·31 : 33 10	10·26 : 33 8
Height overall	m : ft in	4·90 : 16 1	4·90 : 16 1	4·50 : 14 9
Wing area	m² : sq ft	29·17 : 314·0	29·17 : 314·0	29·17 : 314·0
Weight empty	kg : lb	4,074 : 8,982	4,649 : 10,249	4,175 : 9,205
Weight loaded (max)	kg : lb	6,350 : 14,000	6,995 : 15,422	6,654 : 14,670
Max wing loading	kg/m² : lb/sq ft	217·58 : 44·59	239·68 : 49·11	227·99 : 46·72
Max power loading	kg/hp : lb/hp	3·18 : 7·00	2·33 : 5·14	3·17 : 6·99
Max level speed	km/h : mph	671 : 417	694 : 431	718 : 446
at (height)	m : ft	6,065 : 19,900	5,000 : 16,400	7,985 : 26,200
Cruising speed	km/h : mph	293 : 182	306 : 190	346 : 215
S/L rate of climb	m/min : ft/min	881 : 2,890	1,341 : 4,400	1,180 : 3,870
Service ceiling	m : ft	11,245 : 36,900	11,825 : 38,800	12,650 : 41,500
Range (normal)	km : miles	1,633 : 1,015	1,915 : 1,190	1,617 : 1,005

Known as the 'Sweetheart of Okinawa' by its own pilots, and as 'Whistling Death' by the Japanese, the F4U Corsair perpetuated the name of two earlier Vought aircraft. Ordered in June 1938, the XF4U-1 first flew on 29 May 1940, powered by an 1,850hp Pratt & Whitney XR-2800-4 two-row radial engine. The initial contract for five hundred and eighty-four F4U-1s, issued on 30 June 1941, specified two, later three, 0.50in Browning machine-guns in each outer wing. The production F4U-1, first flown on 25 June 1942, was powered by a 2,000hp Double Wasp, and deliveries began on 3 October 1942. Most F4U-1s went to Marine Corps and land-based Navy squadrons, due to early troubles with the landing gear, aggravated by the far-aft position of the cockpit. The unique inverted-gull wing was designed to avoid the ultra-long main-wheel legs that would otherwise have been needed to provide deck clearance for the 13ft 2in (4.01m) propeller – one of the biggest then in use, and driven by the most powerful engine then installed in a piston-engined fighter. The Corsair was the first production US warplane to exceed 400mph (644km/h) in level flight. As the war in the Pacific progressed,

Brewster (which built seven hundred and thirty-five designated F3A-1) and Goodyear (4,007 as the FG-1/1A/1D) were brought in to augment the F4U-1 programme; Vought itself built 4,699. A blown canopy was introduced on models being built by all three companies in August 1943. Vought's F4U-1C (two hundred built) had four 20mm M2 wing cannon to replace the six machine-guns; the F4U-1D (1,375 by Vought), F3A-1D (Brewster) and FG-1D (2,302 by Goodyear) had an R-2800-8W water-injection engine and provision for eight 5in underwing rocket projectiles or 2,000lb (907kg) of bombs. Britain's Fleet Air Arm received 2,012 aircraft (ninety-five F4U-1s, five hundred and ten F4U-1As, four hundred and thirty F3A-1Ds and nine hundred and seventy-seven FG-1Ds) designated Corsair Mks I – IV, with wingtips clipped slightly to ease stowage on British carriers. A further three hundred and seventy F4U-1Ds went to the RNZAF. Twelve F4U-1s were modified by the Naval Aircraft Factory in 1943 to become F4U-2s, with a radar scanner pod on the starboard wing. The F4U-1P was a photo-reconnaissance conversion. The next (and final wartime) production version was the F4U-4

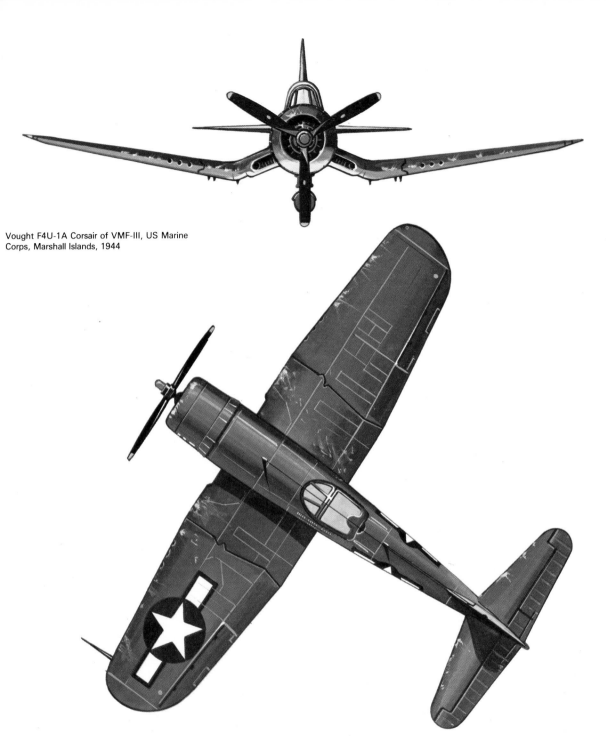

Vought F4U-1A Corsair of VMF-III, US Marine
Corps, Marshall Islands, 1944

(Goodyear FG-4), which first flew on 20 September 1944.
Powered by an uprated Double Wasp engine, it was armed
with six 0.50in machine-guns and could carry two 2,000lb
bombs or large rocket projectiles under the fuselage.
Production of this version continued until 1947, when 2,351
had been completed. They included three hundred F4U-4Cs
(four 20mm cannon); nine converted for photo-reconnaissance as F4U-4Ps; plus other conversions to F4U-4E and
-4N, with APS-4 or APS-6 radar for night fighting. Goodyear
produced five each of the F2G-1 and F2G-2, developed
models with 3,000hp R-4360-4 engines. In US wartime service
the Corsair operated chiefly in the Pacific theatre. It more than

lived up to its Japanese nickname: the highly individual
engine note (caused by air passing through the wing-root
engine cooler inlets) was accompanied by a 'kill ratio' over its
adversaries of approximately eleven to one, including a
considerable toll against *Kamikaze* aircraft and during the
invasions of Iwo Jima and Okinawa. After the war, production
of the Corsair continued until December 1952 with the F4U-5,
F4U-6 (later AU-1) and F4U-7. Total output by Vought reached
7,829, to make with Brewster and Goodyear manufacture a
grand total of 12,571 – the longest continuous production run
of any US fighter of World War 2.

Lancer

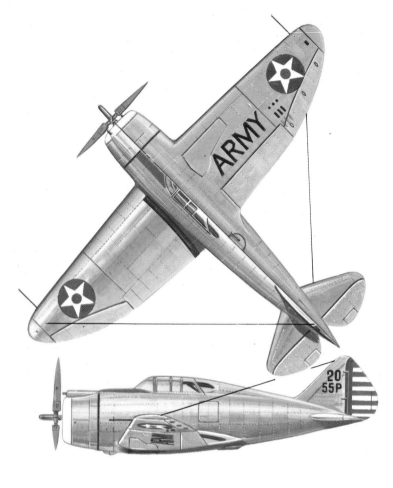

Republic P-43 Lancer of the US Army Air Corps,
1941

Span: 36ft 0in (10.97m)
Length: 28ft 5¼in (8.68m)
Weight: 7,810lb (3,543kg)
Engine: 1×1,200hp Pratt & Whitney
   R-1830-35 Twin Wasp 14-cyl radial
Max speed: 349mph (562kmh)
Operational ceiling: 38,000ft (11,582m)
Range: 800 miles (1,287km)
Arament: 2×0.50in and 2×0.30in,
machine-guns

The seventy-seventh and final aircraft (36-430) on the USAACs contract for Seversky P-35 fighters was completed with a 1,200hp supercharged Twin Wasp radial engine. From this, Seversky designers developed a further prototype, the AP-4, as a private venture, providing this aircraft with a rear-mounted turbo-supercharger and an inward-retracting main landing gear. In May 1939, five months before the Seversky company was renamed Republic Aviation Corporation, the US Army Air Corps ordered thirteen service test fighters, based upon the AP-4 but with detail changes, and these were designated YP-43. They were armed with two 0.50in and two 0.30in machine-guns, and each was powered by a 1,200hp Pratt & Whitney R-1830-35 Twin Wasp radial engine. These were delivered between September 1940 and April 1941, by which time production orders had been given for fifty-four P-43s and eighty P-43As, with the name Lancer. Delivery of these began in May and September 1941 respectively, and

during the same year one hundred and twenty-five P-43A-1s, with four 0.50in guns, were ordered, one hundred and eight of them as Lend-Lease equipment for the Chinese Air Force. The USAAF aircraft were in fact not used as fighters: they were modified as P-43B or C and used for photo-reconnaissance. The other seventeen P-43A-1s were supplied to the Royal Australian Air Force, and were similarly employed. The real purpose of keeping open the P-43 production line was to maintain continuity in readiness, eventually, to manufacture the P-47 Thunderbolt. Meanwhile, in 1939 Republic had proffered two new prototypes, the AP-4J and AP-4L, powered respectively by a 1,400hp Twin Hornet and a 2,000hp Double Wasp engine. The Army ordered eighty of the former model, as the P-44, in September 1939, and promised much larger contracts later for the 2,000hp version. In the event, however, the P-47 Thunderbolt eventually ousted the latter and the eighty P-44s became instead the P-43A's mentioned above.

Douglas SBD Dauntless

Douglas SBD-5 Dauntless of VB-5, US Navy,
USS *Yorktown*, August/September 1943

Span: 41ft 6in (12.65m)
Length: 33ft 0in (10.06m)
Weight: 10,700lb (4,853kg)
Engine: 1,200hp Wright R-1820-60
Cyclone 9-cyl radial
Max speed: 252mph (406kmh) at 13,800ft
(4,200m)
Operational ceiling: 24,300ft (7,400m)
Range: 1,115 miles (1,794km)
Armament: 2×0.50in machine-guns;
2×0.30in machine-guns
Max bomb load: 1,000lb (454kg)
externally

Evolution of the Dauntless began in 1934, when a Northrop team under Ed Heinemann based a Navy dive-bomber on Northrop's Army A-17A. Designated XBT-1, it flew in July 1935. In February 1936 fifty-four BT-1s with 825hp R-1535-94 engines were ordered. The last was completed as the XBT-2, with a 1,000hp R-1830-32 engine; with further modifications, it was redesignated XSBD-1 when Northrop was absorbed by Douglas on 31 August 1937. Perforated dive flaps, a distinctive Dauntless feature, were then introduced. Delivery of fifty-seven SBD-1s to the USMC began in June 1940. Simultaneously, the USN ordered eighty-seven SBD-2s with additional fuel and armour, and autopilots. Both versions had two 0.30in machine-guns in the upper cowling and a 0.30in in the rear cockpit. Bombs up to 1,000lb (454kg) could be carried on a ventral cradle; maximum bomb load was 1,200lb (544kg). Delivery of SBD-2s, from November 1940, was followed from March 1941 by one hundred and seventy-four -3s with R-1830-52 engines and 0.50in front guns. The two models were standard USN carrier-borne dive-bombers at the time of Pearl Harbor; subsequently, the Navy received a further four hundred and ten SBD-3s. In May 1942 SBD pilots were credited with forty of the ninety-one enemy aircraft lost during the Battle of the Coral Sea; at Midway SBDs sank three Japanese carriers and crippled one. Their own attrition rate

was the lowest of any US carrier aircraft in the Pacific, due largely to an outstanding ability to absorb battle damage. Later, Dauntless operated from escort carriers, flying ASW or close-support missions. In October 1942 delivery began of seven hundred and eighty SBD-4s with radar and radio-navigation equipment. The major production model, the SBD-5, with increased engine power, followed. In addition to the 2,965 SBD-5s, sixty SBD-5As were delivered to the USMC: four hundred and fifty SBD-6s completed Dauntless production in July 1944. Production totalled 5,936, including one hundred and sixty-eight A-24s and six hundred and fifteen A-24Bs for the USAAF, delivered from June 1941, these corresponding to the SBD-3 and -3A, -4 and -5 respectively, but had new tailwheels, internal equipment changes and no arrester gear. They were not flown with great combat success, and were used chiefly for training or communications. The RNZAF received eighteen SBD-3s, twenty-seven SBD-4s and twenty-three SBD-5s; thirty-two SBD-5s were supplied to the French Navy, and between forty and fifty A-24Bs to the *Armée de l'Air;* but the latter, like their US Army counterparts, were employed mainly on second-line duties. Nine SBD-5s were delivered to the FAA but were not used operationally.

Skytrain/Skytrooper

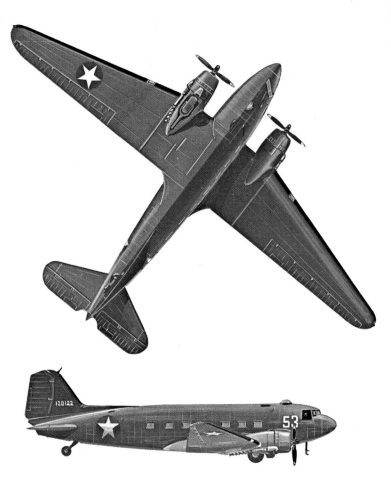

Douglas C-53C Skytrooper of the USAAF, El Kabret, spring 1943

Span: 95ft 0in (28.96m)
Length: 64ft 5½in (19.65m)
Weight: 29,300lb (13,290kg)
Engines: 2 × 1,200hp Pratt & Whitney
  R-1830-92 Twin Wasp radials
Max speed: 210mph (338kmh)
Operational ceiling: 24,100ft (7,346m)
Range: 1,350 miles (2,173km)

First Douglas Commercial transports to be acquired by the US services were a number of DC-2s (Army C-32A and C-34, Navy R2D-1), followed by thirty-five C-39s with DC-2 fuselages and the DC-3s tail surfaces and outer wing panels. The principal wartime versions of the DC-3 were the Twin Wasp-engined C-47 Skytrain, C-53 Skytrooper and the Navy R4D series, differing in minor detail only, except for their function. The first nine hundred and fifty-three C-47s were troop or cargo transports; they were followed in 1942 by four thousand nine hundred and ninety-one C-47As, and from 1943 by three thousand one hundred and eight C-47Bs, all by Douglas. One hundred and thirty-three TC-47Bs were also built, for training duties. The Skytrooper, as its name implied, was specifically a troop transport, of which Douglas produced one hundred and ninety-three C-53s, eight C-53Bs, seventeen C-53Cs and one hundred and fifty-nine C-53Ds from 1941 to 1943. Seventeen C-117A VIP transports were delivered in 1945. Commercial airline DSTs (Douglas Sleeper Transports) or DC-3s impressed for war service included thirty-six with designations C-48 to C-48C, one hundred and thirty-eight C-49 to C-49K, fourteen C-50 to C-50D, one C-51, five C-52 to C-52C, two C-68 and four

C-84. The Skytrooper preceded the C-47 into service (October 1941), despite its higher designation number; the first Skytrains were delivered in January 1942. More than one thousand two hundred were supplied under Lend-Lease to the RAF, by whom they were known as Dakota Mks I to IV. They first entered service with No 31 Squadron in Burma in June 1942. Additional roles included casualty evacuation and glider towing. Total wartime production of military DC-3s, which ended in August 1945, amounted to ten thousand one hundred and twenty-three, mostly built by Douglas. Nor was this all: in addition to about seven hundred supplied to the USSR under Lend-Lease, the Soviet engineer Boris Lisunov spent some time at Douglas prior to initiating production of a Soviet-built version known as the Li-2 (formerly PS-84). Some two thousand were built in the USSR, including some with a gun turret just above and behind the crew cabin. Licence production was also undertaken in Japan, where Showa built three hundred and eighty L2D2s and L2D3s for the JNAF (code-named 'Tabby' by the Allies) and Nakajima completed a further seventy.

Devastator

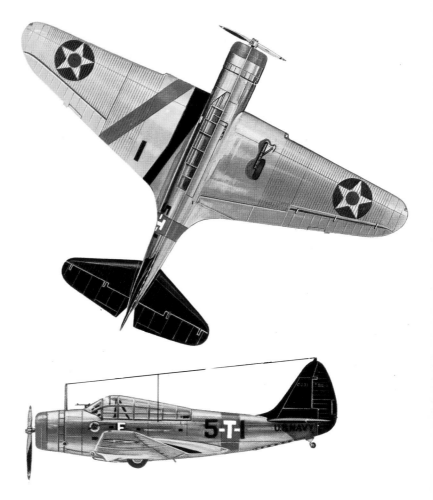

Douglas TBD-1 Devastator, commanding officer's aircraft of US Navy Squadron VT-5, USS *Yorktown*, 1939

Span: 50ft 0in (15.24m)
Length: 35ft 0in (10.67m)
Weight: 10,914lb (4,951kg)
Engine: 1×900hp Pratt & Whitney
K-1830-64 Twin Wasp 14-cyl radial
Max speed: 206mph (332kmh)
Operational ceiling: 19,700ft (6,005m)
Range with torpedo: 435 miles (700km)
Armament: 1×0.30in and 1×0.50in
machine-guns
Max bomb load: 1×21in torpedo or
1×1,000 (454kg) bomb

Two prototype designs were ordered by the US Navy in mid-1934 as the first step towards securing a new generation of single-engined torpedo-bombers to serve in the newly-commissioned aircraft carrier USS *Ranger* and others of her class. One of these prototypes, the Great Lakes XTBG-1 biplane, was rejected on the grounds of instability and inadequate performance. The other contender, the Douglas XTBD-1, was an extremely clean-looking all-metal monoplane with an 800hp XR-1830-60 (Pratt & Whitney Twin Wasp) engine and a retractable main undercarriage. This prototype (9720) flew for the first time on 15 April 1935 and continued to be test-flown for the next two years, gaining experience which was incorporated into the production model. The first production contract was placed in February 1936, and covered the manufacture of one hundred and fourteen TBD-1 Devastators, which thus became the first carrier-based monoplanes to be produced in quantity for the US Navy. The first production Devastator was flown on 25 June 1937, and deliveries began in the following November. The first US Navy Squadron to receive the new aircraft was VT-3, attached to the USS *Saratoga,* and by the time of America's entry into World War 2

Devastators had also been delivered to VT-2 (USS *Lexington*), VT-5 *(Yorktown)*, VT-6 *(Enterprise)*, VT-8 (shore-based at Norfolk, Virginia), VS-42 *(Ranger)* and VS-71 *(Wasp)*. A second batch of TBD-1s ordered in August 1938 brought the overall production total to one hundred and twenty-nine. In 1939 the first production Devastator was fitted with twin Edo floats by the Naval Aircraft Factory. This aircraft was redesigned TBD-1A and used for a variety of test purposes over the next four years, but no series production of this version was undertaken. At the time of the attack on Pearl Harbor the US Navy had a hundred Devastators on strength, of which sixty-nine were in first-line operational service. During the first six months of the war in the Pacific they were flown intensively against Japanese shipping or land targets, establishing a fine record of operational successes that reached their peak in the Coral Sea campaign of May 1942. But a month later, in the Battle of Midway Island, the remaining Devastators were decimated by the heavier and superior Japanese opposition, and thereafter those few which survived were withdrawn to serve out their time in various instructional capacities.

Mars

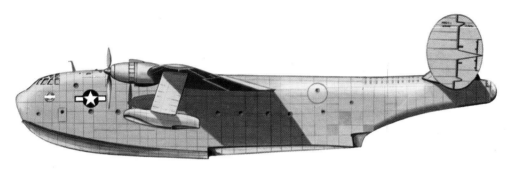

Martin XPB2M-1 Mars prototype, *circa* late 1943

Span: 200ft 0in (60.96m)
Length: 117ft 3in (35.74m)
Weight: 140,000lb (63,500kg)
Engines: 4 × 2,200hp Wright R-3350-18 Duplex Cyclone 18-cyl radials
Max speed: 207mph (333kmh)
Operational ceiling: 17,400ft (5,304m)
Range: 4,375 miles (7,041km)

The largest flying-boat in the world for its time, the Martin Model 170 Mars was designed originally to serve with the US Navy as a long-range maritime patrol bomber. An XPB2M-1 prototype was ordered in August 1938, and this aircraft (serial number 1520) was launched on 5 November 1941, making its first flight (delayed because the aircraft ran aground after an accidental fire in one engine) on 3 July 1942. The huge hull accommodated a two-deck internal layout for a crew of eleven, but as a pre-war design no provision had been made to afford them armour protection, and the only defensive armament comprised power-operated gun turrets in the nose and tail. The conversion and production effort that would have been necessary to bring the aircraft up to wartime combat standards were evidently considered prohibitive, and so its adoption for its intended role was never achieved. Instead, during 1943 the gun turrets were removed and faired over, and the airframe of the prototype was modified and strenthened to enable it to serve as a cargo transport. In this form, redesignated XPB2M-1R, it began operating with the US Naval Air Transport Service in December 1943. On its first cargo mission it flew 4,375 miles (7,041km) non-stop from the Naval Air Station at Patuxent River, Maryland, to Natal, Brazil, with a 13,000lb (5,897kg) payload. On the return trip it carried, over a 1,216 miles (1,957km) stage length, a record payload (then) of 35,000lb (15,876kg), and early in the following year it transported a payload of 20,500lb (9,299kg) over an even longer distance of 4,700 miles (7,564km) on a trip to Hawaii and back. In January 1945 the US Navy ordered twenty examples

of a much-modified version, the JRM-1, exclusively for the cargo transport role. The prototype of this model made its first flight in the summer of 1945, but foundered after an early test flight and the order was subsequently reduced to only five aircraft, which served with Squadron VR-2. The JRM-1 Mars, with a modified hull design and single fin and rudder, was powered by four 2,300hp R-3350-8 engines, had a gross weight of 145,000lb (65,770kg) and a maximum speed of 225mph (362km/hr). Duty and reserve crews, each of four men, could be carried. Plans were made for several commercial passenger-carrying developments, but none of these was realised. For cargo carrying, internal equipment included tie-down rings and a 5,000lb (2,268kg) capacity hoist, and the loading hatches were redesigned and enlarged. Provision was made for the JRM-1 to be converted, if required, to an ambulance aircraft carrying eight-four stretcher cases and twenty-five medical attendants, or to an assault transport carrying one hundred and thirty-two fully-equipped troops, seven Jeeps or other military equipment. The fourth and last JRM-1 was delivered in the summer of 1946. On 19 May 1946 the JRM-1 *Marshall Mars* set up an unofficial world record for the number of people carried in a single flight, when it flew from Alameda to San Diego with a crew of seven and three hundred and one passengers. One final Mars, the JRM-2, was built, and was delivered in the autumn of 1947. This had an improved engine installation and was cleared for operation at an all-up weight of 165,000lb (74,843kg); the JRM-1s were in due course brought up to the same standard and

redesignated JRM-3. Retired from US Navy service in the mid-1950s, the four flying-boats were purchased by Forest Industries Flying Tankers Ltd. They were modified by Fairey Aviation of Canada for operation in that country by their new owners as forest-fire water-bombers, each aircraft having two hull scoops capable of filling four glass-fibre internal tanks with a total water load of 7,000 US gallons (26,500 litres).

Consolidated PBY-6A Catalina

Badge of the US Coast Guard

Consolidated PBY-6A Catalina (BuNo 46642) of
the US Navy, 1943/44

Aircraft type		Consolidated PBY-3	Consolidated PBY-5A	NAF PBN-1
Power plant		2×1,000 hp Pratt & Whitney R-1830-66	2×1,200 hp Pratt & Whitney R-1830-92	2×1,200 hp Pratt & Whitney R-1830-92
Accommodation		8	7/9	7/9
Wing span	m : ft in	31·70 : 104 0	31·70 : 104 0	31·78 : 104 3
Length overall	m : ft in	19·86 : 65 2	19·46 : 63 10	19·71 : 64 8
Height overall	m : ft in	5·64 : 18 6	6·15 : 20 2	6·48 : 21 3
Wing area	m² : sq ft	130·06 : 1,400·0	130·06 : 1,400·0	130·06 : 1,400·0
Weight empty	kg : lb	6,698 : 14,767	9,485 : 20,910	8,749 : 19,288
Weight loaded (max)	kg : lb	13,092 : 28,863	16,012 : 35,300	17,236 : 38,000
Max wing loading	kg/m² : lb/sq ft	100·63 : 20·62	123·02 : 25·21	132·44 : 27·14
Max power loading	kg/hp : lb/hp	6·55 : 14·43	6·67 : 14·71	7·18 : 15·83
Max level speed	km/h : mph	307 : 191	288 : 179	299 : 186
at (height)	m : ft	3,660 : 12,000	2,135 : 7,000	2,040 : 6,700
Cruising speed	km/h : mph	183 : 114	188 : 117	179 : 111
S/L rate of climb	m/min : ft/min	283 : 930	189 : 620	—
Service ceiling	m : ft	7,435 : 24,400	4,480 : 14,700	4,600 : 15,100
Range (normal)	km : miles	3,500 : 2,175	4,096 : 2,545	4,168 : 2,590

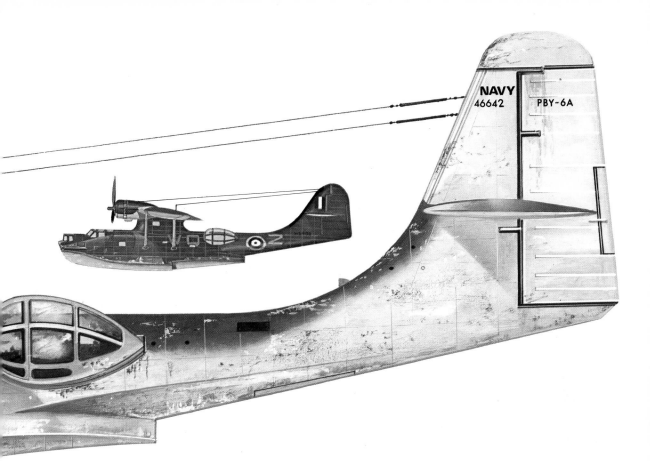

Designed to a 1933 Navy contract, the Consolidated XP3Y-1 prototype flew for the first time on 28 March 1935. Its two 825hp Pratt & Whitney R-1830-54 Twin Wasp radials were later exchanged for -64s of 850hp. Sixty were ordered by the US Navy in June 1935, the original P3Y-1 designation later being changed to PBY-1 to denote a patrol bomber. Deliveries began in October 1936. The PBY-1 could carry up to 2,000lb (907kg) of bombs, and was armed with four single 0.30in machine-guns in nose, ventral and two beam positions. The next Navy contracts were for fifty generally similar PBY-2s, followed by sixty-six PBY-3s, which differed in having 1,000hp R-1830-66 Twin Wasps. Next came the PBY-4, with 1,050hp R-1830-72 engines, incorporating the large blister transparencies amidships which characterised all subsequent versions. Replacing the beam hatches, each blister housed a 0.50in machine-gun and greatly increased the observers' field of vision. The single 0.30in machine-guns in the nose and ventral tunnel were retained. In 1938 the Soviet Union evaluated three PBY-3s, and set up a production line at Taganrog later the same year. This licence version was designated GST *(Gidro-Samolet Transportnyi;* transport hydro-aeroplane), and powered by two 950hp M-87 radial engines, a Soviet development of the French Gnome-Rhône. Well over 200 were manufactured for the Soviet naval air arm. One US Navy PBY-4 was converted in 1939 to amphibian configuration, with a retractable tricycle undercarriage, as the XPBY-5A; thirty-three PBYs then on order were similarly modified, and a further one hundred and thirty-four PBY-5As were ordered as such from the outset. The PBY-5 introduced a redesigned rudder, and 1,200hp R-1830-92 Twin Wasps. Bomb load was increased to 4,000lb (1,814kg) and an extra 0.30in gun was positioned in the nose. Deliveries began in 1940; by December 1941 the US Navy had twenty-one operational PBY squadrons, of which sixteen were equipped with the PBY-5. A similar model was supplied to Britain for

evaluation in mid-1939, and an initial RAF order for 30 was more than doubled in 1940. The RAF name Catalina was also later adopted by the US Navy, and applied to almost all PBY variants. More than six hundred and fifty assorted PBYs were purchased by the RAF, or delivered under Lend-Lease, as Catalina Marks I to VI. These included ninety-seven aircraft fitted with anti-submarine and anti-shipping radar, serving with Coastal Command as Catalina Mk IVAs. The Royal Australian Air Force was equipped with most of the Mks V and VI. It was a Catalina Mk I of No 209 Squadron RAF which, on 26 May 1941, sighted the German battleship *Bismarck.* She had, since sailing, managed to avoid both naval and air search, threatening enormous losses to Allied convoys. The next production model (one hundred and sixty-five built) was the PBN-1 Nomad developed by the US Naval Aircraft Factory. This had a modified fuselage, a taller fin and rudder, strengthened wings and increased fuel capacity. Deliveries began in February 1943. The final US production model was the PBY-6A, generally similar to the PBN-1 except for a radome above the cockpit and a twin-gun ball-turret in the nose, plus 0.50in waist and 0.30in ventral machine-guns. Many PBY-6As were supplied to the Soviet Union under Lend-Lease. During World War 2, Catalinas were operated by the air forces of Australia (one hundred and sixty-eight), Canada (about seventy), New Zealand (more than thirty), France (thirty) and the Netherlands East Indies (thirty-six). Total US/Canadian production of all models was approximately 3,290, of which seven hundred and forty-one were built in Canada by Canadian Vickers (three hundred and seventy-nine) and Boeing Canada (three hundred and sixty-two). The RCAF amphibious version was named Canso. All variants of the PBY/PBN were extensively used in both the Pacific and Atlantic theatres, and also off the coasts of North and South America.

Vought F4U Corsair

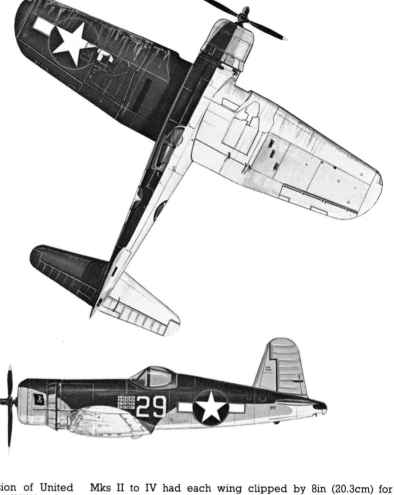

Vought F4U-1A Corsair of VF-17, US Navy, summer 1943

Span: 40ft 11¾in (12.49m)
Length: 33ft 4½in (10.17m)
Weight, normal take-off: 11,093lb
  (5,032kg)
Engine: 2,000hp Pratt & Whitney
  R-2800-8 Double Wasp 18-cyl radial
Max speed: 417mph (671kmh) at 19,900ft
  (6,065m)
Operational ceiling: 36,900ft (11,245m)
Range, normal: 1,015 miles (1,633km)
Armament: 6×0.50in Browning machine-
  guns
Max bomb load: 1,000lb (227kg)

Originating with the Vought-Sikorsky Division of United Aircraft Corpn, the Vought V-166B, designated XF4U-1, flew on 29 May 1940. It was the first US warplane to exceed 400mph. It remained in production until 1953; 12,571 were built. The initial USN contract was for five hundred and eighty-four F4U-1s; delivery began in September 1942 to USMC/USN land-based squadrons, due to difficulties in operating from carriers, and the first operational missions were flown by VMF-124, USMC in February 1943. The gull-wing was used to avoid the need for long undercarriage legs to clear the large-diameter propeller. But the far-aft cockpit position gave a poor view when landing; hence, from the F4U-1, a raised canopy was introduced. The Vought F4U-1C had four 20mm wing cannon instead of six machine-guns; the F4U-1D and the similar Goodyear FG-1D had a water-injection R-2800-8W and provision for eight underwing RPs or two 1,000lb (454kg) bombs. Brewster, after manufacturing seven hundred and thirty-five F3A-1s, ceased production in 1944. Goodyear built 4,014 FG-1s and -1Ds and Vought 4,669 F4U-1s to -1Ds. The FAA received 1,977 as Corsair Mks I to IV, the RNZAF 425.

Mks II to IV had each wing clipped by 8in (20.3cm) for stowage aboard carriers, and preceded US F4Us into carrier service, entering action in April 1944. In 1943, twelve F4U-1s were modified to F4U-2s with four wing guns and radar in a starboard wingtip fairing; others became F4U-1P PR aircraft. The F4U-4 (Goodyear FG-4) had six 0.50in wing guns and a 2,100hp R-2800-1W. Delivery began late in 1944. Despite large cuts in orders after VJ-day, Vought completed 2,356 F4U-4s and Goodyear two hundred FG-4s, including radar-equipped F4U-4E and -4N night fighters. Goodyear built five F2G-1s and five F2G-2s, with 3,000hp R-4360-4 Wasp Majors. During World War 2 US Corsairs operated mostly from land bases in the Pacific. The note of the airstream through the cooler inlets, and their 11:1 'kill ratio', led the Japanese to nickname them 'Whistling Death'. The postwar versions – F4U-5, AU-1 (F4U-6) and F4U-7 – served with distinction in the Korean War. Postwar, France's *Aéronavale* operated F4U-7s until 1964. Until the late 1960s F4U-5s equipped a Salvadorean air force fighter-bomber squadron, and about sixty equipped the 2nd Air Attack Squadron of Argentina's naval air arm.

Seagull

Curtiss SOC-4 Seagull of the US Coast Guard, Port Angeles (USA) 1938-39. Data apply to SOC-1 Seaplane

Span: 36ft 0in (10.97m)
Length: 31ft 7½in (9.63m)
Weight: 5,437lb (2,466kg)
Engine: 1×600hp Pratt & Whitney
  R-1340-22 Wasp 9-cyl radial
Max speed: 165mph (266kmh)
Operational ceiling: 14,900ft (4,542m)
Range: 675 miles (1,086km)
Armament: 2×0.30in machine-guns
Max bomb load: 1×116lb (53kg)

The versatile Seagull has received less attention among aircraft of the inter-war years than it deserves, perhaps due to the prosaic nature of the duties it was required to perform. Yet it was built in substantial numbers and carried out a decade of useful service, outlasting the aircraft designed to replace it and, at the end, never being replaced at all. The prototype (serial number 9413), first flown in April 1934, was conceived initially purely for the observation role, being designated XO3C-1. It was powered by a Pratt & Whitney Wasp radial engine, seated two occupants in tandem in open cockpits and had a landing gear comprising a single central amphibious float and two stabilising floats beneath the outer lower wing panels. In March 1935 it was reclassified as a scout observation type, receiving the new designation XSOC-1, and an initial contract for one hundred and thirty-five production SOC-1 Seagulls was placed by the US Navy. Delivery began later that year, the first aircraft being assigned to the cruiser USS *Marblehead* in November. Forty more SOC-1s were ordered in May 1936; these were redesignated SOC-2 late in 1937, signifying a different-model Wasp engine and a wheels-only landing gear. The SOC-3 had interchangeable wheel or (non-amphibious) float gear, but was otherwise similar to the SOC-2; eighty-three were built by Curtiss and forty-four (designated SON-1) by the Naval Aircraft Factory at Philadelphia. Production (totalling three hundred and six, including the original prototype) was completed by three floatplane Seagulls built for the US Coast Guard. These were given SOC-4 designations in 1943 when they came under Navy jurisdiction. During their career the Curtiss Seagulls served aboard every aircraft carrier, battleship and cruiser in the US Fleet, as well as a number of lesser vessels. They were flown, *inter alia,* by US Navy Squadrons VO-1 to VO-5, VCS-7, VCS-9, VS-5B, VS-6B, and VS-9S to VS-12S; one was used as personal aircraft of the C-in-C, US Fleet. Two hundred and seventy-nine Seagulls were still in service in mid-1940, and three years later twenty-seven US cruisers were still equipped with these aircraft. During the war the addition of arrester gear brought the new designations SOC-2A and SOC-3A. The Seagull's intended replacement, the SO3C, proved a disappointing type, and when it was withdrawn early in 1944 the surviving Seagulls were returned to an operational status which they maintained until the war was over.

Consolidated-Vultee PB4Y-2 Privateer

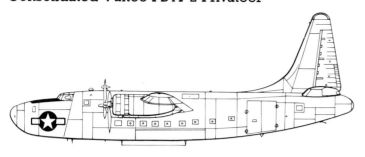

Consolidated RY-3 transport version of the
PB4Y-2 used by the US Navy and RAF
Transport Command

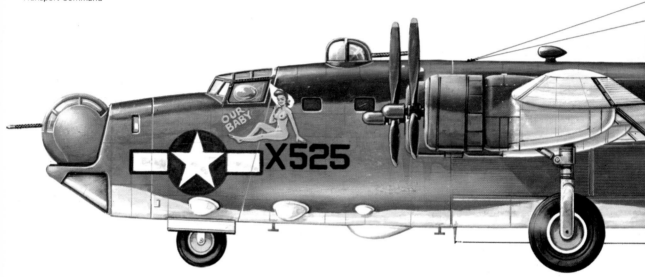

Aircraft type		Consolidated PB4Y-2
Power plant		4 × 1,350 hp Pratt & Whitney R-1830-94
Accommodation		11
Wing span	m : ft in	33·53 : 110 0
Length overall	m : ft in	22·73 : 74 7
Height overall	m : ft in	8·89 : 29 2
Wing area	m² : sq ft	97·36 : 1,048·0
Weight empty	kg : lb	16,967 : 37,405
Weight loaded	kg : lb	29,030 : 64,000
Max wing loading	kg/m² : lb/sq ft	298·17 : 61·07
Max power loading	kg/hp : lb/hp	5·38 : 11·85
Max level speed	km/h : mph	398 : 247
at (height)	m : ft	4,265 : 14,000
Cruising speed	km/h : mph	254 : 158
S/L rate of climb	m/min : ft/min	302 : 990
Service ceiling	m : ft	5,945 : 19,500
Range	km : miles	4,235 : 2,630*

*with 1,814 kg (4,000 lb) bomb load

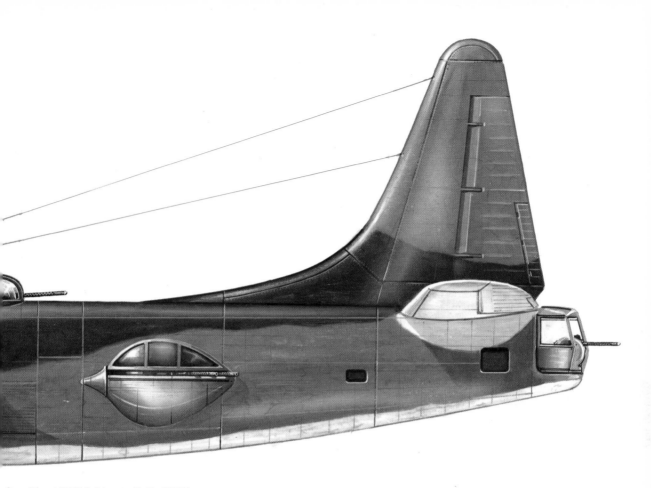

Consolidated PB4Y-2 Privateer (BuNo 59525)
of the US Navy

The Privateer, developed from the highly successful Liberator series, resulted from the US Navy's need for a purpose-built land-based patrol bomber to augment the PB4Y-1 (B-24D) Liberators transferred from the Army Air Forces. Consolidated-Vultee converted three B-24Ds into XPB4Y-2 prototypes, the first of which flew on 20 September 1943. They had a longer fuselage, with a single highfin and rudder, and were powered by non-turbocharged 1,350hp Pratt & Whitney R-1830-94 engines in redesigned nacelles. The wings and undercarriage of the Liberator were retained. Designed for low-level patrol bombing duties, the Privateer was armed with twelve 0.50in in Browning machine-guns in four power-operated turrets (nose, tail and two dorsal) and two waist positions; it could carry a maximum short-range bomb load of 12,800lb (5,806kg). Two production orders were placed, for six hundred and sixty and seven hundred and ten PB4Y-2s, but total production after end-of-war cancellations amounted to only seven hundred and thirty-six aircraft. Privateers saw limited combat service towards the end of the war, mostly in the Pacific, with the Navy and Marine Corps. Navy Squadron VP-24 was equipped with the PB4Y-2B, converted to carry a pair of underwing ASM-N-2 Bat radar-homing, anti-shipping glide bombs. A transport model, designated RY-3, was also produced. Of the forty-six manufactured, twenty-seven went to the RAF under Lend-Lease as Liberator C Mk IXs, operating in Canada with Transport Command.

Curtiss P-40

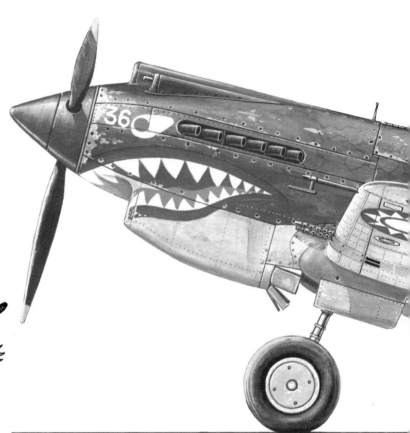

'Flying Tiger' emblem of the American Volunteer Group

Aircraft type		Curtiss P-40C	Curtiss P-40F	Curtiss P-40N
Power plant		1×1,040 hp* Allison V-1710-33	1×1,300 hp* Packard (Merlin) V-1650-1	1×1,200 hp Allison V-1710-81
Accommodation		1	1	1
Wing span	m : ft in	11·38 : 37 4	11·38 : 37 4	11·38 : 37 4
Length overall	m : ft in	9·68 : 31 9	10·16 : 33 4	10·16 : 33 4
Height overall	m : ft in	3·76 : 12 4	3·76 : 12 4	3·76 : 12 4
Wing area	m² : sq ft	21·93 : 236·0	21·93 : 236·0	21·93 : 236·0
Weight empty	kg : lb	2,636 : 5,812	2,989 : 6,590	2,722 : 6,000
Weight loaded (max)	kg : lb	3,655 : 8,058	4,241 : 9,350	4,014 : 8,850
Max wing loading	kg/m² : lb/sq ft	166·62 : 34·14	193·34 : 39·62	183·00 : 37·50
Max power loading	kg/hp : lb/hp	3·52 : 7·75	3·26 : 7·19	2·95 : 6·51
Max level speed	km/h : mph	555 : 345	586 : 364	608 : 378
at (height)	m : ft	4,570 : 15,000	6,095 : 20,000	3,200 : 10,500
Cruising speed	km/h : mph	435 : 270	467 : 290	463 : 288
Time to height		1·0 min to 820 m (2,690 ft)	7·6 min to 4,570 m (15,000 ft)	6·7 min to 4,570 m (15,000 ft)
Service ceiling	m : ft	8,990 : 29,500	10,485 : 34,400	11,580 : 38,000
Range	km : miles	1,175 : 730	604 : 375**	386 : 240*

*at 4,570 m (15,000 ft) performance figures are for gross weight of 3,323 kg (7,327 lb)

*at 3,660 m (12,000 ft) **with 500 lb bomb

*with 500 lb bomb

Curtiss P-40B of the 2nd Pursuit Squadron,
American Volunteer Group, Chinese Air Force,
Toungoo (Burma), December 1941

Curtiss refitted the tenth production P-36A in July 1937 with a supercharged 1,160hp Allison V-1710-19 engine, and the XP-40 (Model 75P) was born: the first of a fighter series that eventually reached a production total of 13,738 and served with ten Allied nations during World War Two. The USAAC (or USAAF, as it became in June 1941) gave the name Warhawk to all P-40 variants. Flown for the first time on 14 October 1938, the XP-40 was followed in April 1939 by a USAAC contract for five hundred and twenty-four production aircraft (1,040hp Allison V-1710-33 engines). The first three were used as prototypes; the initial flight by a true production P-40 (Curtiss Model 81-A) was made on 4 April 1940. The order had meanwhile been reduced to two hundred; deliveries began in May 1940. Two 0.30in guns were installed above the nose, in the engine cowling. France, already a major customer for the Hawk 75A, ordered one hundred and forty Hawk 81-A1s (similar to the P-40), but its government surrendered before these could be delivered. Diverted to the RAF, they became operational with No 2 Squadron in August 1941, for low-level tactical reconnaissance. Given the RAF name Tomahawk Mks I/IA/IB, they were armed with four 0.303in Browning machine-guns (two in the cowling; one in each wing). The next USAAF production version (one hundred and thirty-one built) was the P-40B, with the same powerplant, armour protection for the pilot, an extra 0.30in gun in each wing, and the calibre of the nose guns increased to 0.50in. One hundred and ten similar Model 81-A2s, intended for France, went instead to the RAF, which named

them Tomahawk Mk IIA. The P-40C was similar to the B except for a further 0.30in gun in each wing and improved self-sealing fuel tanks. It first flew on 10 April 1943, and one hundred and ninety-three were built for the USAAF. Yet another batch intended for France, of six hundred and thirty-five similar Model 81-A3s, went to the RAF, becoming Tomahawk Mk IIBs. A further two hundred and ninety-five of this version, supplied to the RAF under Lend-Lease, were handed on to China (one hundred) and the USSR (one hundred and ninety-five). In 1941 Curtiss introduced major design changes which justified the new Model number 87. Powered by a 1,150hp Allison V-1710-39 engine, this version was fitted with a modified propeller reduction gear, permitting the fuselage to be shortened by 6in (0.15m). Other changes included shorter main-wheel legs, redesigned rear fuselage and a deeper nose radiator. Provision was made for carrying a 500lb bomb or 52 US gallon drop-tank under the fuselage; smaller bombs could be carried under the wings. Armament was reduced to two 0.50in machine-guns in each wing, the over-nose guns being deleted. Most of these new fighter-bomber versions went to the RAF, which received five hundred and sixty Model 87-A1s as Kittyhawk Mk Is. Twenty-three similar Model 87-A2s were built for the USAAF as the P-40D, and Curtiss retained two for further development. Six 0.50in guns were installed in the Model 87-A3, of which 1,500 were allocated to the RAF as Kittyhawk Mk IAs and eight hundred and twenty delivered to the USAAF as the P-40E.

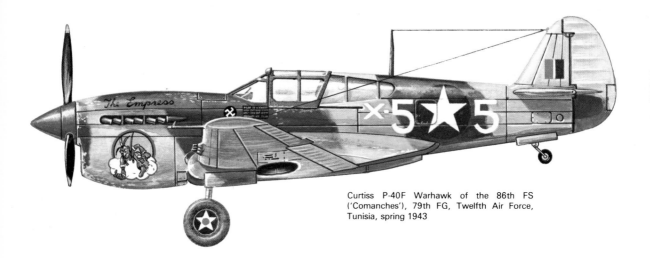

Curtiss P-40F Warhawk of the 86th FS ('Comanches'), 79th FG, Twelfth Air Force, Tunisia, spring 1943

TP-40N tandem-seat duel control combat trainer version of the Warhawk

Meanwhile, one of Curtiss's two development P-40Ds became the XP-40F (Model 87-D) after fitting with a Rolls-Royce Merlin 28; this made its first flight on 30 June 1941. Performance at altitude was much better than with the Allison, and 1,311 Merlin-engined P-40Fs were built for the USAAF. The first two hundred and sixty or so had the old-style P-40 fuselage, but later models had a 20in (0.51m) longer rear fuselage, redesigned to improve low-speed stability. They had the Packard-built V-1650-1 version of the Merlin, a cowling without the air intakes that had been a trademark of the earlier P-40s, and provision for a 170 US gallon drop-tank under the fuselage. A batch of two hundred and fifty was allocated to the RAF as the Kittyhawk Mk II, but was not delivered. Sixty P-40Gs were converted from the original P-40s in late 1940, by bringing them up to six-wing-gun standard. The P-40H and J projects never left the drawing-board; the latter was to have had a turbocharged Allison engine. The next, and heaviest, Warhawk was the P-40K; built in parallel with the P-40F, it had the lengthened fuselage of the later F models, and a small dorsal fin. Twenty-one P-40Ks were delivered to the RAF as Kittyhawk Mk IIIs, and 1,279 to the USAAF. This version was followed by the 'Gipsy Rose Lee', so called because it was a 'stripped' development of the P-40F, but known more formally as the P-40L. It had four wing guns only, reduced fuel capacity, and no armour protection, but the weight thus saved was only some 250lb (113.5kg); USAAF production was, therefore, limited to six hundred, in a mixture of long- and short-fuselage models – all powered by V-1650-1 Packard

Merlins. Similar to the K, except for a 1,200hp Allison V-1710-81, the P-40Ms were transferred mostly to the RAF (five hundred and ninety-five, also known as Kittyhawk Mk IIIs), only five being delivered to the USAAF. The last production Warhawk was also numerically the greatest: the P-40N of 1943. The USAAF received 4,634, and five hundred and eighty-six went to the RAF as Kittyhawk Mk IVs. Most were powered by 1,200hp Allison V-1710-81 or -99 engines, but the final two hundred and twenty had a 1,360hp V-1710-115. Armament comprised four 0.50in wing guns on early examples, and six on later ones, which were equipped also to carry a 1,500lb (680kg) bomb load. Thirty P-40Ns were converted to two-seat advanced trainers. Three hundred P-40Fs and Ls were refitted with V-1710-81 engines and redesignated P-40R1 and R2 respectively. Two XP-46 improved P-40s were more highly powered but still inferior to the Merlin models. Production ended in November 1944, by which time Curtiss had built a total of 1,704 Model 81s and 12,034 Model 87s. In addition to widespread use by the USAAF in the European, North African and Pacific theatres, Lend-Lease and ex-French Warhawks allocated to the RAF (1,180 Tomahawks and 3,262 Kittyhawks) were also employed by the Canadian, South African, Australian and New Zealand air forces; these too served in Europe, the Far East, the Western Desert and Italy. The USSR received 2,097 P-40s under Lend-Lease, and others were supplied to China. Annual output of Warhawks reached its highest points in 1942 (when 4,453 were built) and 1943 (4,258).

Liberator

Unadulterated: the B-24A initial production Liberator for the USAAC

The Ford Motor Co made a major contribution to Liberator production, including 1,587 of these B-24Js

The Liberator originated from a USAAC request in January 1939 that Consolidated should develop an advanced bomber to supersede the B-17. It was expected to demonstrate improved range, speed and operational ceiling. The resulting Model 32 had a cantilever monoplane shoulder-wing; a deep fuselage with a bomb bay that could accommodate 8,000lb (3,629kg); a tail unit with large oval endplate fins; tricycle-type landing gear; and power plant comprising four 1,200hp Pratt & Whitney R-1820-33 engines. A high aspect ratio 'Davis' wing was used to attain long range, and this incorporated leading-edge slots and Fowler trailing-edge flaps to ensure good take-off and landing characteristics. First flown on 29 December 1939, the XB-24 prototype performed satisfactorily, but there was little improvement over the B-17. Changes in the seven pre-production YB-24s included deletion of the leading-edge slots, introduction of de-icing boots for both wing and tail unit leading-edges, and a gross weight increase. In 1940, thirty-six examples of the first B-24A production model were ordered, and Consolidated also received an order for one hundred and twenty aircraft from a French Purchasing Mission; shortly after, a British Mission ordered one hundred and sixty-four for service with the RAF. These latter aircraft were designated Liberator by the RAF, a name later adopted by the USAAF. Before any production aircraft were ready France capitulated, and the French order was added to those for Britain; the first were flown across the North Atlantic in March 1941. Designated LB-30A by Consolidated (Liberator to British specification), they were used first by BOAC, later RAF Ferry Command, to carry aircrew across the Atlantic. Only nine B-24As were completed as such, these having two 0.30in and six 0.50in machine guns, and increased gross weight. When delivered they were used from 1 July 1941 by the USAAFs Ferrying Command for trans-Atlantic ferry services. Re-engined with turbocharged R-1830-41 engines, the XB-24 became redesignated XB-24B; with resited oil coolers, and a dorsal and tail turret each with two 0.50in guns, nine were bulit as B-24Cs. First major production version for the USAAF, however, was the generally similar B-24D with R-1830-43 engines, gross weight increased to 56,000lb (25,401kg), and armament in later production aircraft comprised ten 0.50in machine-guns and a maximum bomb load of 12,800lb (5,806kg). A total of 2,696 were built, 2,381 and three hundred and five by Consolidated at San Diego and Fort Worth respectively, and ten by Douglas. Some later production B-24Ds had R-1830-65 engines, and these powered some of the seven hundred and ninety-one similar B-24Es built by Consolidated (one hundred and forty-four), Douglas (one hundred and sixty-seven) and Ford (four hundred and eighty). The main alteration in this version was a change of propellers; some retained R-1830-43 engines. Delivery of B-24Gs began in 1943, four hundred and thirty being built by North American. The first twenty-five were similar to B-24Ds, but the remainder introduced a twin 0.50in gun upper nose turret which was intended to provide more positive defence against head-on attack. Very similar aircraft were built as B-24H by Consolidated (seven hundred and thirty-eight) with an

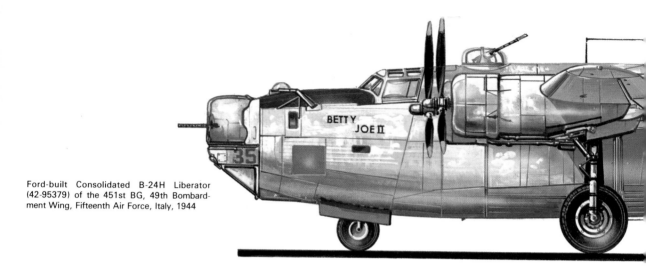

Ford-built Consolidated B-24H Liberator (42-95379) of the 451st BG, 49th Bombardment Wing, Fifteenth Air Force, Italy, 1944

Liberandos, a B-24D (42-40664) of the 376th BG, Ninth Air Force, at an air base in Cyrenaica after a raid on the Ploesti oilfields in Romania

Emerson nose turret, Douglas (five hundred and eighty-two) with Consolidated nose turret, and Ford (1,780) with the latter turret. Most extensively built was the similar B-24J, but this had a Motor Products nose turret, and later production examples had an autopilot and bomb-sight of the same manufacture. When B-24G/Hs were re-equipped with this bomb-sight they too were designated B-24J. Production totalled 6,678, contributed by Consolidated San Diego (2,792), Consolidated Fort Worth (1,558), Douglas (two hundred and five), Ford (1,587), and North American (five hundred and thirty-six). Final production versions were the B-24L with a tail gun station of Consolidated design, housing two manually-controlled 0.50in guns, in lieu of the tail turret; and the B-24M with Motor Products tail turret. In other respects both versions were similar to the B-24J, and construction comprised four hundred and seventeen B-24L and nine hundred and sixteen B-24M from Consolidated, and 1,250 and 1,677 respectively from Ford. Variants included one XB-24F with a thermal de-icing system; an XB-24K with single fin and rudder; XB-24N and YB-24N prototype and pre-production examples respectively of the 1,350hp R-1830-75 powered B-24N which was cancelled after VE-day; and a few RB-24L gunnery trainers. A single XB-41 was produced by conversion of a B-24D, equipped with a total of fourteen 0.50in machine-guns to serve as a bomber escort, but it proved unsuccessful. Photo-reconnaissance versions of the Liberator included an initial XF-7 with additional fuel capacity and up to eleven cameras, followed by similar F-7s, and six-camera F-7A and F-7Bs. Transport

versions included two hundred and eighty-five C-87s with fuselage windows and accommodation for twenty-five passengers and five crew, and six C-87As, each with ten executive sleeping berths. Five C-87s were converted, under the designation AT-22, to serve as flying class-rooms for flight engineers; the final USAAF transport version was the C-109 tanker, developed especially to carry aviation fuel over the Himalayas from India to China. US Navy interest in the Liberator was more than academic, a total of nine hundred and seventy-seven being acquired as PB4Y-1s; a mix of B-24D and B-24J versions, most were received in August 1943 when the USAAF handed over its anti-submarine units. The equivalent to USAAF C-87 and C-87A transports were acquired as RY-2 and RY-1 respectively. A number of Navy aircraft were modified as PB4Y-1Ps for reconnaissance duties. Specially built for the Navy was the PB4Y-2 Privateer; seven hundred and thirty-six were received. These had 1,350hp R-1830-94 engines without turbochargers, changed engine nacelles, lengthened fuselage, and the single fin and rudder of the XB-24K. Britain also received many Liberators, most of them under Lend-Lease. These included: Liberator Mk Is, equivalent to the B-24A, some with ASV radar; Liberator Mk IIIs, similar to the B-24C, one of which, named *Commando,* was used by Winston Churchill; Liberator Mk IIs, equivalent to the B-24D, (Lend-Lease supplies were designated Liberator Mk IIIA); B-24Es, B-24Gs and B-24H/Js were designated Liberator Mks IV, V and VI respectively. Liberator Mk VIs specially modified for service with Coastal Command

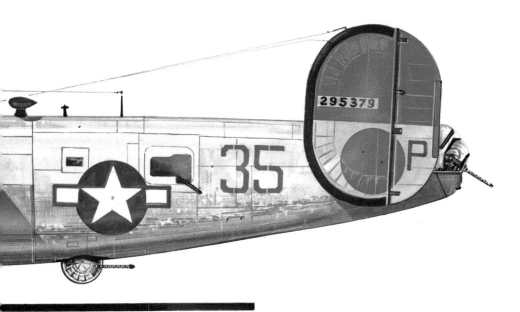

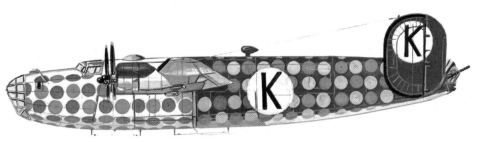

B-24D Liberator 'lead ship' of the 458th BG,
Eighth Air Force, European Theatre of
Operations, 1944

became Liberator Mk VIIIs, and transports equivalent to the
USAAF C-87 and Navy RY-3 became C Mk VII and C Mk IX
respectively. When production ended in 1945, approximately
19,260 of these valuable aircraft had been built.

A PB4Y-1 (BuNo 123928)

Squadron art on the nose of a B-24J of the
448th BS, 93rd BG, Eighth Air Force, UK, 1943

Helldiver

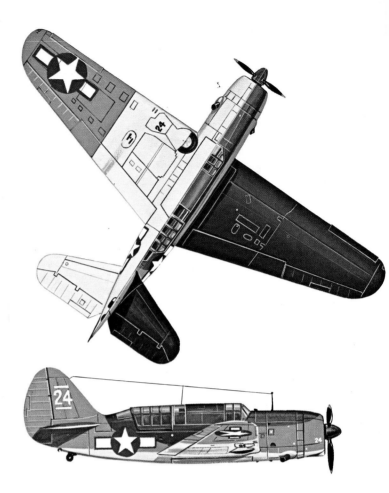

Curtiss SB2C-1C of Squadron V8-8. VSS
Bunker Hill, June 1944

Span: 49ft 8⅛in (15.15m)
Length: 36ft 8in (11.18m)
Weight: 14,760lb (6,695kg)
Engine: 1 × 1,700hp Wright R-2600-8
    Cyclone radial
Max speed: 281mph (452kmh)
Operational ceiling: 24,700ft (7,529m)
Range: 1,895 miles (3,050km)
Armament: 2 × 20mm cannon, 2 × 0.30in
    machine-guns
Max bomb load: 1,000lb (454kg)

The XSB2C-1 Helldiver prototype, following its first flight on 18 December 1940, was lost in a crash early in the following year – an inauspicious beginning to the career of perhaps the most successful dive bomber ever to enter U.S. Navy service. The initial Navy order, placed in November 1940, was later increased until nine hundred and seventy-eight SB2C-1s had been completed, the first of which was delivered in June 1942. They were succeeded by one thousand one hundred and twelve SB2C-3s, two thousand and forty-five SB2C-4s and nine hundred and seventy SB2C-5s. The SB2C-3 had the 1,900hp R-2600-20 model of the Cyclone engine, while the SB2C-4 introduced search radar in an under-wing fairing and provision for an external warload of 1,000lb (454kg) of bombs or eight 5in rocket projectiles. The SB2C-5 was essentially a longer-range variant of the -4. Nine hundred Helldivers purchased by the USAAF, and built by Curtiss and Douglas with the Army title A-25A Shrike, were mostly transferred to

the Marine Corps as SB2C-1As. Starting in the summer of 194 the Canadian Car and Foundry Co built eight hundred and ninety-four SBW-1, -3, -4 and -5 Helldivers, including twenty six supplied to the British Fleet Air Arm. Fairchild in Canad contributed three hundred SBF-1, -3 and -4 versions to bring the overall Helldiver production total to seven thousand two hundred aircraft. The British machines were not used on active service, but the American Helldivers, perpetuating the name given to Curtiss's earlier SBC biplane dive bomber played a prominent part in the Pacific war, operating from the USS *Bunker Hill, Enterprise, Essex, Independence* and other carriers. Their first major action was the Rabaul campaign in November 1943, and they took part in virtually every major naval/air action during the rest of the war. One SB2C-1 wa fittted experimentally with twin floats as the XSB2C-2, and an SB2C-5 with 2,100hp R-2600-22 engine became the sole XSB2C-6, but neither version went into production

Douglas A-26/B-26 Invader

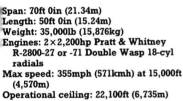

Douglas A-26B Invader of the US Ninth Air Force, Europe, 1944-45

Span: 70ft 0in (21.34m)
Length: 50ft 0in (15.24m)
Weight: 35,000lb (15,876kg)
Engines: 2 × 2,200hp Pratt & Whitney R-2800-27 or -71 Double Wasp 18-cyl radials
Max speed: 355mph (571kmh) at 15,000ft (4,570m)
Operational ceiling: 22,100ft (6,735m)
Range: 1,400 miles (2,253km)
Armament: 10 × 0.50in machine-guns
Max bomb load: 4,000lb (1,814kg) internally

The Douglas Invader's design was begun in January 1941. It was initiated as a successor to the Douglas A-20 Havoc and designated in the 'A' for attack series. In June 1941 the USAAF ordered three prototypes each to a different configuration, the first flying on 10 January 1942. The XA-26 was an attack bomber, with a 3,000lb internal bomb load, twin guns, in a transparent nose and two each in dorsal and ventral turrets; the XA-26A night fighter had radar in a solid nose four cannon in a ventral tray and four 0.50in guns in a dorsal turret; the XA-26B had a short nose mounting a 75mm cannon. The initial production model, the A-26B, additionally had six 0.50in wing machine guns, and the bomb load increased. Later batches introduced R-2800-79 engines with water injection, boosting power and performance at altitude, eight nose guns; and additional gun-packs, RPs or 2,200lb (907kg) of bombs could be carried beneath the wings. To concentrate fire-power, the dorsal guns could be locked forward and fired by the pilot. Douglas built five hundred and thirty-five water-injection Bs, following the initial eight hundred and twenty-five. The A-26 made its European operational debut in autumn 1944, and its first Pacific appearance early in 1945. The A-26C, appearing in

1945, saw limited war-service. Similar to the B, this had the twin-gun transparent 'bombardier' nose. After VJ-day, large numbers of orders were cancelled, but even so, 1,091 A-26Cs were completed. In Europe alone, Invaders flew over 11,000 sorties and dropped more than 18,000 tons of bombs for the loss of sixty-seven aircraft in combat; curiously, they destroyed only seven enemy aircraft. Postwar, redesignated B-26 as a bomber after the Martin B-26 Marauder was withdrawn in 1958, they became a standard USAF type. In the Korean War the Invader proved ideal for close support and night intruder operations. Its usefulness in limited war engagements was emphasised in Vietnam, and On Mark Engineering brought forty B-26Bs up to B-26K standard for the COIN role. Modifications included installing higher-powered engines and airframe strengthening to permit carriage of a 6,000lb ordnance load on eight underwing points, in addition to the internal load. Until the late 1960s Invaders, either Bs or Cs, though not first-line equipment, served with the French, Indonesian and Turkish air forces, but were operated in their original roles by Brazil, Chile, the Dominican Republic, Guatemala, Peru, Saudi Arabia and South Vietnam.

Douglas Havoc

Douglas A-20G Havoc (43-9407) of the 675th
BS, 417th BG(L), Fifth Air Force, New Guinea,
circa summer 1944

One of the classic combat aircraft, the Douglas DB-7 evolved into two basic families: the two-seat night fighter/intruder (RAF Havoc, USAAF P-70), and three-seat attack bomber (RAF Boston, US Army A-20 Havoc). There were also 46 US Army F-3A two-seat photo-reconnaissance versions, converted from A-20Js and A-20Ks. The Douglas Aircraft Company had already begun the design of a twin-engined attack bomber before receiving, in 1938, a USAAC specification calling for such an aircraft. This Model 7A design was submitted in July 1938, Douglas becoming one of four companies to build prototypes for competitive evaluation. The design was refined further during prototype construction, the resulting Model 7B flying for the first time on 26 October 1938. Of shoulder-wing configuration, it was powered by two 1,100hp Pratt & Whitney R-1830C radial engines and featured a retractable tricycle landing gear. First customer for the new aircraft was a French Purchasing Commission which ordered 100 DB-7s (Douglas Bomber) on 15 February 1939. These differed from the 7B in having mid-mounted wings due to a deeper, narrower fuselage, with a more streamlined nose; two 1,100hp R-1830-SC3G engines in longer, underslung nacelles; armament of six 7.5mm machine-guns, four forward-firing from two-gun blisters on each side of the nose, and one each in dorsal and ventral positions, plus a 1,764lb (800kg) internal bomb load. France placed a second contract for one hundred and seventy DB-7s with 1,200hp R-1830-S3C4G engines on 14 October 1939; only one hundred and forty were

so powered. These first two hundred and seventy aircraft were, apart from the prototype 7B, the only DB-7s to have Twin Wasp engines: all subsequent models, bringing overall production to 7,477 by September 1944, had variants of the Wright R-2600 Cyclone. By the summer of 1940 Douglas had received orders totalling 1,198 from Britain, France, and Holland; not counting the original two hundred and seventy on order, these included one hundred DB-7A (1,600hp R-2600-A5Bs) and four hundred and eighty DB-7Cs for France (the latter taken over by Britain to DB-7B standard); three hundred DB-7Bs (R-2600-A5Bs and 0.303in guns) for Britain; and forty-eight similar DB-7Cs for Holland. Production to US government orders began with a contract of 24 June 1939 for sixty-three A-20 attack bombers, similar to DB-7Bs but with 1,600hp R-2600-7 turbocharged engines. Subsequent orders included one hundred and forty-three A-20As (unsupercharged R-2600-3s); nine hundred and ninety-nine A-20Bs (DB-7A standard, R-2600-11s); nine hundred and forty-eight A-20Cs (1,600hp R-2600-23s); one hundred and forty built by Boeing); 2,850 similarly-powered A-20Gs; four hundred and twelve A-20Hs (1,700hp R-2600-29s); four hundred and fifty A-20Js (R-2600-23s); and four hundred and thirteen A-20Ks (R-2600-29s). No accurate records exist of the eventual deployment of all these DB-7 variants. Most of the aircraft ordered by France and Holland were delivered to Britain, and both Britain and the Soviet Union received large numbers of these aircraft under Lend-Lease.

All-black Douglas P-70, with under-fuselage gun pack

Aircraft type		Douglas A-20G	Douglas A-20K	Douglas P-70
Power plant		2×1,600 hp Wright R-2600-23	2×1,700 hp Wright R-2600-29	2×1,600 hp Wright R-2600-11
Accommodation		3	3	3
Wing span	m : ft in	18·69 : 61 4	18·69 : 61 4	18·69 : 61 4
Length overall	m : ft in	14·63 : 48 0	14·73 : 48 4	14·50 : 47 7
Height overall	m : ft in	5·36 : 17 7	5·36 : 17 7	5·36 : 17 7
Wing area	m² : sq ft	43·11 : 464·0	43·11 : 464·0	43·11 : 464·0
Weight empty	kg : lb	7,250 : 15,984	7,764 : 17,117	7,272 : 16,031
Weight loaded (max)	kg : lb	12,338 : 27,200	12,247 : 27,000	9,645 : 21,264
Max wing loading	kg/m² : lb/sq ft	286·07 : 58·62	283·97 : 58·19	223·64 : 45·83
Max power loading	kg/hp : lb/hp	3·86 : 8·50	3·60 : 7·94	3·02 : 6·65
Max level speed	km/h : mph	546 : 339	510 : 317	529 : 329
at (height)	m : ft	3,780 : 12,400	3,260 : 10,700	4,265 : 14,000
Cruising speed	km/h : mph	438 : 272	414 : 257	435 : 270
Time to height		7·1 min to 3,050 m (10,000 ft)	8·8 min to 3,050 m (10,000 ft)	8·0 min to 3,660 m (12,000 ft)
Service ceiling	m : ft	7,865 : 25,800	7,040 : 23,100	8,610 : 28,250
Range (normal)	km : miles	1,754 : 1,090	1,609 : 1,000	1,706 : 1,060

*with 907 kg (2,000 lb)
bomb load

Marauder

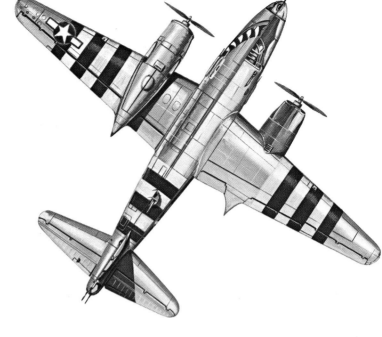

Martin B-26B-55 Marauder of the 598th
Bomber Squadron, 397th Bomber Group, US
Ninth Air Force, June 1944

Span: 71ft 0in (21.64m)
Length: 58ft 3in (17.75m)
Weight: 37,000lb (16,783kg)
Engines: 2 × 1920hp Pratt & Whitney
R-2800–43 Double Wasp radials
Max speed: 282mph (454kmh)
Operational ceiling: 21,700ft (6,614m)
Range: 1,150 miles (1,851km)
Armaments: 11 × 0.50in and 1 × 0.30in
machine-guns
Max bomb load: 5,200lb (2,359kg)

Finishing the war with a combat loss rate of less than one per cent, the Marauder more than vindicated its early reputation as a 'widow maker', which arose chiefly from the high accident rate created by inexperienced pilots handling an unfamiliar and unusually heavy aeroplane. As the Martin 179, its design was entered for a 1939 US Army design competition and was rewarded by an immediate order for two hundred and one aircraft without the usual prototype preliminaries. The first B-26, flown on 25 November 1940, exhibited a modest armament, compared with later models, of only five defensive guns. Delivery to USAAC units began in 1941, in which year there also appeared the B-26A, with heavier calibre nose and tail guns, provision for extra fuel tanks in the bomb bay and for carrying a torpedo beneath the fuselage. One hundred and thirty-nine B-26As were completed, making their operational debut from Australian bases in the spring of 1942. The B-26 also appeared in action from Alaskan and North African bases. Then followed the B-26B, with uprated engines and increased armament. Of the one thousand eight hundred and eighty-three built, all but the first six hundred and forty-one B-26Bs also introduced a new, extended-span wing and taller tail. The B-26B made its operational debut in Europe in May 1943, subsequently becoming one of the hardest-worked Allied medium bombers in this theatre. One thousand two hundred and ten B-26Cs were built, essentially similar to the later B models. These were succeeded by the B-26F (three hundred built), in which the wing incidence was increased with the purpose of improving take-off performance and reducing the accident rate. The final model was the B-26G, which differed only slightly from the F; nine hundred and fifty G models were completed, the last being delivered in March 1945. Of the overall US production supplies to the RAF under Lend-Lease included fifty-two B-26As (as Marauder Is), two hundred B-26Fs (Marauder II) and one hundred and fifty B-26Gs (Marauder III). Many other Marauders were completed for the USAAF as AT-23 or TB-26 trainers, and some for the US Navy as JM-1s.

Lodestar

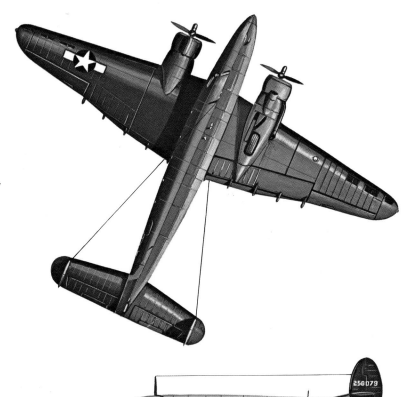

Lockheed C-60A Lodestar of the USAAF, 1943-44

Span: 65ft 6in (19.96m)
Length: 49ft 9⅛in (15.19m)
Weight: 18,500lb (8,392kg)
Engines: 2×1200hp Wright R-1820-87
   Cyclone radials
Max speed: 266mph (428kmh)
Operational ceiling: 27,000ft (8,230m)
Range: 1,660 miles (2,672km)

The pre-war Model 18 Lodestar commercial transport was selected by the US Army for wartime production, three hundred and twenty-five being built as standard Army and Navy paratroop transports with the designation C-60A. A proposed freighter version with large cargo-loading doors was to have been built in even large numbers, but this contract was cancelled. However, a variety of assorted civil Model 18s were acquired for war service under several separate designations. Those in USAAF service included thirty-six C-56 to C-56E; thirteen C-57 and seven C-57A; ten C-59; thirty-six C-60; and one C-66. The US Navy designations R50-1, -2, -5 and -6 correspond to the USAAFs C-56, C-59, C-60 and C-60A, while the R50-3 and -4 were 4-seat and 7-seat executive transports respectively. Many of the impressed commercial Model 18s were returned to their former owners during 1943-44, very few remaining in service beyond this date. Although not in service in great numbers, the Lodestar performed a wide range of duties that included troop and cargo transport, casualty evacuation and glider training. More then two dozen civil Lodestars were also impressed into service with the RAF, to whom Lend-Lease deliveries included ten Mk IA and seventeen Mk II. Twenty aircraft corresponding to the American C-56B version were supplied to the Royal Netherlands Indies Army Air Corps.

Martin B-26 Marauder

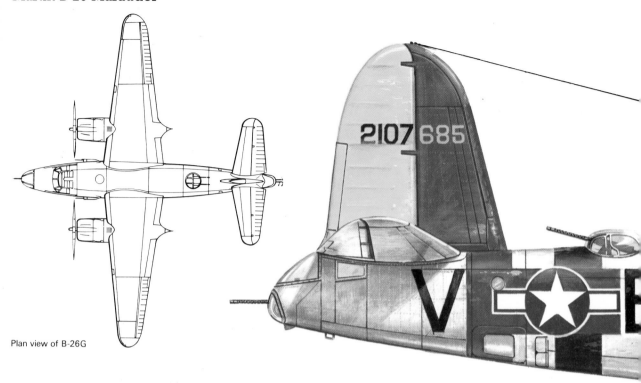

Plan view of B-26G

Martin B-26C-45 (42-107685) of the 451st BS
(322nd BG), Ninth Air Force, UK June 1944

Aircraft type		Martin B-26B	Martin B-26G
Power plant		2×2,000 hp Pratt & Whitney R-2800-41	2×2,000 hp Pratt & Whitney R-2800-43
Accommodation		7	7
Wing span	m : ft in	19·81 : 65 0	21·64 : 71 0
Length overall	m : ft in	17·75 : 58 3	17·09 : 56 1
Height overall	m : ft in	6·05 : 19 10	6·20 : 20 4
Wing area	m² : sq ft	55·93 : 602·0	61·13 : 658·0
Weight empty	kg : lb	10,151 : 22,380	10,795 : 23,800
Weight loaded (max)	kg : lb	15,422 : 34,000	17,327 : 38,200
Max wing loading	kg/m² : lb/sq ft	275·61 : 56·48	283·31 : 58·05
Max power loading	kg/hp : lb/hp	3·86 : 8·50	4·33 : 9·55
Max level speed	km/h : mph	510 : 317	455 : 283
at (height)	m : ft	4,420 : 14,500	1,525 : 5,000
Cruising speed	km/h : mph	418 : 260	348 : 216
Time to height		12·0 min to 4,570 m (15,000 ft)	8·0 min to 1,525 m (5,000 ft)
Service ceiling	m : ft	7,165 : 23,500	6,035 : 19,800
Range	km : miles	1,851 : 1,150*	1,770 : 1,100*

*with 1,361 kg (3,000 lb) bomb load   *with 1,814 kg (4,000 lb) bomb load

94

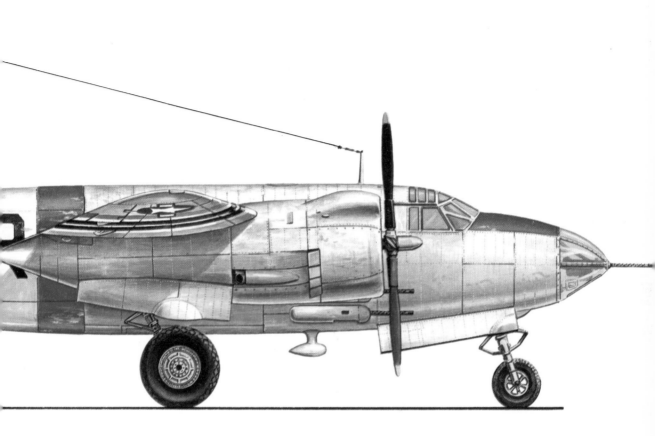

Designed to meet a USAAC requirement of 1939 for a medium bomber, Martin's Model 179 gained almost immediate acceptance and a contract for two hundred and one B-26 production aircraft, without recourse to prototype or pre-production examples for evaluation. The initial B-26 had a wing loading of 45.2lb/sq ft (220.6kg/m²), needing a long take-off run, and landed at more than 100 mph (161km/h). The first B-26, flown on 25 November 1940, served in effect as the prototype. Deliveries of the remaining two hundred began in February 1941. Powered by two 1,850hp Pratt & Whitney R-2800-5 engines, the B-26 could carry two 2,000lb bombs internally, or a maximum load of 4,800lb (2,177kg) in smaller sizes, and defensive armament included three 0.50in and one, or two, 0.30in guns. The B-26A (one hundred and thirty-nine built) appeared in October 1941, the first thirty with identical engines to the B-26, the remainder with similarly-rated R-2800-39s. Internal bomb load was limited to 2,000lb (907kg) to allow introduction of an auxiliary fuel tank in the bomb bay. The RAF received fifty-two late-production B-26As, designating them Marauder, a name adopted also by the USAAF. Production of the B-26B began in April 1942, the first six hundred and forty-one with 2,000hp R-2800-41 engines, improved armour, and twin tail guns in a lengthened rear fuselage. By then the Marauder's reputation had resulted in a board of enquiry to determine why so many were being lost in training accidents. Primary reasons were inexperienced crews and the high wing loading, and wisely the board decided to continue with production, but to modify the

training programme and introduce design changes. These modifications appeared on the B-26C in 1942, consisting of a new wing of greater span and area, and a taller fin and rudder. The first of 1,210 B-26Cs was delivered in August 1942, and a further 1,242 B-26Bs were completed to virtually the same standard. Power plant of the late-production B-26B models and the B-26C were 2,000hp R-2800-43 engines. Maximum bomb load was 5,200lb (2,359kg), but it was more usual to restrict it to 4,000lb (1,814kg) and carry an auxiliary fuel tank. Subsequent armament improvements resulted in some aircraft with up to 15 machine-guns. The RAF received nineteen B-26Bs as Marauder Mk IA, and was allocated one hundred and twenty-three B-26Cs as Marauder Mk IIs, though about twenty-five less were delivered. A B-26, converted to test a wing de-icing system that used hot engine bleed air, was designated XB-26D. Next production version was the B-26F, similar to the B-26B, but with 3½° increased wing incidence to improve take-off. The RAF received two hundred as Marauder Mk IIIs, and one hundred and fifty others as Mk IIIs equivalent to B-26Gs. The latter (eight hundred and ninety-three built) had the longer fuselage and -43 engines of late B/C models, but was otherwise similar to the B-26F. The B-26 remained operational in Europe until May 1945, but in the Pacific was replaced from spring 1944 by late-model B-25 Mitchells. Interspersed among earlier B-26B/C production were five hundred and eighty-three trainer/target tugs designated AT-23A (two hundred and eight built) and AT-23B (three hundred and seventy-five).

Boeing B-17 Flying Fortress

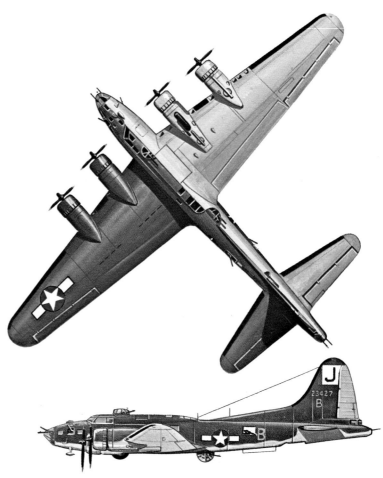

Douglas-built Boeing B-17F-60-DL of the 390th
BG, US Eighth Air Force, UK, 1943-45

Span: 103ft 9⅜in (31.63m)
Length: 74ft 8⅝in (22.78m)
Weight: 55,000lb (24,948kg)
Engines: 4 × 1,200hp Wright R-1820-97
    Cyclone 9-cyl radials
Max speed: 299mph (481kmh) at 25,000ft
    (7,620m)
Operational ceiling: 37,500ft (11,430m)
Range with 6,000lb (2,722kg) bomb load:
    1,300 miles (2,092km)
Armament: 8 × 0.50in Browning machine-
    guns, 1 × 0.303in Browning machine-
    gun
Max bomb load (short range): 12,800lb
    (5,806kg) internally, plus 8,000lb
    (3,629kg) externally

In August 1934 Boeing began to develop their Model 299 bomber design to meet a 1934 USAAC requirement for an offshore anti-shipping bomber. The prototype, powered by four 750hp Pratt & Whitney radials, flew on 28 July 1935. Just over three weeks later it began USAAC evaluation trials but was destroyed on 30 October 1935 in a take-off accident. However, it had shown sufficient potential and in January Boeing received a contract for thirteen YB-17 and one Y-1B-17A for more exhaustive service trials, these differing from the prototype in having 930hp Wright Cyclones, those of the Y1B-17A being turbo-supercharged. Twelve Y1B-17s entered service with the Army's 2nd BG, with whom they remained as B-17s after completing service trials. In 1938 a production contract was placed for the modest quantity of thirty-nine. These incorporated a number of improvements, notably a modified nose and a larger rudder, and were designated B-17B. The thirty-eight B-17Cs had increased armament and more powerful Cyclones; twenty were supplied to the RAF in 1941 as the Fortress Mk I; forty-two B-17Ds had a tenth crew member, self-sealing fuel tanks and no external bomb racks. Most of the USAAF's remaining B-17Cs were converted to D standard. The last variant to appear before Pearl Harbor was the B-17E, which first flew in

September 1941. It introduced the huge ventral fin and rudder that characterised subsequent Fortresses; firepower was considerably increased by ventral and dorsal power turrets, a tail gun position and a multi-gun nose, bringing defensive armament to thirteen guns. Boeing built five hundred and twelve B-17Es, including forty-five RAF Fortress Mk IIs. B-17s carried out the first raids on European targets made by the 8th US Air Force in August 1942; this version also served extensively in the Pacific theatre. The B-17F was sub-contracted to Douglas and Lockheed-Vega factories which, with Boeing, built 3,405; nineteen were supplied to the RAF as Fortress Mk IIs, and forty-one were converted to F-9 PR aircraft. These companies built 8,680 of the last production model, the B-17G; eighty-five became Fortress Mk IIIs with RAF Coastal Command, and ten were converted to F-9Cs. The B-17G was characterised by its 'chin' turret with two 0.50in machine-guns, also added to later B-17Fs in service. The USN and USCG were allotted forty-eight B-17Gs for ASR or early warning patrol duties, designated PB-1G and PB-1W respectively. About fifty B-17s, adapted to carry a lifeboat under the fuselage, were redesignated B-17H and employed on ASR.

Mariner

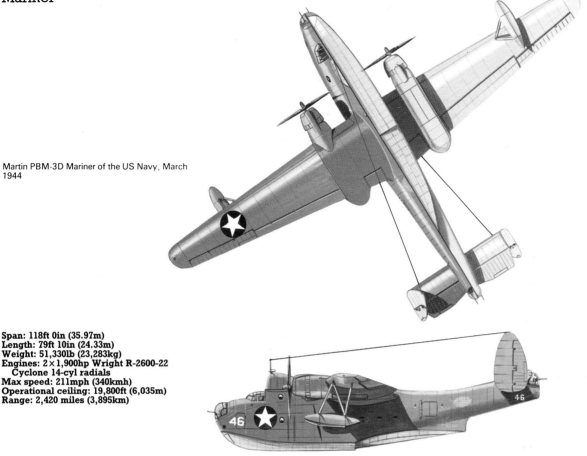

Martin PBM-3D Mariner of the US Navy, March 1944

Span: 118ft 0in (35.97m)
Length: 79ft 10in (24.33m)
Weight: 51,330lb (23,283kg)
Engines: 2 × 1,900hp Wright R-2600-22 Cyclone 14-cyl radials
Max speed: 211mph (340kmh)
Operational ceiling: 19,800ft (6,035m)
Range: 2,420 miles (3,895km)

The Mariner (Martin Model 162) design for a maritime reconnaissance bomber was initiated in 1937, and to test its aerodynamic and hydrodynamic qualities Martin built a Model 162A quarter-scale single-seat 'prototype'. A full-size prototype, designated XPBM-1, was ordered in June 1937 by the US Navy, and in the following December a contract was placed for twenty PBM-1 production aircraft, differing principally in having dihedral tailplanes. First flight of the XPBM-1 (serial number 0796) was made on 18 February 1939, and delivery of production aircraft, mostly to Squadron VP-74, began in 1940. Powerplant of this initial model was two 1,600hp Wright R-2600-6 Cyclone radial engines, and the PBM-1 carried a crew of seven, a bomb load of 2,000lb (907kg), including depth charges, and a defensive armament of one 0.30in and five 0.50in machine-guns in nose, tail, dorsal and waist positions. Shortly after this version entered service substantially larger orders were placed for improved models of the Mariner. These appeared from 1942, and were designated in the PBM-3 series, the XPBM-2 having been a prototype with additional fuel tankage and provision for catapult launching. Whereas the PBM-1 had had retractable wingtip floats, those of the PBM-3 models were larger, non-retractable and braced by struts. Engine nacelles were lengthened to accommodate depth charges or bombs. Variants included the PBM-3B (thirty-two built for Lend-Lease supply to the RAF); PBM-3C (two hundred and seventy-four for the US Navy); PBM-3D (two hundred and one for the USN);

PBM-3R (fifty for the US Naval Air Transport Service); and PBM-3S (one hundred and fifty-six for the USN). The PBM-3B, -3C, -3R and -3S were powered by 1,700hp R-2600-12 Cyclones, the PBM-3D having uprated R-2600-22 engines of 1,900hp each. Except for their power-plant the -3C and -3D combat models were essentially similar, having increased armour protection internally, power-operated nose and dorsal turrets and search radar in a large fairing above and behind the flight deck. Bomb load of the PBM-3D was 8,000lb (3,629kg). The PBM-3S, produced for a more specialised anti-submarine role, was structurally similar to the -3C but had less armour protection, a total armament of four hand-held guns and increased fuel capacity. All armament was deleted from the PBM-3R, which served as a transport accommodating twenty troops or an equivalent freight load. No examples were built of the PBM-4, a proposed version with R-3350-8 Cyclone engines. In May 1943 there flew the first of two prototypes of the PBM-5, a more powerful version with 2,100hp Pratt & Whitney R-2800-34 Double Wasp radial engines, eight 0.50in guns and a smaller APS-15 search radar in a bullet-shaped fairing mounted on a pylon above and behind the flight deck. Deliveries began in September 1944. More than a thousand of this version were ordered, but after VJ-day cancellations the total number of PBM-5s built (including prototypes) was five hundred and ninety-one. Some of these, re-equipped after the war with more modern gear, were then redesignated PBM-5E.

Consolidated B-24 Liberator

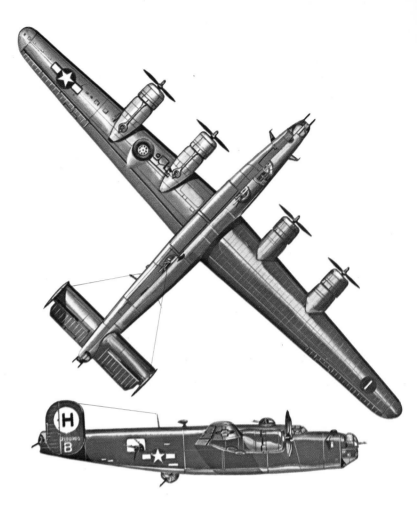

Convair B-24J-95-CO of the 448th BG, US Eighth Air Force, UK, *circa* November/December 1943

Span: 110ft 0in (33.53m)
Length: 67ft 2in (20.47m)
Weight: 56,000lb (25,401kg)
Engines: 4 × 1,200hp Pratt & Whitney R-1830-65 Twin Wasp 14-cyl radial
Max speed: 290mph (467kmh) at 25,000ft (7,620m)
Operational ceiling: 28,000ft (8,535m)
Range at max overload weight: 2,100 miles (3,380km)
Armament: 10 × 0.50in Browning machine-guns
Max bomb load: 5,000lb (2,268kg) internally

The Liberator was built in greater numbers and more variants than any other World War 2 US aircraft and served in more combat theatres, over a longer period, than any heavy bomber. The exceptionally high aspect ratio Davis wing gave it prodigious range and the capacious fuselage permitted a large bomb or cargo-load. The XB-24 Consolidated Model 32 (prototype) flew on 29 December 1939, followed by seven service trials YB-24s and thirty-six production B-24As. The French order one hundred and twenty, which were diverted to Britain, the first few, LB-30 or -30A, being used by BOAC for transatlantic ferrying; twenty went to RAF Coastal Command as Liberator Mk 1s, with ASV radar. B-24A deliveries to the USAAF began in June 1941, followed by nine B-24Cs with turbo-supercharged engines and revised armament. The first US version to serve in the bomber role was the B-24D, similar to the C except for R-1830-43s and increased gross weight; production, including ten by Douglas, totalled 2,738; the RAF received two hundred and sixty as Mks III and IIIA and one hundred and twenty-two as Mk Vs with radar and Leigh searchlights for Coastal Command. In mid-1943 the USAAF anti-submarine patrol B-24Ds were transferred to the USN and redesignated PB4Y-1. Convair (as Consolidated became), Douglas and Ford built seven hundred and ninety-one B-24Es,

distinguishable from the D by different propellers: North American built four hundred and thirty B-24Gs, some with a powered nose turret. An Emerson nose turret and R-1830-65s characterised the H; Convair, Douglas and Ford built 3,100, and then, with North American, manufactured 6,678 B-27Js, with Motor Products nose turret and Briggs ventral ball turret. The RAF received 1,278 as Mks VI (bomber) and VII (general reconnaissance); nine hundred and seventy-seven went to the USN, designated PB4Y-1, most with radar replacing the ventral turret. Armament variations characterised the B-24L and M (1,667 and 2,593 respectively, by Convair and Ford). Ford completed seven single-finned YB-24Ns, and forty-six similar RY-3s, for the USN, before contracts for over 5,000 B-24Ns were cancelled in May 1945. The Liberator shared the day bombing of Europe with the Boeing B-17 but was even more prominent in the Pacific where its range was particularly valuable. It gave considerable service as a transport, two hundred and seventy-six B-24Ds being completed as C-87s; and some one hundred B-24s became F-7 PR aircraft. The RCAF and Commonwealth air forces operated considerable numbers. Liberator production, ending on 31 May 1945, totalled 18,188.

Grumman F6F Hellcat

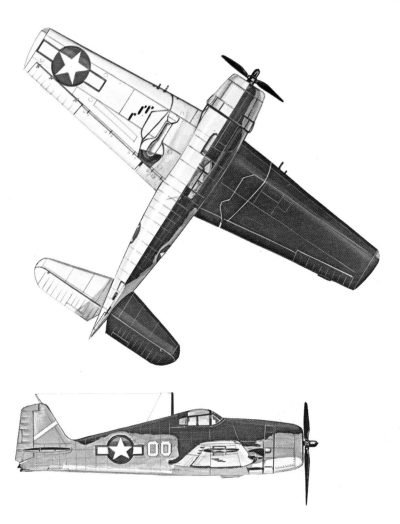

Grumman F6F-3 Hellcat of VF-9, US Navy, USS
Yorktown, September 1943

Span: 42ft 10in (13.06m)
Length: 33ft 7in (10.24m)
Weight, normal take-off: 12,441lb
(5,643kg)
Engine: 2,000hp Pratt & Whitney
R-2800-10 Double Wasp 18-cyl radial
Max speed: 375mph (604kmh) at 17,300ft
(5,273m)
Operational ceiling: 37,300ft (11,370m)
Range: 1,090 miles (1,754km)
Armament: 6×0.50in Browning M-2
machine-guns

The Hellcat, essentially a larger and more powerful development of the F4F Wildcat, flew in its original XF6F-1 form on 26 June 1942, with a 1,700hp Wright R-2600-10 Cyclone engine. It was then re-engined with a 2,000hp Pratt & Whitney R-2800-10 Double Wasp to become the XF6F-3, flying in this form on 30 July 1942. Production F6F-3s were virtually unchanged from this aircraft. They began to appear early in October 1942, making their operational debuts with the FAA in July 1943, and with the USN in the attack on Marcus Island on 31 August by F6F-3s from USS *Essex, Yorktown* and *Independence.* The F6F rapidly replaced the Wildcat aboard USN attack carriers. FAA Hellcats participated in anti-shipping strikes off the Norwegian coast and in the attack on the *Tirpitz;* they were also operated extensively in the Far East. Production for the USN totalled 4,646 F6F-3s, including eighteen F6F-3E and two hundred and five F6F-3N night fighters; a further two hundred and fifty-two were supplied to the FAA as the Hellcat Mk I, under Lend-Lease. Aerodynamic and control-surface improvements were introduced on the

F6F-5, which entered production in 1944 and was able to operate in the fighter-bomber role with under wing weapons. The F6F-5 was powered by an R-2800-10W capable of 2,200hp using water-injection, and was both the principal and the last production Hellcat model. By November 1945, when production ended, 12,272 Hellcats had been manufactured. Of these, 6,436 were of the F6F-5 model, nearly a fifth of which were F6F-5N night fighters; and nine hundred and thirty others were essentially similar Hellcat Mk IIs for the FAA. Whereas its predecessor, the Wildcat, had been widely used in both the Atlantic and Pacific war areas, the Hellcat operated with the USN and the FAA predominantly in the Pacific, but was used aboard escort carriers in the Atlantic against U-boats. In service with land-based USMC units as well as carrier-based squadrons, it was officially credited with 4,947 victims, some eighty per cent of the 6,477 enemy aircraft destroyed in air-to-air combat by USN carrier pilots during the war, plus two hundred and nine by USMC pilots.

Boeing B-29 Superfortress

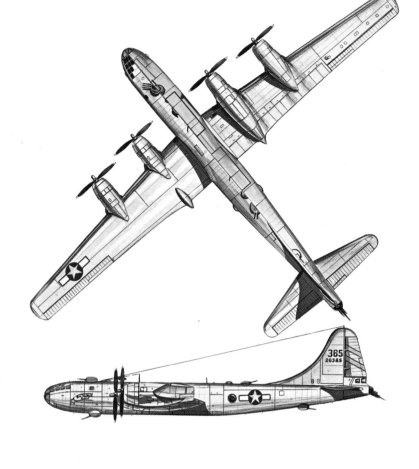

Boeing B-29 Superfortress of the 795th BS, 468th BG, US 20th Air Force, China-Burma-India theatre, early autumn 1944

Span: 141ft 3in (43.05m)
Length: 99ft 0in (30.18m)
Weight: 135,000lb (61,235kg)
Engines: 4×2,200hp Wright R-3350-23 Cyclone 18-cyl radials
Max speed: 357mph (575kmh)
Operational ceiling: 33,600ft (10,240m)
Range with 10,000lb (4,536kg) bomb load: 3,250 miles (5,230km)
Armament: 1×20mm cannon; 10×0.50in machine-guns
Max bomb load: 20,000lb (9,072kg) internally

Design of the Superfortress began well before America's entry into World War 2, when the Boeing Model 345 was developed to a USAAC requirement of February 1940 for a 'hemisphere defense weapon'. In August 1940 two prototypes, designated XB-29, were orderd by the USAAF, and the first was flown on 21 September 1942. A much larger aeroplane than Boeing's earlier B-17, it had a circular-section, pressurised fuselage, remote controlled gun turrets and four 2,200hp Wright R-3350-13 Cyclone radial engines. By the time of the first flight, nearly 1,700 B-29s had been ordered. The first pre-production YB-29 Superfortress flew on 26 June 1943, and squadron deliveries began in the following month to the 58th BW. The first operational B-29 mission was carried out on 5 June 1944, and the first attack upon a target in Japan on 15 June 1944. It was during this month that the B-29s moved to the bases in the Marianas Islands, from whence they subsequently mounted a steadily increasing bombing campaign against Japan. Apart from the direct damage caused by this campaign, it was responsible for many Japanese aircraft from other Pacific battle fronts being withdrawn for home defence duties, although comparatively few types were capable of effective combat at the altitudes flown by the American

bombers. B-29s also carried out extensive minelaying in Japanese waters; one hundred and eighteen others became F-13/F-13A photo-reconnaissance aircraft. Finally, two B-29 brought the war to its dramatic close with the dropping of atomic bombs on Hiroshima and Nagaski on 6 and 9 August 1945 by *Enola Gay* and *Bockscar*. Shortly after VJ-day over 5,000 were cancelled, but when B-29 production ended early in 1946 the three Boeing factories had completed 2,756 B-29s and B-29As; in addition, six hundred and sixty-eight B-29s were manufactured by Bell, and five hundred and thirty-six B-29s by Martin; three hundred and eleven of the Bell machines were converted to B-29Bs with reduced armament. In 1945, an order was placed for two hundred B-50s, improved B-29s with 3,500hp R-4360 Wasp Major engines, but cut to sixty after VJ-day. The principal external difference was the increased height of the fin; improvements included a lighter wing. In total eighty B-50As, forty-five B-50Bs, two hundred and twenty-two B-50Ds (with in-flight refuelling), and twenty-seven TB-50H bomber trainers were built. Conversions included strategic reconnaissance aircraft for SAC, crew trainers, weather reconnaissance aircraft and tankers. The B-50 also serve with the RAF, as the Washington.

Goose

Grumman JRF-5 Goose of the US Navy, *circa* 1945

Span: 49ft 0in (14.94m)
Length: 38ft 4in (11.68m)
Weight: 8,000lb (3,629kg)
Engines: 2×450hp Pratt & Whitney
R-985-AN6 Wasp Junior 9-cyl radials
Max speed: 201mph (323kmh)
Operational ceiling: 21,300ft (6,492m)
Range: 640 miles (1,030km)

A general-purpose utility transport amphibian which is still giving plenty of useful service more than thirty years after its first appearance, the Goose originated in 1936 as the G-21, a 6/7-seat aircraft for both civil and military use. The prototype, powered by two 450hp Pratt & Whitney R-985-SB Wasp Junior radial engines, was flown for the first time in June 1937, and about a score of the G-21A model (higher-powered R-985-SB2 engines and increased gross weight) were sold to civilian customers prior to the out-break of World War 2. One G-21 was acquired by the US Navy in 1938, and evaluated as the XJ3F-1 for the 'general utility' role. It was, however, decided to order the type as a utility transport, in which capacity it was designated JRF-1. An initial order for twenty was placed, ten of these (delivered from late 1939) being JRF-1s and the other ten JRF-4s with provision for carrying two 250lb (113kg) bombs or depth charges beneath the wings. Five of the JRF-1s were subsequently adapted for aerial photography and target-towing as JRF-1As. Prior to the Navy order the US Army Air Corps had also placed a contract in 1938 for twenty-six as utility aircraft; these were given the designation OA-9, as were five civil G-21s impressed for war service in 1942. During 1939-40 ten more were purchased by the USN (seven JRF-2s and three JRF-3s) for use by the US Coast Guard in an air/sea rescue capacity. The JRF-3 version, intended for use in northern waters, was fitted with anti-icing equipment and an autopilot. Major production version of the Grumman design,

of which one hundred and eighty-five were built, was the JRF-5. In its basic form this was fitted out with cameras and other equipment for aerial survey work, and fifty were ordered for the RAF by the British Purchasing Commission in 1940. These, however, were requisitioned by the US Navy, to whom deliveries began in 1941. Six, designated JRF-5G, were assigned to the US Coast Guard for rescue duties; another six were supplied to the RAF, which named them Goose I, a name which was later adopted for all G-21 models in service; twenty-nine were delivered to the Royal Canadian Air Force for use on navigation training and other duties; and a further number were supplied to the Portuguese Navy. Internal changes were the main features of the JRF-6 (new radio and electrical equipment) and JRF-6B (navigation training equipment). Of these versions, thirty-seven were supplied to the US Navy and fifty in 1943 to the RAF as the Goose IA. The latter were employed variously for transport duties with No. 24 Squadron, for air/sea rescue, or for ferry duties with the Air Transport Auxiliary. Five other aircraft were employed by the USAAF; these comprised three commercial G-21As, impressed in 1942 as OA-13As, and two OA-13Bs which were JRF-5s acquired from the US Navy. Among post-war forces to employ ex-American G-21As was France's *Aéronavale*, whose *Escadrille* 8S was equipped with JRF-5s for maritime reconnaissance until the end of the 1950s, and those of the Portuguese Navy were also still in service at that time.

Lockheed P-38/F-4/F-5 Lightning

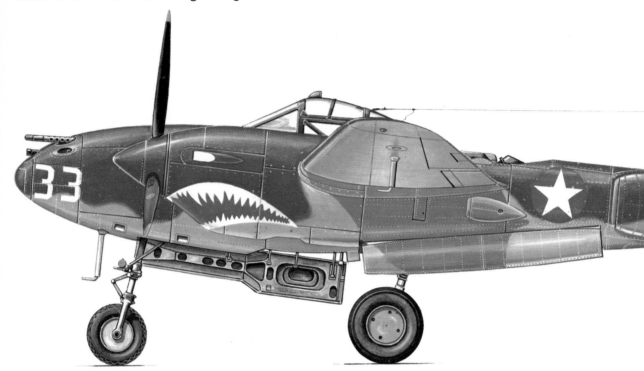

Lockheed P-38E Lightning of the 347th FG, attached to the thirteenth Air Force, Guadalcanal, early 1943

Aircraft type		Lockheed P-38D	Lockheed P-38H	Lockheed P-38J
Power plant		2×1,150 hp Allison V-1710-27/29	2×1,425 hp Allison V-1710-89/91	2×1,425 hp Allison V-1710-89/91
Accommodation		1	1	1
Wing span	m : ft in	15·85 : 52 0	15·85 : 52 0	15·85 : 52 0
Length overall	m : ft in	11·53 : 37 10	11·53 : 37 10	11·53 : 37 10
Height overall	m : ft in	3·00 : 9 10	3·00 : 9 10	3·00 : 9 10
Wing area	m² : sq ft	30·43 : 327·5	30·43 : 327·5	30·43 : 327·5
Weight empty	kg : lb	5,343 : 11,780	5,615 : 12,380	5,797 : 12,780
Weight loaded (max)	kg : lb	7,031 : 15,500	9,208 : 20,300	9,798 : 21,600
Max wing loading	kg/m² : lb/sq ft	230·97 : 47·33	302·46 : 61·98	321·84 : 65·95
Max power loading	kg/hp : lb/hp	3·06 : 6·74	3·23 : 7·12	3·44 : 7·58
Max level speed	km/h : mph	628 : 390	647 : 402	666 : 414
at (height)	m : ft	7,620 : 25,000	7,620 : 25,000	7,620 : 25,000
Cruising speed	km/h : mph	483 : 300	483 : 300	467 : 290
Time to height		8·0 min to 6,095 m (20,000 ft)	1·0 min to 808 m (2,650 ft)	7·0 min to 6,095 m (20,000 ft)
Service ceiling	m : ft	11,885 : 39,000	13,410 : 44,000	13,410 : 44,000
Range	km : miles	644 : 400*	483 : 300*	724 : 450*
		*normal	*normal	*with 1,451 kg (3,200 lb) bomb load

102

Five-camera nose of the F-5G Lightning

Perspex bomb aiming nose (P-38L)

P-38L night fighter with radar pod

The Lightning evolved to meet a USAAC specification for a bomber interceptor capable of 360mph (579kmh) at 20,000ft (6,100m), attaining that height in six minutes, with an endurance of one hour at that speed. Only a twin-engined aircraft could achieve such a performance, and Lockheed adopted a twin-boom layout enabling the Allison V-1710 engines, turbochargers, radiator baths and main landing gear units to be housed in the booms. The central nacelle accommodated pilot, nosewheel and armament. One XP-38 prototype was ordered in 1937, flying first on 27 January 1939, then powered by 960hp non-supercharged Allison V-1710-11/15 engines with 'handed' (each turning outward) propellers. Armament comprised four 0.50in machine-guns and one 37mm cannon. On 11 February 1939 the XP-38 was destroyed in an accident, but before that the USAAC had ordered thirteen YP-38s for service trials. These had 1,150hp V-1710-27/29 turbocharged engines and a new 37mm cannon. The first YP-38 flew in September 1940, and all were completed by June 1941, when the first of sixty-six P-38 production aircraft were delivered. Only the first thirty were P-38 configuration, the remainder being delivered as P-38Ds with amended tailplane incidence and self-sealing fuel tanks. First US production fighter in the 'over-400mph' class, the P-38 gained an early reputation for shedding its tail unit. The zero (instead of negative) tailplane incidence of the P-38D corrected this. The P-38D was also the first to adopt the name Lightning, following an order from Britain for one hundred and forty-three. The first three arrived in the UK in December

1941 but, powered by 1,040hp non-supercharged and non-handed engines (against Lockheed's advice), their performance was so poor that the RAF rejected them. The one hundred and forty outstanding were retained by the USAAF, as P-322s, and used for training. Similarly, five hundred and twenty-four Mk IIs ordered by the RAF were retained for USAAF use. Production continued with two hundred and ten P-38Es, similar to the P-38D except that a 20mm cannon replaced the 37mm. The following P-38F fighter-bombers carried up to 2,000lb (907kg) of stores under the inner wing sections, and introduced 1,325hp V-1710-49/53 engines and manoeuvring flaps: the P-38s high wing loading was a combat disadvantage, and the flaps improved its rate of turn. Basically similar to the P-38F, except for 1,325hp V-1710-51/55 engines and detail changes, P-38G fighter-bomber production totalled 1,082. Load-carrying ability of the two underwing pylons increased to 3,200lb (1,451kg) on the P-38H (1,425hp Allison V-1710-89/91s) and some had improved GEC superchargers. The P-38J of 1943 introduced 'chin' radiator scoops beneath the engines, boosted aileron controls and, on the last 1,400 of 2,970 built, additional fuel. Late P-38Js had a self-ferry endurance of twelve hours. After an experimental P-38K high-altitude fighter, which had 1,425hp V-1710-75/77s and larger-diameter propellers, Lockheed built the P-38L, the last and most numerous (3,810) production model. Vultee had completed only one hundred and thirteen of 2,000 when the contract was cancelled.

Republic P-47/F-47 Thunderbolt

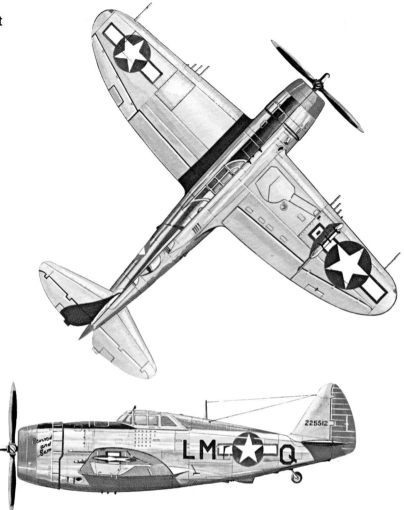

Republic P-47D-21-RE Thunderbolt of the 62nd
FS, 56 FG, USAAF, UK, May 1944

Span: 40ft 9⅜in (12.43m)
Length: 36ft 1¾in (11.02m)
Weight, normal take-off: 13,500lb
(6,123kg)
Engine: 2,300hp Pratt & Whitney
R-2800-21 Double Wasp 18-cyl radial
Max speed: 433mph (697kmh) at 30,000ft
(9,144m)
Operational ceiling: 40,000ft (12,190m)
Range, normal: 640 miles (1,030km)
Armament: 8 × 0.50in Browning M-2
machine-guns
Max bomb load: 2,500lb (1,134kg)

In the light of the early air fighting in Europe Alexander Kartveli almost completely redesigned the XP-47 light fighter projected early in 1939, resulting in the XP-47B. It was almost twice as heavy and a Double Wasp radial engine replaced the XP-47s Allison in-line. In September 1940, one hundred and seventy-one P-47Bs and six hundred and two P-47Cs were ordered. The XP-47B flew on 6 May 1941. The B and C models were similar, but the C had a slightly longer fuselage to improve manoeuvrability. Thunderbolts entered USAAF service in March 1942, becoming operational with 8th Air Force units over Europe in April 1943 and in the Pacific theatre some two months later. Huge orders had been placed for the P-47D, which was initially a refined C. To this configuration, Republic manufactured 5,423 P-47Ds and Curtiss three hundred and fifty-four designated P-47G. From the P-47D-25 the cockpit view was vastly improved by cutting down the rear fuselage and fitting a 'teardrop' canopy. The weight saved allowed extra fuel to be carried. Production batches from P-47D-27 had a dorsal fin fillet to offset the reduced keel area. Bubble-canopied P-47Ds served widely as a fighter and

fighter-bomber in Europe; 8,179 were completed at Farmingdale and Evansville. The RAF received two hundred and forty Thunderbolt Mk Is (early P-47D) and five hundred and ninety Mk IIs (later P-47D); two hundred and three were allocated to the Soviet Air Force uncer Lend-Lease and eighty-eight to Brazil. The next production model (following various experimental variants) was the P-47M; this utilised the 2,800hp R-2800-57 with which the XP-47J had flown at 504mph (811kmh), in the P-47D airframe. An improvised version produced hastily to counter the V1 flying-bomb attacks on Britain, only one hundred and thirty were built. The last and heaviest production Thunderbolt was the P-47N, a very long-range escort and fighter-bomber variant; Republic built 1,816. Production, ending in December 1945, totalled 15,660 aircraft. About two-thirds survived the war. The Thunderbolt was one of the principal types supplied under the 1947 Rio Pact to many Latin American countries, including Bolivia, Brazil, Colombia, the Dominican Republic, Ecuador, Honduras, Nicaragua and Peru, a few serving until the late 1960s.

North American P-51/F-51 Mustang

North American P-51D-5-NA of the 339th
Fighter Group, 66th Fighter Wing US Eighth Air
Force, interned in Sweden August 1944 and
later purchased by the RSWAF

Span: 37ft 0¼in (11.29m)
Length: 32ft 3¼in (9.84m)
Weight: 10,100lb (4,581kg)
Engine: 1×1,490hp Packard-built
   V-1650-7 (Rolls Royce Merlin) Vee-
   type
Max speed: 437mph (703kmh)
Operational ceiling: 41,900ft (12,771m)
Range: 950 miles (1,529km)
Armament: 6×0.50in machine-guns
Max bomb load: 1×1,000lb (454kg) 5×5in
   rocket projectiles or three bazooka-
   type launching tubes beneath each
   wing

North American P-51 Mustang

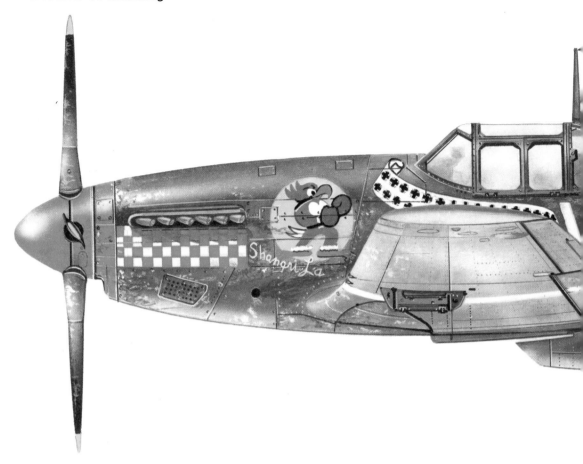

Aircraft type		North American A-36A	North American P-51B	North American P-51D
Power plant		1×1,325 hp* Allison V-1710-87	1×1,380 hp Packard (Merlin) V-1650-3	1×1,490 hp Packard (Merlin) V-1650-7
Accommodation		1	1	1
Wing span	m : ft in	11·28 : 37 0	11·28 : 37 0	11·28 : 37 0
Length overall	m : ft in	9·83 : 32 3	9·83 : 32 3	9·83 : 32 3
Height overall	m : ft in	3·71 : 12 2	3·71 : 12 2	3·71 : 12 2
Wing area	m² : sq ft	21·65 : 233·0	21·65 : 233·0	21·65 : 233·0
Weight empty	kg : lb	2,998 : 6,610	3,168 : 6,985	3,232 : 7,125
Weight loaded (max)	kg : lb	4,536 : 10,000	5,352 : 11,800	5,262 : 11,600
Max wing loading	kg/m² : lb/sq ft	209·44 : 42·92	247·14 : 50·64	242·95 : 49·79
Max power loading	kg/hp : lb/hp	3·42 : 7·55	3·88 : 8·55	3·53 : 7·79
Max level speed	km/h : mph	573 : 356	708 : 440	703 : 437
at (height)	m : ft	1,525 : 5,000	9,145 : 30,000	7,620 : 25,000
Cruising speed	km/h : mph	402 : 250	583 : 362	583 : 362
Time to height		—	12·5 min to 9,145 m (30,000 ft)	13·0 min to 9,145 m (30,000 ft)
Service ceiling	m : ft	8,230 : 27,000	12,740 : 41,800	12,770 : 41,900
Range	km : miles	885 : 550**	1,448 : 900*	3,701 : 2,300*

*at 915 m (3,000 ft)
**with two 500 lb bombs

*at cruising speed

*with two 416 litre (110 USG) drop-tanks

North American P-51B Mustang (43-6913) of
the 336th FS (Capt Don S. Gentile), 4th FG,
Eighth Air Force, UK 1944

XP-51 Mustang prototype, with Allison
V-1710-39 engine

One of the few aircraft to be conceived, developed, built and used extensively within the compass of World War 2, the Mustang originated in 1940 when the British Purchasing Commission negotiated with North American to design and build a new fighter for the RAF, to British specifications. North American designed and built the NA-73X in four months, but the new 1,100hp Allison V-1710-39 engine did not arrive until later. The NA-73X incorporated many new features, based on NACA data, notably a laminar-flow wing, and a low-drag radiator scoop below the centre fuselage. After ground trials, the NA-73X flew on 26 October 1940 at Mines Field, piloted by Vance Breese. It had a remarkably encouraging test programme, although a crash delayed it. The first production Mustang Mk I flew on 23 April 1941. The second production example reached Britain 24 October 1941, soon followed by a steady flow from the original order for four hundred. RAF evaluation of its new fighter showed it to be fast and highly manoeuvrable at low level, but disappointing at altitude, as the power output of the Allison engine fell off rapidly as it climbed. It was, therefore, unsuitable for operational use as a fighter in the European theatre. It was suitable, however, for use in a tactical reconnaissance or ground attack role, and the RAFs aircraft were equipped initially for photo-reconnaissance, and were used in this role for the first time in May 1942. They eventually equipped twenty-three squadrons of Army Co-operation Command for this purpose. North American's development and production of this aircraft for the UK had needed US government blessing. A condition of approval stipulated the supply of two aircraft to the USAAC for evaluation, these being designated XP-51 on delivery. Before this happened, however, the US Army procured one hundred and fifty Mustangs for supply to Britain under Lend-Lease. They differed from Mustang Mk Is by having self-sealing tanks, and armament of four 20mm cannon instead of eight machine-guns. Britain received ninety-three as Mk IAs, and fifty-five were diverted to the USAAF as tactical reconnaissance F-6As. Two with Packard Merlin engines went to the Army, initially designated XP-78 but later XP-51B. USAAF testing of its two XP-51s confirmed RAF findings, and five hundred were ordered as A-36A close-support aircraft with 1,325hp Allison V-1710-87 engines, dive brakes, and underwing racks. They were the first Mustangs to be used operationally by the USAAF, in the Middle East during 1943. Ordered at about the same time as the A-36As were three hundred and ten P-51As with 1,200hp V-1710-81 engines, four 0.50in guns, and underwing racks for up to 1,000lb (454kg) of bombs or two 75 or 150 US gallon (284 or 568 litre) drop-tanks. Of these, fifty went to the RAF as Mustang Mk IIs and thirty-five to the USAAF after conversion as F-6Bs. Soon after the first Mustangs had been received in Britain, it was decided to install Rolls-Royce Merlin engines experimentally. Early testing of converted Mk Is showed startling performance improvements, and information was given to North American without delay. At the same time installation by NAA of 1,430hp Packard Merlin V-1650-3s in two P-51s had resulted in the XP-78/XP-51Bs. Early testing confirmed a maximum speed of

North American P-51As (*Mrs Virginia* nearest camera) in Burma theatre markings

Early-production P-51A with an oxidation problem

441mph (710kmh) at optimum altitude: one climbed to 20,000ft (6,100m) in 5.9 minutes. The USAAF was suitably impressed, ordering such large numbers that a second production line was established at Dallas, Texas. Production of the new model began in the summer of 1943, the P-51B (Inglewood) and P-51C (Dallas) being virtually identical but differing from the P-51/51A by a strengthened fuselage, new ailerons, and detail changes. Armament comprised four 0.50in guns. Construction of P-51Bs (1,988) and P-51Cs (1,750) introduced the 1,490hp V-1650-7 Merlin to some 2,100 of that total. RAF Lend-Lease allocations numbered nine hundred and ten, two hundred and seventy-four P-51Bs and six hundred and thirty-six P-51Cs entering service from February 1944. They entered USAAF service slightly earlier, being used operationally for the first time on 13 December 1943 by the Eighth Air Force on a long-range escort mission to Kiel. Of the 2,828 P-51B/51Cs received by the USAAF, ninety-one were converted to F-6Cs. Major production version was the P-51D, with Dallas building 1,454 and Inglewood 6,502. They introduced a 'bubble' canopy, cut-down rear fuselage, and armament of six 0.50in guns. F-6D conversions totalled one hundred and thirty-six. The last 1,100 from Inglewood were equipped to carry 5in rocket projectiles, and late production aircraft from both lines introduced a small dorsal fin. Then followed 1,500 P-51Ks, differing in having a smaller diameter propeller; one hundred and sixty-three were converted to F-6K. RAF allocations as

Mustang Mk IV were two hundred and eighty-one P-51D and five hundred and ninety-four P-51K. Three XP-51Fs and two XP-51Gs were prototypes for lightweight experimental construction, with substantial weight saving achieved by redesign, structural simplification, deletion of surplus equipment, and introduction of lightweight materials, including plastics. At the same time, a reduction in drag was achieved by use of a new wing section, elongation of the cockpit canopy, and substitution of a shallow heat exchanger for the under-fuselage oil cooler. Powerplant of these XP-51Fs and XP-51Gs were respectively V-1650-7s and Rolls-Royce Merlin 145Ms with combat ratings of 1,695hp and 1,910hp. Two later XP-51J prototypes were similar to the XP-51F, but were powered by Allison V-1710-119s which had a rating of 1,720hp at optimum altitude. With experience gained from these prototypes, North American built the P-51H final production version, fastest of all the Mustangs, able to attain 487mph (784kmh) at optimum altitude. Power Plant was the 1,380hp V-1650-9 engine which, with water injection, had a combat rating of 2,218hp at 10,200ft (3,110m). Generally similar to the XP-51F, it had a taller fin added, from the 21st aircraft. Armament comprised six 0.50in guns, plus two 1,000lb bombs, or ten 5in rockets. Only five hundred and fifty-five P-51Hs were built before VJ-day brought contract cancellations, bringing the final construction total to 14,819.

Lockheed P-38 Lightning

Lockheed P-38J-15-LO Lightning of the 55th FS, 20th FG, US Eighth Air Force, UK, early 1944

Span: 52ft 0in (15.85m)
Length: 37ft 10in (11.53m)
Weight, normal take-off: 17,500lb (7,938kg)
Engines: 2×1,425hp Allison V-1710-89/91 12-cyl V-type
Max speed: 414mph (666kmh) at 25,000ft (7,620m)
Operational ceiling: 44,000ft (13,410m)
Range (on internal fuel): 1,175 miles (1,880km)
Armament: 1×20mm Hispano M2 cannon; 4×0.50 Colt-Browning machine-guns
Max bomb load: 3,200lb (1,452kg); or 10×5in rocket projectiles

Few would dispute the P-38s claim to epitomise the successful realisation of the long-range tactical fighter in World War 2. Design work began early in 1937 to meet an exacting USAAC requirement. Lockheed's Model 22 won the competition and in June 1937 one prototype, designated XP-38, was ordered. It flew on 27 January 1939, followed on 16 September 1940 by the first of thirteen YP-38 evaluation aircraft with more powerful V-1710 engines and nose armament of four machine-guns and a 37mm cannon. Delivery of production P-38s began in June 1941; thirty were built, one modified to an XP-38A with a pressurised cabin. The next production model was the P-38D (thirty-six built), with self-sealing fuel tanks, and airframe modifications. The RAF ordered the type in 1940, naming it Lightning, but only three Mk Is with non-supercharged engines were delivered; a contract for five hundred and twenty-four Mk IIs was cancelled. The remaining one hundred and forty Mk Is were repossessed as the P-322 by the USAAF, which also acquired the Mk IIs; many were later converted to P-38Fs or Gs. Meanwhile, the USAAFs next version, the P-38E, entered production (two hundred and ten built) with a 20mm replacing the 37mm cannon. Increased power was the major improvement in the F and G models, enabling the carriage of external weapons or fuel tanks for the first time. Production of five hundred and twenty-seven P-38Fs and 1,082 P-38Gs, deliveries beginning during 1942, heralded a marked expansion in the P-38s deployment in the major theatres of the war. The P-38H of 1943 had further increased power; six hundred and one P-38Hs were delivered. The 2,970 P-38Js were similar, but introduced 'chin' air cooler intakes; increased internal fuel raised endurance (with drop-tanks) to 12 hours. Even greater numbers were built of the rocket-carrying P-38L, with 1,600hp V-1710-111/113 engines and a maximum speed of 414mph (666kmh). Lockheed manufactured 3,810 P-38Ls, 2,000 were ordered from Vultee, who completed one hundred and thirteen before the remainder were cancelled when the Pacific war ended. P-38s converted for other duties included a few P-38M night fighters from P-38Ls, a few TP-38L conversion trainers, and the undesignated 'Droop Snoot' and 'Pathfinder' (formerly J or L models). The most widely used single photo-reconnaissance aircraft of World War 2, nearly 1,400 E, F, G, H, J and L models were converted to F-4s or F-5s.

Northrop P-61 Black Widow

Northrop P-61A Black Widow *Tabitha*
(42-5569) of the 425th Night Fighter Squadron
USAAF, France, summer 1944

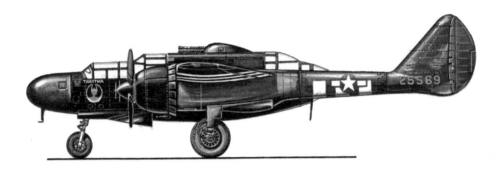

Aircraft type		Northrop P-61A	Northrop P-61B
Power plant		2×2,040 hp Pratt & Whitney R-2800-65	2×2,040 hp Pratt & Whitney R-2800-65
Accommodation		3	3
Wing span	m : ft in	20·12 : 66 0	20·12 : 66 0
Length overall	m : ft in	14·91 : 48 11	15·11 : 49 7
Height overall	m : ft in	4·47 : 14 8	4·47 : 14 8
Wing area	m² : sq ft	61·69 : 664·0	61·69 : 664·0
Weight empty	kg : lb	9,510 : 20,965	9,979 : 22,000
Weight loaded (max)	kg : lb	14,696 : 32,400	17,236 : 38,000
Max wing loading	kg/m² : lb/sq ft	238·12 : 48·80	279·28 : 57·23
Max power loading	kg/hp : lb/hp	3·67 : 8·10	4·31 : 9·50
Max level speed	km/h : mph	594 : 369	589 : 366
at (height)	m : ft	6,095 : 20,000	6,095 : 20,000
Cruising speed	km/h : mph	518 : 322	515 : 320
Time to 6,095 m (20,000 ft)		10·3 min	12·0 min
Service ceiling	m : ft	10,090 : 33,100	10,090 : 33,100
Range (max)	km : miles	2,334 : 1,450	4,828 : 3,000

One of the rare specialised night fighter designs of 1939-45, the Black Widow began when the USAAC ordered two XP-61 prototypes in January 1941. Thirteen YP-61s for service trials were ordered two months later, and five hundred and sixty production aircraft by February 1942. The first XP-61 flew on 21 May 1942, armed with four 20mm nose cannon and a dorsal barbette containing four 0.50in machine-guns, but the latter was deleted after the first thirty-seven production P-61As, reappearing (eventually in modified form) in mid-production of the later P-61B. Two hundred P-61As were built, the first forty-five having 2,000hp R-2800-10 engines, the others the 2,040hp -65 version. Twenty P-61As had underwing attachments for four 1,600lb bombs or two 300 US gallon drop-tanks, and this provision was standardised on the P-61B (four hundred and fifty built) and P-61C (forty-one built, four hundred and seventy-six others cancelled). Powerplant of the P-61C was the 2,100hp R-2800-73. Despite rapid completion of the early test aircraft, production Black Widows did not appear until towards the end of 1943, and did not become operational until early summer 1944, making their debut with the USAAFs 18th Fighter Group in the Pacific. Subsequently they served also as night fighters in Europe. Twelve P-61Bs were transferred to the Marine Corps as F2T-1N night fighter crew trainers. Two P-61As became XP-61D testbeds for turbocharged R-2800-77s, and two P-61Bs were converted to two-seat XP-61Es, with a ventral pack of four 20mm guns (instead of the dorsal barbette), increased fuel, and no nose radar. One XP-61E later became the prototype XF-15 Reporter, a post-war photo-reconnaissance development of which thirty-six examples were completed in 1946.

Grumman TBF/TBM Avenger

Eastern-built TBM-3 Avenger of Air Group 38,
US Navy, August 1945

Span: 54ft 2in (16.51m)
Length: 40ft 0½in (12.19m)
Weight: 18,250lb (8,278kg)
Engine: 1,900hp Wright R-2600-20
    Cyclone 14-cyl radial
Max speed: 267mph (430kmh) at 15,000ft
    (4,570m)
Operational ceiling: 23,400ft (7,130m)
Range: 2,530 miles (4,072km)
Armament: 3×0.50in machine-guns;
    2×0.30in machine-guns
Max bomb load: 1×22in torpedo or
    1×2,000lb bomb internally

The Avenger was a pre-war design, two XTBF-1 prototypes of which were ordered by the USN in April 1940. The first made its maiden flight on 1 August 1941, by which time a substantial first order had been placed. The first production TBF-1s were delivered to VT-8 late in January 1942, and the Avenger made its combat debut early in the following June at the Battle of Midway. The aircraft had typical Grumman lines, the most noticeable feature being the very deep fuselage, which enabled the torpedo or bomb load to be totally enclosed. The TBF-1C had two wing-mounted 0.50in machine-guns in addition to the nose, dorsal and ventral guns of the original TBF-1, and could carry auxiliary drop-tanks. Both models were 3-seaters and were powered by the 1,700hp R-2600-8 engine. Up to December 1943 Grumman built 2,293 TBF-1/-1C Avengers, including the two original prototypes, one XTBF-2 and one XTBF-3; four hunded and two of them were supplied to the Royal Navy as Avenger Mk Is (TBF-1B) and sixty-three to the RNZAF. The British aircraft were briefly known as Tarpon,

but the US name was later standardised. Meanwhile, in the USA production had also begun in September 1942 by the Eastern Aircraft Division of General Motors, which built 2,882 as the TBM-1 and -1C, of which three hundred and thirty-four went to the FAA as Avenger Mk IIs. The 'dash 2' variant was not built by either company, but Eastern completed a prototype and 4,664 TBM-3s with uprated Cyclone engines and their wings strengthened to carry rocket projectiles or a radar pod; two hundred and twenty-two of these became the British Avenger Mk III. Further strengthening of the airframe produced the XTBM-4, but production of this model was cancelled when the war ended. This did not, however, end the Avenger's long and productive career; those of the USN were not finally retired until 1954, and postwar variants served with some foreign naval air forces for several years after this. During the major part of World War 2 the Avenger was the standard USN torpedo bomber, operating from carriers and shore bases, mostly in the Pacific theatre.

Bell P-59 Airacomet

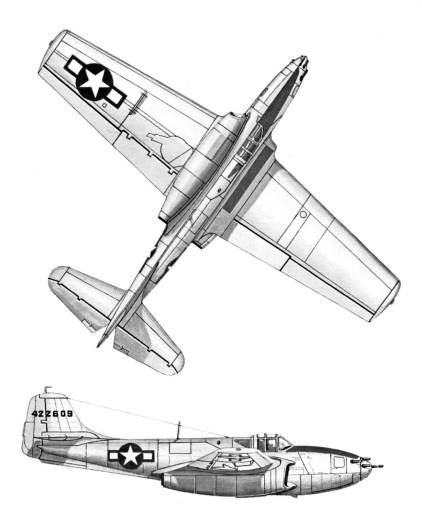

Bell P-59A (first production aircraft) of the USAAF, Murac Field late 1943

Span: 45ft 6in (13.87m)
Length: 38ft 1½in (11.62m)
Weight: 10,822lb (4,909kg)
Engines: 2×2,000hp (907kg) st General Electric J31-GE-3 turbojets
Max speed: 409mph (658kmh)
Operational ceiling: 46,200ft (14,082m)
Range: 240 miles (386km)
Armament: 1×37mm cannon and 3×0.50in machine-guns

The first aeroplane to be designed in the US to acquire experience of the Whittle-type gas turbine engine, the Airacomet project was initiated in the autumn of 1941, the first of three XP-59A prototypes being flown on 1 October 1942. These three machines, bearing for security reasons the designation originally allotted to an entirely different piston-engined Bell fighter project, were powered by two General Electric I-A turbojets, derived from the Whittle W.2B engine. A higher-rated engine, the 1,400lb (635kg) st I-16, was installed in the thirteen YP-59A service trials aircraft which followed. Two of these machines were evaluated by the US Navy, and a third was sent to the UK in exchange for one of the first Gloster Meteors. In addition to operating problems encountered with the early jet engines, the Airacomet's performance and stability were also below expectations; as a result, the original production order for one hundred aircraft was later reduced, and most of those built were employed for training, engine development and other non-operational duties. Although it took no active part in World War 2, the Airacomet served the primary purpose of establishing the jet fighter concept, paving the way for the P-80 Shooting Star and subsequent fighters with the new form of propulsion. Twenty P-59As were built with J31-GE-3 engines, and thirty P-59Bs with J31-GE-5s, additional internal fuel capacity and detail airframe modifications.

Piasecki HRP-1 Rescuer

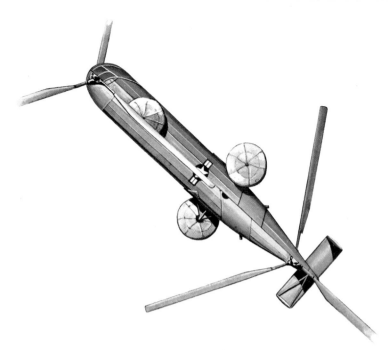

Piasecki HRP-1 Rescuer of the US Navy *circa* 1949

Rotor Diameter: (each) 41ft 0in (12.50m)
Length: 48ft 0in (14.63m)
Weight: 6,900lb (3,130kg)
Engine: 1×600hp Pratt & Whitney
R-1340-AN-1 Wasp 9-cyl radial
Max speed: 99mph (159kmh)
Operational ceiling: 10,400ft (3,170m)
Range: 265 miles (426km)

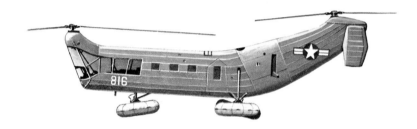

Although it was built only in modest numbers and had an unspectacular (though useful) service career, the Piasecki HRP-1 has its place in the history of rotorcraft by virtue of being the world's first practical tandem-rotor helicopter and, at the time of its appearance, the world's largest helicopter of any kind. Frank N. Piasecki, holder of the first helicopter pilot's licence to be issued in the United States, became interested in rotorcraft development before America's entry into World War 2, and in 1943 he formed a company known as the P.V. Engineering Forum whose first design, the PV-2, was a single-seat, single main rotor helicopter with a 90hp Franklin engine. This machine, which flew for the first time on 11 April 1943, was Piasecki's first and only single-rotor helicopter, for on 1 February 1944 he received a contract to develop a tandem-rotor utility transport and rescue aircraft for the US Navy. Given the factory designation PV-3, this machine, powered by a Wright R-975 piston engine, made a successful first flight at Morton, Pennsylvania, in March 1945 and was followed by two XHRP-1 prototypes, one for US Navy flight trials and the other for static and dynamic tests. The test programme was completed in the spring of 1947, by which time the company title had changed to Piasecki Helicopter Corporation, and work had already begun on an initial batch of ten HRP-1 Rescuers ordered by the US Navy in June 1946. The first of these flew on 15 August 1947, and a second batch of ten was built later; they served with US Navy Squadrons HMX-1 and VX-3, the final machine being delivered in 1949.

These were powered by 600hp Pratt & Whitney R-1340-An-1 engines. Twelve of the HRP-1s were eventually assigned to the US Marine Corps for assault training, while three others, as HRP-1Gs, were used as rescue craft by the US Coast Guard. After withdrawal of the Rescuer from military service in the early 1950s, about six appeared on the US civil register. The tandem-rotor layout offered a wider choice of c.g. positions, together with a small frontal area and a large lifting area; thus the HRP-1 was able to register a significant step forward, from craft whose main purpose had been to prove the flight principles of the helicopter, to a vehicle capable of doing a real job of work. Nicknamed – for obvious reasons – the 'flying banana', the HRP-1 carried a crew of two sitting in tandem, and its 400 cu ft (11.33 cu m) cabin could accommodate eight passengers, 2,000lb (907kg) of cargo or six stretchers. The single engine was mounted in the rear part of the fuselage, with a clutch and gearbox amidships from which drive shafts ran to reduction gearboxes below each of the rotor hubs. In June 1948 the US Navy ordered five examples of the much-developed PV-17 with the designation HRP-2. This had a considerably longer, redesigned fuselage with an all-metal skin (the HRP-1s front half was fabric-covered), a more roomy crew cabin with side-by-side seats, and modified rotor heads. This version formed the basis of the later PD-22 model which became the highly successful military Vertol H-21 series described separately.

Vertol Retriever

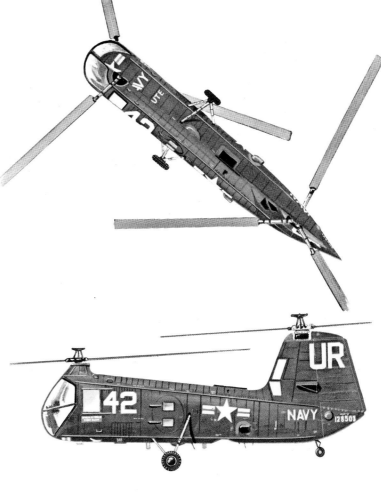

Vertol HUP-2 Retriever of the US Navy *circa* 1956

Rotor Diameter: (each) 35ft 0in (10.67m)
Length: 32ft 0in (9.75m)
Weight: 5,750lb (2,608kg)
Engine: 1×550hp Continental R-975-46
    9-cyl radial
Max speed: 108mph (174kmh)
Hovering ceiling: 7,000ft (2,134m)
Range: 340 miles (547km)

This tandem-rotor design was evolved by Piasecki Helicopter Corporation to meet a Bureau of Aeronautics requirement, issued in 1945, for a utility helicopter to be based aboard aircraft carriers and other large warships of the US Navy for search and rescue, plane guard and general transportation duties. The proposed aircraft was given the works designation PV-14 and two XHJP-1 prototypes (37976 and '77) were completed for US Navy evaluation. In 1948 work began on thirty-two PV-18s, or HUP-1 Retrievers, as the production version was known. They differed little from the original XHJP-1, the major apparent change being the addition of inward-sloping endplate fins to the horizontal stabilisers below the rear rotor head. Both sets of three-blade rotors could be folded for shipboard stowage and the HUP-1, powered by a single 525hp Continental R-975-34 piston engine, could accommodate four/five passengers or three casualty litters in addition to the 2-man crew. Successful tests with a Sperry autopilot in the XHJP-1 enabled the next model, the HUP-2, to be built without tail surfaces and the more powerful Continental R-975-42 was installed in this and all subsequent production models. Another feature of the Retriever was a large rectangular rescue hatch offset to starboard in the floor of the front fuselage, through which a winch inside the cabin could lift weights of up to 400lb (181kg) at a time. One hundred and sixty-five HUP-2s were built for the US Navy; fifteen were supplied to France's Aéronavale, and the US Navy also operated about a dozen HUP-2S submarine-hunting aircraft with dunking sonar equipment. Another HUP-2 was given a sealed, watertight hull and outrigged twin floats for waterborne tests. US Navy units, which included HU-1 and HU-2, began to receive the Retriever in February 1949. In 1951 the US Air Force, on behalf of the Army, ordered a version of the HUP-2 with a reinforced cabin floor and hydraulically boosted controls, for general support and evacuation work. Seventy of these were delivered as H-25A Army Mules from 1953, as were fifty similar Naval HUP-3s (including three for the Royal Canadian Navy) for ambulance and light cargo duties. Production of the last aircraft was completed in July 1954. A proposal to boost the speed, range and payload of all H-25/HUP aircraft still in service by refitting them with 700hp Wright R-1300-3 engines did not take place, and by the time the new tri-service designation system was introduced in July 1962 only the HUP-2 and HUP-3 remained in service; these became the UH-25B and UH-25C respectively.

Stratotanker/Stratolifter/ Boeing E-3A

Boeing KC-135A of the 93rd Air Refueling Squadron, USAF Stategic Air Command, Castle AFB, California, *circa* spring 1957

Span: 130ft 10in (39.88m)
Length: 136ft 3in (41.53m)
Weight: 297,000lb (134,717kg)
Engines: 4×13,750lb (6,237kg) st Pratt & Whitney J57-P-59W turbojets
Max speed: 530mph (853kmh)
Service ceiling: 50,000ft (15,240m)
Range: 1,150 miles (1,850km)

The military counterpart of the Boeing 707 airliner, which has the Boeing Model number 717, is in use by the US Air Force in a considerable variety of roles, its total production having amounted to eight hundred and six. By far the most prolific version is the KC-135A flight refuelling tanker, which first flew on 31 August 1956; an overall total of seven hundred and thirty-two KC-135As were built before production ended in December 1964. They have been in service since June 1957, and are currently able to refuel other aircraft by the probe-and-drogue method as well as by the familiar 'butterfly boom' beneath the rear fuselage. The KC-135A can be used as a long-range transport, but there were also specialised transport models. These included fifteen new and three converted C-135As (first flight 19 May 1961) and thirty fan-engined C-135Bs (first flight 12 February 1962) the latter's capacity being one hundred and twenty-six troops, forty-four casualty litters or 87,100lb (39,508kg) of freight. Twelve C-135F tankers, generally similar to the A model, were supplied to the Armée de l'Air to act as a tanker fleet for the Mirage IV-A bomber force. The last USAF production model of the Boeing 717 (seventeen built) was the EC-135C (originally KC-135B) airborne command post. Boeing Model number 739 identifies four RC-135A and ten RC-135B built, respectively, for the Air Photographic and Charting Service of MAC and for electronic reconnaissance. Aircraft converted for special functions have resulted in many new designations, including EC-135A (six, airborne command post/communications relay), JKC-135A and NKC-135A (special test), VC-135B (eleven, VIP transport),

WC-135B (ten, weather reconnaissance), RC-135C (ten, electronic reconnaissance), RC-135D (four ditto), RC-135E (one, ditto), EC-135G (four, airborne command post/communications relay), EC-135H (five, airborne command post), EC-135J (three ditto), EC-135K (one ditto), EC-135L (three, airborne command post/communications relay), RC-135M (special mission), EC-135N (eight, radio/telemetry for Apollo space programme), EC-135P (five, airborne command post), KC-135Q (tanker for SR-71), KC-135R (special reconnaissance), KC-135S (ditto), KC-135T (ELINT collection), and RC-135U (special reconnaissance). In addition to the above, several examples of the commercial Boeing 707 have been supplied to meet military orders. These have included three short-fuselage 707-153S as VC-137A (VC-137B after conversion to turbofans) and one Presidential 707-353 (VC-137C) for the USAF; and other 707-320 series to the Argentine Air Force (one), Federal German Luftwaffe (four), Canadian Armed Forces (five, designated CC-137), Imperial Iranian Air Force (six), Israeli Defence Force (five), Portuguese Air Force (two) and USAF (one). Two other Boeing 707-320 airframes have undergone conversion to become EC-137D aerodynamic prototypes of Boeing's new AWACS (Airborne Warning and Control System) patrol aircraft for the USAF. The first of them (71-1407) flew for the first time in the new form on 9 February 1972, and their main purpose was to flight test the large prototype radars developed by Hughes and Westinghouse and mounted in the huge circular radome above the rear fuselage of the EC-137D. After selection of

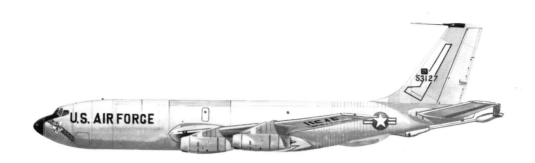

Boeing C-135B of Military Airlift Command, USAF, *circa* 1966

Span: as per KC-135A
Length: 134ft 6in (41.00m)
Weight: 275,500lb (122,700kg)
Engines: 4 × 18,000lb (8,165kg) st Pratt &
    Whitney TF-33-P-5 turbofans
Max speed: 604mph (972kmh)
Operational ceiling: 45,000ft (13,725m)
Range: 4,625 miles (7,445km)

Westinghouse for the radar contract, the second development phase involves four genuine E-3A prototypes, each powered by four 21,000lb (9,525kg) st Pratt & Whitney TF33-P-7 turbofan engines. The third (production) phase is dependent upon finance and the outcome of trials during the earlier phases; if approved, it is expected to involve thirty-four aircraft, including the bringing up of the prototypes to production standard.

Boeing EC-137D (second prototype for E-3A), 1973

Span: 145ft 9in (44.42m)
Length: 152ft 11in (46.61m)
Weight: 330,000lb (149,690kg)
Engines: 4 × 19,000lb (8,618kg) st Pratt &
    Whitney JT3D-7 turbofans
Max speed: approx 605mph
Operational ceiling: approx 39,000ft
    (11,885m)
Range: 1,150 miles (1,850km)

Bell HSL-1

Bell HSL-1 of the US Navy, 1957

Rotor Diameter: (each) 51ft 6in (15.70m)
Length: 39ft 2¾in (11.96m)
Weight: 26,500lb (12,020kg)
Engine: 1×2,400hp Pratt & Whitney
   R-2800-50 Double Wasp 18-cyl radial
Max speed: 138mph (222kmh)
Range: 350 miles (563km)

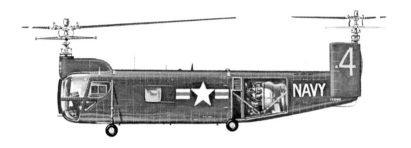

The Bell HSL-1, although not a notably successful aeroplane, was the first helicopter designed from the outset for the submarine hunter/killer role. As the Bell Model 61, it was announced the winner of a US Navy design competition in June 1950, and an evaluation batch of three XHSL-1s (129133 to '35) was ordered shortly afterwards. It was Bell's first and only design to feature a tandem rotor layout, having a Pratt & Whitney R-2800-50 radial engine mounted at the rear and driving a transmission shaft to the front pylon. Standard Bell 2-blade rotors were fitted fore and aft, with provision for folding them for stowage on board ship. The first XHSL-1 made its maiden flight on 4 March 1953. Equipment on board the HSL-1 included electronic tracking gear and dunking sonar and its 4,000lb (1,814kg) cargo load could include

bombs, depth charges or Fairchild AUM-N-2 Petrel air-to-underwater missiles. The crew was made up of two pilots and two sonar operators. Production orders were given for seventy-eight HSL-1s, of which eighteen were scheduled for delivery to the Fleet Air Arm under the Mutual Defense Assistance Program; but the Korean war had ended by the time the XHSL-1 test programme was completed, with the result that the British machines were not delivered and only fifty of those for the US Navy were completed. Delivery of these began in January 1957, to Squadron HU-1, but they spent most of their brief career on training duties. The HO4S, which the HSL-1 had been intended to replace, remained in service until the appearance of the HSS-1 anti-submarine version of the Sikorsky S-58.

Iroquois

Bell UH-1B Iroquois of the US Army with experimental armament of six Nord AS-11 wire-guided missiles.

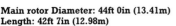

Main rotor Diameter: 44ft 0in (13.41m)
Length: 42ft 7in (12.98m)
Weight: 8,500lb (3,856kg)
Engine: 1 × 960shp Lycoming T53-L-5
    turboshaft
Max speed: 138mph (222kmh)
Service ceiling: 14,000ft (4,267m)
Range: 230 miles

Total orders to date have amounted to more than six thousand Model 205s, and the latest versions have double the power and carrying capacity of the original prototypes. These were three XH-40 test aircraft, ordered in 1955 and each powered by a 700shp Lycoming T53 engine; the first XH-40 (55-4459) was flown on 22 October 1956. Six YH-40s then followed for service trials, these having longer cabins and landing skids and 770shp engines. From June 1959 the US Army began to receive the first of nine pre-production HU-1s for field tests, which were followed by seventy-four of the initial production version, the HU-1A. The 'HU' designation (inverted to UH in 1962) gave rise to the nickname 'Huey' which is more often used than the aircraft's official name of Iroquois. The HU-1A was followed by four YHU-1Bs with 960shp T53-L-5 engines, redesigned rotor blades and an enlarged cabin seating two crew members and seven passengers or three stretchers. Total production orders for HU-1Bs subsequently exceeded seven hundred aircraft, the 1,100shp T53-L-11 engine being fitted in the later batches. In the late autumn of 1962 armed HU-1Bs (and some of the HU-1As) became operational with the US forces in Vietnam, the HU-1B being equipped with four 7.62mm M-60 machine-guns and two pods of air-to-ground unguided rockets. The HU-1B was superseded in 1965 by the faster and more manoeuvrable UH-1C, which has a new Bell-developed 'door-hinge' rotor and a T53-L-11 engine. The UH-1C was preceded into service (in May 1963) by the UH-1D, easily the most numerous version with more than a thousand being built. The UH-1D has the Bell Model number 205 and features a much-enlarged cabin accommodating twelve-fourteen troops or six casualty litters and a medical attendant in addition to the crew. Production examples were preceded by seven YHU-1Ds, the first of which flew on 16 August 1961; powerplant is the T53-L-11. The UH-1D became the workhorse helicopter of the Vietnam campaign, where it has been used for a wide variety of roles including trooping and armed patrol or escort. It has been ordered by the air forces of many countries, and three hundred and fifty-two were ordered by the Federal German forces, these being built in Germany with Dornier the principal contractor. The UH-1E broadly resembles the UH-1B and C, but has special equipment including a rescue hoist and was built for the US Marine Corps as an assault transport helicopter with two M-60 gun pods and up to thirty-six 2.75 in HVAR rockets. Delivery began in February 1964. The US Air Force ordered one hundred and forty-six examples of the UH-1F, with 1,100shp (derated) T58-GE-3 engines, for missile site support duties, together with a number of TH-1F trainer versions; first flight of a UH-1F was made on 20 February 1964, and delivery began in September 1964. No. G model was announced, the next model being the UH-1H, six hundred and nineteen being ordered for the US Army, thirty for the USAF, thirteen for the RNZAF, and ten CUH-1H for the Canadian Armed Forces. The UH-1H replaces the UH-1D, to which it is identical except for a 1,400shp T53-L-13 engine.

Martin P6M SeaMaster

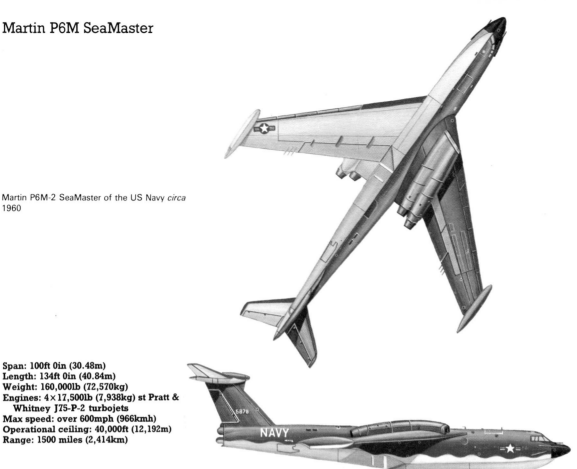

Martin P6M-2 SeaMaster of the US Navy *circa* 1960

Span: 100ft 0in (30.48m)
Length: 134ft 0in (40.84m)
Weight: 160,000lb (72,570kg)
Engines: 4 × 17,500lb (7,938kg) st Pratt & Whitney J75-P-2 turbojets
Max speed: over 600mph (966kmh)
Operational ceiling: 40,000ft (12,192m)
Range: 1500 miles (2,414km)

The eclipse of the military flying-boat after World War 2, in favour of shore-based aircraft for the maritime patrol function, was temporarily deferred by a few post-war designs in which much of the experience gained during the war from the operation of water-borne aircraft was put to good effect. In particular, this minor resurgence was made possible by a better knowledge of the hydrodynamic problems involved, resulting in the use of higher length/beam hull ratios which did much to close the performance gap between the flying boat and its land-based counterparts. It led to the appearance in the USA in the late 1940s and early 1950s of such types as the Martin Model 237 Marlin, first flown on 30 May 1948 and built as the P5M-1 (one hundred and fourteen) and P5M-2 (about one hundred) for the US and French Navies. In 1952 the US Navy held a design competition for a new flying-boat, to carry out the role of mine-layer and to be powered by turbojet engines. Both Convair and Martin submitted proposals, and the latter company's Model 275 was selected as the winner. Two XP6M-1 prototypes, named SeaMaster, were ordered; the first of these flew on 14 July 1955, followed by the second on 18 May 1956. Characteristics of the design were the high-mounted 'T' tail (reminiscent of that of the P5M-2 version of the Marlin), the high length/beam ratio (more than 13:1) of the streamlined hull, and the grouping of the 13,000lb (5,897kg) st

Allison J71-A-4 afterburning jet engines in pairs above the sharply-swept wings to keep the intakes from ingesting spray during take-off and landing. The XP6M-1 carried a crew of four, and had a pair of 20mm guns in a remotely-controlled tail turret as the only defensive armament. In the underside of the hull was installed a watertight rotary bomb door, on the inside of which could be mounted a weapon load of mines or bombs, a camera pod or other equipment. The intention was to employ the SeaMaster in small, widely-dispersed numbers, with refuelling and other services provided by submarines or other small, mobile Naval units. However, both XP6M-1s crashed during flight testing, due to faults in the tail and tailplane-actuating mechanism, and of the Navy's order for six YP6M-1s and twenty-four P6M-2 production aircraft only the YP6M-1s and three P6M-2s were completed. The former were basically similar to the prototypes, except for redesigned intakes and a modified fin fairing, and the first example was flown on 20 January 1958. Four 17,500lb (7,938kg) st Pratt & Whitney J75-P-2 turbojets were installed in the P6M-2s, the first of which was flown on 17 February 1959; in the following August the US Navy terminated the SeaMaster programme, and the completed aircraft served only with a single squadron, based at Harvey Point Naval Air Station, North Carolina.

Sikorsky HR2S-1

Sikorsky HR2S-1W of the US Navy, 1958

Main rotor diameter: 72ft 0in (21.95m)
Length: approx. 66ft 6in (20.27m)
Weight: 31,000lb (14,061kg)
Engines: 2 × 1,900hp Pratt & Whitney
  R-2800-50 Double Wasp 18-cyl radials
Max speed: 122mph (196kmh)
Operational ceiling: 8,000ft (2,438m)
Range: 220 miles (354km)

The Sikorsky S-56 came into being as an asault transport for the US Marine Corps, although some sixty per cent of those eventually built were to meet US Army orders. The original requirement was for an assault transport helicopter capable of air-lifting twenty-six troops or an equivalent weight of military equipment. The S-56 was Sikorsky's first twin-engined helicopter, although the traditional single main rotor layout was retained. For many years the S-56 was the western world's largest and fastest military helicopter, and held two height-with-payload records from 1956-59. It was also the first production helicopter to have a retractable main under-carriage. Loading of the aircraft was via clamshell nose doors, giving access beneath the flight deck to the 1,900 cu ft (53.80 cu m) cabin. A winch capable of hoisting 2,000lb (907kg) at a time was fitted in the cabin roof to assist the loading of cargo. The US Navy placed an order in May 1951 for a prototype XHR2S-1, which was flown for the first time on 18 December 1953. Three more XHR2S-1s followed, and the first of fifty-five production HR2S-1s was flown on 25 October 1955, deliveries to Marine Corps Squadron HMX-1 starting in July 1956. Two aircraft were modified as HR2S-1W patrol aircraft with a huge AN/APS-20E search radar under the nose and additional crew members for radar picket duties. In 1954 an HR2S-1, redesignated YH-37, was evaluated by the US Army, from which followed orders for ninety-four similar aircraft as H-37A Mojaves for general transport duties. Delivery of the last S-56 was made in May 1960, but Sikorsky was engaged until the end of 1962 in converting all but four of the H-37As to H-37B (later CH-37B) standard. Improvements in this version included the installation of Lear autostabilisation equipment and the ability to load and unload while the helicopter was hovering. The Navy and Marine S-56s became CH-37Cs under the 1962 designation system. Some later production S-56s had 2,100hp R-2800-54 engines. The S-56s rotor and transmission systems were utilised in the development of the abortive Westland Westminster and Sikorsky's own S-60 and S-64 crane helicopters, but hopes of selling the S-56 on the commercial market were not realised, due mainly to the high operating costs of a piston-engined machine of this size. A proposal to fit Lycoming T55 turboshaft engines was not adopted.

Bell 47

Bell 47G of the Sheriff's Department, County of Los Angeles, California, 1961

Main rotor diameter: 35ft 1½in (10.71m)
Length: 31ft 7in (9.62m)
Weight: 2,350lb (1,066kg)
Engine: 1×200hp Franklin 6V4-200-C32
  6-cyl vertically-oppposed type
Max speed: 100mph (161kmh)
Operational ceiling: 10,900ft (3,322m)
Range: 215 miles (346km)

In one form or another the Bell 47 has been in continuous production since late 1945, the total output by Bell and its foreign licensees having reached around five thousand of these remarkably long-lived aircraft by the end of 1967, to make the type the world's most widely-built helicopter by a comfortable margin. Production was still continuing in 1972. The original Bell 47 was the production version of Bell's first helicopter, the experimental Model 30. The first of five Bell 30 prototypes, all with 165hp Franklin engines, was flown in 1943, and the first of an initial ten Bell 47s, with a 178hp Franklin, was flown on 8 December 1945. The CAA type approval certificate granted to this aircraft on 8 March 1946 was the first ever awarded to a commercial helicopter anywhere in the world. Large-scale production, initiated in 1946, began with the military Bell 47A and civil 47B, both with 178hp Franklins. Sixteen 47As were completed for the USAAF, with the designation YR-13; ten similar HTL-1s were tested by the US Navy. A car-type enclosed cabin seating two crew members side by side was standard on most early A and B models, but a utility/agricultural version, the 47B-3, had open crew positions. From this was developed the Bell 47D, first variant to introduce the 'goldfish bowl' moulded canopy, and this new model was certificated by the FAA on 25 February 1948. It also formed the subject of the first substantial military order, the US Army receiving sixty-five H-13Bs, of which it had sixteen converted to an ambulance version as the H-13C, and the US Navy ordering twelve HTL-2s. In 1949 the Bell 47D-1 appeared with an openwork tail-boom (as on the H-13C) and

an underfin. Eighty-seven 2-seat H-13D's and four hundred and ninety 3-seat dual-control H-13Es to this configuration were supplied to the US Army, their US Navy counterparts being the HTL-4 (forty-six) and HTL-5 (thirty-six). The Navy's HTL-3 (nine delivered) corresponded to the Model 47E, a 2-seater with a 200hp Franklin 6V4-200-C32 engine; while the Army's XH-13F (Bell Model 201) was a solitary test-bed for a Continental T51 turbine engine. It was the 200hp Franklin engine, combined with the 3-seat capacity of the 47D-1, that gave rise to the Model 47G, which was granted an FAA type certificate in June 1953 and was still in production in its later forms in 1972. The US Army's H-13G (now OH-13G), two hundred and sixty-five of which were built, corresponds to this model, as does the Navy's HTL-6, of which forty-eight were built. The first departure from the use of Franklins appeared in the 1955 Bell 47G-2, whose 200hp Lycoming VO-435 enabled it to operate at higher weights without losing performance. The Bell 47G series are named Sioux by the US Army, which received more than four hundred and fifty of the G-2 model designated H-13H (now UH-13H). Two of these were later converted to G-3 standard as H-13Ks. A more powerful VO-435 of 240hp was installed in the G-2A, which was followed in 1963 by the similarly powered 47G-2A-1 having a wider cabin with separate seats, improved rotor blades and extra fuel tankage. Boosted variants included the G-3 (supercharged Franklin 6VS-335-A of 225hp) and G-3B (turbosupercharged Lycoming TVO-435 of 280hp).

Northrop T-38 Talon

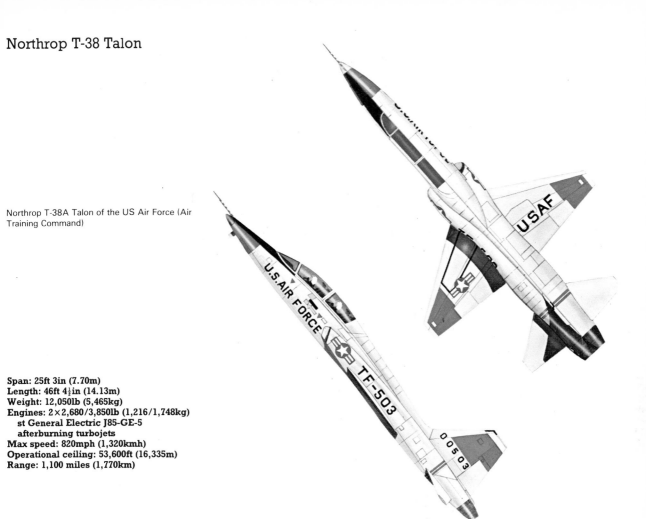

Northrop T-38A Talon of the US Air Force (Air Training Command)

Span: 25ft 3in (7.70m)
Length: 46ft 4½in (14.13m)
Weight: 12,050lb (5,465kg)
Engines: 2×2,680/3,850lb (1,216/1,748kg)
st General Electric J85-GE-5
afterburning turbojets
Max speed: 820mph (1,320kmh)
Operational ceiling: 53,600ft (16,335m)
Range: 1,100 miles (1,770km)

Possessing the distinction of being the first training aeroplane to be designed from the outset for flight at supersonic speeds, the Talon entered service in March 1961 with Air Training Command of the USAF. The Talon, whose first YT-38 prototype (58-1191) was flown on 10 April 1959 with non-afterburning YJ85-GE-1 engines, set out as a supersonic replacement for the veteran Lockheed T-33A, but is capable of covering all stages of advanced and tactical training previously conducted with the Cessna T-37, the T-33 and the F-86F Sabre or F-100F Super Sabre. Final familiarisation is given on the 2-seat version of the type which the trainee will fly operationally. The Talon is also employed by NASA, which acquired twenty-four to give spaceflight readiness training to America's astronauts; and five USAF aircraft were procured by the US Navy. The Federal German Luftwaffe ordered forty-six which, delivered in 1967, fly in the USA in USAF markings and are used to train German student pilots. The thousandth T-38A was delivered in January 1969; one thousand one hundred and eighty-nine were built, the last being delivered in January 1972. Although it clearly has much in common with the Northrop F-5 strike fighter which was evolved from it, the Talon has lower-powered engines and lacks the F-5s wing leading-edge flaps. It has the outstanding initial climb rate of 30,800ft (9,388m) per minute, which secured for it several climb-to-height records in 1961.

McDonnell Douglas F-4 Phantom II

McDonnell Douglas F-4B Phantom II of the US Navy (Squadron VF-84, USS *Independence*), circa 1961

Span: 38ft 5in (11.70m)
Length: 58ft 3in (17.76m)
Weight: 54,600lb (24,766kg)
Engines: 2 × 10,900/16,500lb
  (4,944/7,484kg) st General Electric
  J79-GE-8 afterburning turbojets
Max speed: 1,584mph (2,550kmh)
Operational ceiling: 71,000ft (21,640m)
Range: over 900 miles

There is nothing even remotely wraith-like about McDonnell Douglas's second Phantom, whose warload alone is greater than that of a World War 2 Lancaster or B-29. This solid, ugly interceptor, strike and reconnaissance aeroplane serves with three US air arms, several other air forces, and is the subject of one of the largest post-war programmes yet, in any country; more than four thousand four hundred Phantoms had been completed by 1974. It originated to a US Navy specification for a single-seat carrier-based attack fighter, and when ordered in 1954 was designated AH-1. In 1955 the USN altered its requirement to specify a missile-armed fighter, changing the designation to F4H-1. Twenty-three F4H-1s were ordered for test purposes, the first of these flying on 27 May 1958 with two J79-GE-3A engines. Evaluation of these aircraft led to a number of modifications, notably the introduction of dihedral on the outer wing panels, anhedral on the all-moving tailplane, a blown-flap system of boundary layer control and the adoption of more powerful J79 engines. The trials batch, and the first twenty-four production Phantom IIs, became F4H-1Fs when fitted with J79-GE-2 or -2A turbojets, and parallel versions were ordered by the USAF – adopting a production Navy fighter for the first time in its history – as the F-110A and photo-reconnaissance RF-110A. In 1962, when the US services adopted a unified designation system, the F4H-1F became the F-4A, the definitive F4H-1 (with J79-GE-8 engines) became the Navy/Marine Corps F-4B (six hundred and thirty-five built), the proposed F4H-1Ps 'camera job' became the USMCs RF-4B, and the USAF versions became F-4C and RF-4C

respectively. The USAF eventually received five hundred and eighty-three F-4Cs, for service with Tactical Air Command, Pacific Air Force and US Air Forces Europe. Thirty-six of this version were supplied to the Spanish Air Force. The first F-4C was flown on 27 May 1963; deliveries were completed in 1966, by which time 29 USN squadrons were operating the F-4B. Production of the RF-4C was continuing in 1974, by which time more than five hundred had been completed. The F-4D, first flown on 8 December 1965, was a USAF model with J79-GE-15 engines and improved radar and electronics; eight hundred and twenty-five F-4Ds were built, sixty-four of this version being supplied to the Imperial Iranian Air Force and eighteen to South Korea. Further improvements in equipment and operational capability resulted in the F-4E, a multi-role version for the US Air Force first flown on 30 June 1967. This has more powerful J79-GE-17 engines, a permanent installation of an M61 20mm multi-barrel cannon under the nose and extra fuel capacity. It has been exported to Greece (thirty-six), Iran, Israel and Turkey (forty), and Mitsubishi is building one hundred and twenty-eight for the Japan Air Self-Defence Force. The RF-4E is a multi-sensor reconnaissance version ordered originally by Federal Germany (eighty-eight), and which flew for the first time in October 1970. Japan has ordered fourteen of these as the RF-4EJ, and others have been ordered by Iran. Israel has ordered one hundred and sixty-eight F-4Es and RF-4Es. The F-4F is a version with leading-edge slats for the German Luftwaffe, which has ordered a hundred and seventy-five.

Raven

Hiller OH-23C Raven of the US Army, California National Guard, 1962

Main rotor diameter: 35ft 0in (10.67m)
Length: 27ft 6in (8.38m)
Weight: 2,500lb (1,134kg)
Engine: 1 × 200hp Franklin 6U4-200-C33
 6-cyl vertically opposed type
Max speed: 87mph (140kmh)
Operational ceiling: 10,500ft (3,200m)
Range: 135 miles (217km)

In 1944, at the age of 18, Stanley Hiller Junr designed and built his first helicopter, the XH-44. This aircraft (NX30033) was America's first helicopter successfully to employ co-axial twin rotors, but after a year or two studying this and similar designs Hiller began to seek something lighter and cheaper. He therefore turned to a single main rotor layout in a design known as the United Helicopters UH-5, and in this machine also developed the 'Rotor-Matic' rotor control system which was installed in his first production helicopter. Known originally as the Hiller Model 360, this appeared in 1948 as a 3-seater, powered by a 178hp Franklin 6V4-178-B33 and having a fully enclosed fuselage and cabin. This structure was simplified on the production version, known as the Model 12, which retained the enclosed tailboom but had an open cockpit and engine bay. The Model 12 received FAA Type Approval on 14 October 1948 and in 1949 an aircraft of this type made the first trans-continental flight in the USA by a commercial helicopter. With new-type rotor blades and minor modifications the 1950 version became the Model 12A, later versions of which were powered by 200hp 6V4-200-C33 or 210hp 6V-335-B Franklin engines. Single examples of the Model 12A were evaluated by the US Army and Navy, leading to a small order for sixteen HTE-1 trainers for the Navy and a more substantial one for one hundred H-23A Ravens for the Army. In all, one hundred and ninety-four civil and military examples of the Model 12 and 12A were built, including five H-23As for evaluation by the US Air Force. Operational experience with the H-23A in Korea led to an improved

model, the 12B, four hundred and fifty-three of which were eventually built. Two hundred and seventy-three of these were Army H-23Bs including two hundred and sixteen assigned to the Primary Helicopter School at Fort Wolters, Texas, for training. The Model 12Bs were powered by 200 or 210hp Franklin engines and normally had a skid or float landing gear, although a 4-wheel undercarriage was fitted to the US Navy's thirty-five HTE-2s. The major design changes in the 1955 Model 12C (200hp Franklin) were its all-metal rotor blades and one-piece 'goldfish-bowl' cabin hood. Of two hundred civil and military Model 12Cs completed, one hundred and forty-five were delivered from 1956 as US Army H-23Cs (later redesignated OH-23C). The civil model was certificated by the FAA on 12 December 1955. The Model 12D, first flown on 3 April 1956, was exclusively a military version, four hundred and eighty-three being built for the US Army as the H-23D (later OH-23D) with 250hp Lycoming O-540 engines, new rotor transmission and drive systems, higher gross weight and a substantially longer overhaul life. One additional machine, designated H-23D-2, was fitted with a 305hp VO-540 Lycoming and used by Hiller to develop the automatic stabilising gear for the later L4. This engine also powered the Hiller 12E (originally UH-12E). Certificated by the FAA in January 1959, the Hiller 12E was offered in civil form as the L3 with a 305hp Lycoming VO-540-C2A or as the SL3 with a supercharged 315hp TIVO-540-A2A engine. Both had the new rotor system and automatic stabilisation equipment.

Boeing-Vertol 107-II

Boeing-Vertol 107-II of New York Airways Inc.,
1962

Rotor diameter: (each) 50ft 0in (15.24m)
Length: 44ft 7in (13.59m)
Weight: 19,000lb (8,618kg)
Engines: 2 × 1,250shp General Electric
CT-58-110-1 turboshafts
Max speed: 157mph (253kmh)
Operational ceiling: 13,000ft (3,960m)
Range: 109 miles (175km)

Soon after the former Piasecki Helicopter Corporation changed its title to Vertol Aircraft Corporation in March 1956, a design study programme was initiated to evolve a medium transport helicopter, with civil and military applications, to be powered by a pair of the lightweight, economical gas turbine engines then becoming available. The project was given the works Model number 107 and construction of a prototype (N74060) was put in hand in May 1957. Later that year flight tests were conducted with two H-21 helicopters in which a twin-turbine powerplant had been installed, and on 22 April 1958 the prototype Vertol 107 made its maiden flight. Powered by two 860shp Lycoming T53 turboshaft engines, it was designed to seat twenty-five passengers with a stewardess and a flight crew of two. However, the first interest came from the US Army, which in July 1958 ordered ten modified aircraft as YHC-1As. The first of these (58-5514) was flown on 27 August 1959. With the ordering of the YHC-1B Chinook test batch two months before this, the YHC-1A order was cut back to three aircraft, and the third YHC-1A, with 1,050shp General Electric T58-GE-6 engines and rotors of increased diameter, was later converted to a commercial configuration as the Vertol 107-II-1. It flew in its new form on 25 October 1960, by which time Vertol had become a division of The Boeing Company. This was followed on 19 May 1961 by the first flight of N6671, a company-sponsored production prototype, with square cabin windows and taller rotor pylons and 1,250shp CT58-110-1 engines, tailored to the requirements of New York

Airways. This airline subsequently ordered five of these aircraft under the production designation 107-II-10 and, following FAA certification of the commercial passenger version in January 1962, opened regular services with its 107s on 1 July. Three more were purchased by Pan American and leased to NYA. A modified version of the YHC-1A, the Boeing-Vertol 107M, was in February 1961 declared winner of a design competition held to find a medium assault transport helicopter for the US Marine Corps, and this aircraft was ordered into production as the HRB-1 (CH-46A from July 1962) with the name Sea Knight. The modest initial batch of fourteen was subsequently increased until by the end of 1970 six hundred Sea Knights had been ordered. This total includes CH-46Ds, with 1,400shp T58-GE-10 engines and slightly bigger diameter rotors with cambered blades; and CH-46Fs, which are similar but carry additional electronic equipment. The CH-46 models carry a flight crew of three and up to twenty-five troops (or fifteen casualty litters and two medical attendants), have a rear loading ramp and power-folding for the rotor blades. They serve, or have served, as assault or logistics transports with Marine Corps squadrons in the Atlantic, Pacific and Mediterranean as well as in Vietnam. The US Navy has corresponding models designated UH-46A (twenty-four built) and UH-46D based aboard its Fast Combat Support Ships for the 'vertical replenishment' of supplies to combat vessels at sea.

McDonnell Douglas A-4 Skyhawk

Douglas A-4C (A4D-2N) Skyhawk of VA-153,
US Navy, USS *Constellation, circa* 1962

Span: 27ft 6in (8.38m)
Length (excluding probe): 42ft 10¾in
(13.07m)
Weight, normal take-off: 17,295lb
(7,845kg)
Engine: 7,700lb (3,493kg) st Wright
J65-W-164 turbojet
Max speed: 680mph (1,094kmh) at sea
level
Range: 1,150 miles (1,850km)
Armament: 2×20mm Mk 12 cannon
Max bomb load: 5,000lb (2,268kg)
externally

The Skyhawk, jet successor to the Douglas Skyraider attack bomber, was an extremely effective exercise by designer Ed Heinemann in weight saving and compact design, small enough to fit into USN carrier lifts without wing folding, yet powerful and with great load carrying capability. The USN placed a contract for one prototype XA4D-1 in June 1952; this first flew on 22 June 1954 (the only prototype). The A4D-1 (one hundred and sixty-five built, including nineteen YA4D-1s) initial production model with 7,700lb (3,500kg) st Wright J65-W-4 or 4B, entered USN service in October 1956. The A4D-2 (five hundred and forty-two built) had an in-flight refuelling probe. The A4D-2N (six hundred and thirty-eight built; first flown 21 August 1959) was a limited all-weather version with radar equipment in a slightly longer nose. All had J65 turbojets, two 20mm cannon in the wing roots, and one stores point under the fuselage and two underwing. The next major production model was the A4D-5 (four hundred and ninety-six built), introducing important changes, chiefly the 8,500lb (3,855kg) st Pratt & Whitney J52-P-6A, increasing range twenty-five per cent, and four stores pylons underwing; the first flew on 12 July 1961. When the USN and USAF adopted a unified designation system in 1962, the A4D-1, -2, -2N and -5 became the A-4A, B, C and E, A-4D being avoided to prevent confusion. Early in 1964 the USN ordered two TA-4Es, a tandem 2-seat operational trainer with lengthened fuselage. Deliveries of the production version, the TA-4F, began in 1966; a simplified trainer, the TA-4J, flew in May 1969. The A-4F (one hundred and forty-six built), flown on 31 August 1966, was

an updated single-seat attack model, with operational and avionics improvements including a 'saddle-back' dorsal avionics fairing, wing-spoilers, a zero-zero ejection seat and pilot armour. Several previous marks were updated to A-4F standard. The A-4M Skyhawk II for the USMC has an 11,200lb (5,080kg) st J52, deeper canopy, square-top fin, brake parachute, increased cannon ammunition, five stores points, and other refinements. Deliveries began in November 1971. Gaps in the sequence are filled by converted and/or exported versions. The Argentine Air Force and Navy, respectively, received seventy-five and sixteen ex-USN A-4Bs, redesignated A-4P and Q respectively. The RAN received sixteen A-4Gs and four TA-4Gs, half ex-USN, half new. The A-4H for Israel (ninety, plus ten TA-4H), is based on the A-4E but has a brake parachute, square-top fin, and 30mm DEFA cannon. Israel also acquired about thirty A-4Es, some converted later to A-4F standard. Ten A-4Ks and four TA-4Ks, corresponding to the F, went to the RNZAF in 1970; Kuwait received thirty A-4KU and six TA-4KU. One hundred A-4Cs brought up to A-4K standard for the USN Reserve are designated A-4L. The A-4N Skyhawk II, flown on 8 June 1972, is an A-4M with twin 30mm DEFA cannon, and an updated navigation and weapons delivery system; Israel ordered one hundred and seventeen. The A-4S is a refurbished A-4B; Singapore ordered forty. First in action during the 1958 Lebanon crisis, the Skyhawk was extensively used in Vietnam for ground-attack and support. Extended many times, production ceased in 1979.

Douglas Skywarrior

Douglas A-3B Skywarrior of the US Navy Squadron VAH-6 *circa* 1962

Span: 72ft 6in (22.10m)
Length: 76ft 4in (23.27m)
Weight: 73,000lb (33,112kg)
Engines: 2 × 12,400lb (5,624kg) st Pratt & Whitney J57-P-10 turbojets
Max speed: 610mph (982kmh)
Operational ceiling: 41,000ft (12,500m)
Range: 1,050 miles (1,690km)

The Skywarrior has a long history, having resulted from a 1947 US Navy requirement for a carrier-based attack aircraft to combine jet power with the ability to deliver nuclear weapons. After some two years of preliminary design work Douglas was awarded a contract in March 1949 to develop and build two prototypes. The first of these (125412), the XA3D-1, was flown for the first time on 28 October 1952, powered by two 7,000lb (3,175kg) st Westinghouse XJ40-WE-3 turbojets in underwing pods. Because of the ultimate abandonment of the J40 engine programme, a switch was made to the 9,700lb (4,400kg) st Pratt & Whitney J57-P-6, the YA3D-1 production prototype flying with this powerplant on 16 September 1953. Two hundred and eighty production Skywarriors were built subsequently; these (with their pre-1962 designations in parentheses) comprised fifty A-3A (A3D-1), on hundred and sixty-four A-3B (A3D-2), thirty RA-3B (A3D-2P), twenty-four EA-3B (A3D-2Q) and twelve TA-3B (A3D-2T). The A-3As were delivered from March 1956, the first US Navy unit to receive them being VAH-1. Conversions included five to EA-3A (A3D-1Q), with electronic counter-measures (ECM) gear in the tailcone in place of the A-3As twin 20mm remote-controlled guns; one to YRA-3A (A3D-1P) as a photo-reconnaissance prototype; and others to TA-3A (A3D-1T) dual-control trainers. The definitive Navy version was the A-3B, with more powerful J57-P-10 engines, a modified weapons bay to carry a greater variety of stores, and provision for in-flight refuelling; like the A-3A, it carried a crew of three. Deliveries of the A-3B, to Squadron VAH-2, began in January 1957, and eventually eight heavy attack squadrons, on board the 'Essex' and 'Midway' class carriers, were equipped with the A-3B. Whereas, in the A-3A and A-3B, only the crew compartment was pressurised, the whole fuselage became so in the three subsequent production models. This was brought about by their specialised roles, which called for 'mission kits' and appropriate additional crew members to be installed in the weapons bay. The photo-reconnaissance RA-3B, first flown on 22 July 1958, thus carried two operators and twelve vertical or oblique cameras in this position; the EA-3B, first flown on 10 December 1958, carried ECM equipment and four operators, making a crew total of seven; the TA-3B, first flown on 29 August 1959, was essentially an operational trainer for the EA-3B and carried a pilot, one instructor and six trainees. One TA-3B was converted to VA-3B, equipped as an executive transport. By 1971 those Skywarriors still in service were employed primarily in the electronics reconnaissance role in Vietnam or as KA-3B or EKA-3B flight refuelling tankers. In February 1952 the US Air Force decided to adapt the Skywarrior to meet its own requirement for the tactical light bomber and reconnaissance roles. Although considerable internal redesign was involved, additional prototypes were not considered necessary. Instead, the USAF ordered five RB-66A Destroyers for service evaluation.

Delta Dagger

Convair F-102A Delta Dagger of the US Air Forces Europe (525th Fighter Interceptor Squadron), *circa* 1962

Span: 38ft 1½in (11.62m)
Length: 68ft 4¾in (20.84m)
Weight: 27,700lb (12,565kg)
Engine: 1×11,700/17,200lb
   (5,307/7,802kg) st Pratt & Whitney
   J57-P-23 afterburning turbojet
Max speed: 825mph (1,328kmh)
Operational ceiling: 54,000ft (16,460m)
Range: 1,350 miles (2,175km)

The F-102A, which entered service with the USAF in 1956, can trace its history back to the small, delta-winged XF-92A which first flew on 18 September 1948. When, two years later, the USAF issued a specification for a supersonic interceptor, the basic concept of the XF-92A was scaled up to yeild the YF-102. The first of ten YF-102s made its maiden flight on 24 October 1953, but was patently incapable of exceeding Mach I and for a time its future seemed in jeopardy. Successful application of the area rule principle to the aircraft's body, however, resulted in the YF-102A (four built) which first flew on 20 December 1954 and fully met the USAFs requirements; and the long and satisfactory service given by the eight hundred and seventy-five F-102As subsequently built more than vindicated the aircraft's uncertain start. The first fifty-three F-102As had a somewhat smaller fin and rudder. A further

sixty-three aircraft were built as 2-seat TF-102A combat proficiency trainers (first example flown on 8 November 1955), fully capable of normal operational missions. Production was completed in April 1958. Both models were modernised while in service, with more advanced electronics for greater efficiency at all altitudes, and in-flight refuelling. The first gun-less US interceptor, the Delta Dagger carries four Hughes Falcon air-to-air missiles and twenty-four 2.75in folding-fin unguided aerial rockets. It has full all-weather capability, and served with the US Air Forces Europe, the Pacific Air Force and Air Defense Command units in the USA. By 1973 it no longer equipped front-line USAF units, but nine fighter-interceptor groups of the Air National Guard still operated the type, and others have been supplied to the air forces of Greece and Turkey.

Rockwell Sabreliner

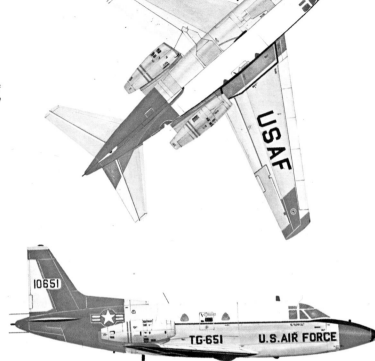

Rockwell (North American) T-39A Sabreliner of the US Air Force (Air Training Command), *circa* 1962

Span: 44ft 5½in (13.54m)
Length: 43ft 9in (13.34m)
Weight: 17,760lb (8,056kg)
Engines: 2×3,000lb (1.361kg) st Pratt & Whitney J60-P-3A turbojets
Max speed: 540mph (869kmh)
Operational ceiling: 39,000ft (11,890m)
Range: 1,950 miles (3,140km)

Although preceding Britain's Hawker Siddeley Dominie by several years, the Sabreliner fulfils a similar function with the US forces and both aircraft follow a twin rear-jet layout. The NA-246 Sabreliner was developed as a private venture to a USAF specification for a utility aircraft and 'combat readiness' trainer, to have a performance akin to that of the Sabre fighter – hence its name. The Sabreliner prototype (N4060K) was flown on 16 September 1958, and the first T-39A on 30 June 1960, deliveries to the USAF Air Training Command beginning later the same year. These had Pratt & Whitney J60-P-3 turbojet engines, compared with the 2,500lb (1,134kg) General Electric J85 engines of the prototype. One hundred and forty-three T-39As were completed for the USAF, three of these being converted later to T-39F electronic warfare trainers for F-105G personnel. Six T-39Bs were completed for Tactical Air Command, with Doppler radar and NASARR

(North American Search and Ranging Radar) in a modified nose and a simulated F-105D cockpit on the starboard side of the cabin, for the training of Thunderchief crews. These entered service in 1961. The US Navy version, for maritime radar training, is the T-39D, of which forty-two were built, the T-39C being a project only. The CT-39E is the US Navy designation for nine off-the-shelf commercial Sabreliner 40s purchased for 'rapid-response' transport of high-priority passengers, ferry pilots and cargo; five of the longer Sabre 60s have been purchased, for the same role, as CT-39Gs. The US Coast Guard has ordered eight Sabre 75As for a marine pollution surveillance and search role, under the designation HT-39H. The Sabreliner (now simply called Sabre) has continued in production by Rockwell for the commercial market as an executive transport.

Lockheed Super Constellation

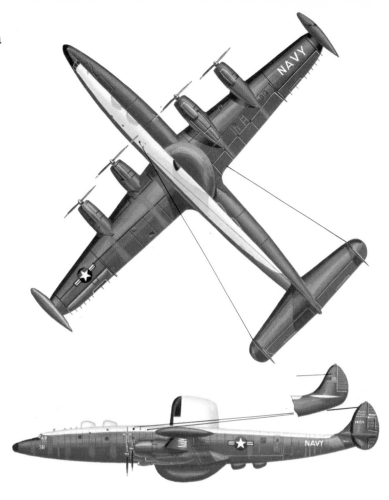

Lockheed EC-121K Super Constellation of the US Navy Pacific Missile Range Squadron, *circa* 1963

Span: 123ft 5in (37.62m)
Length: 116ft 2in (35.41m)
Weight: 143,600lb (65,135kg)
Engines: 4 × 3,400lb Wright R-3350-34 or -42 Turbo-Compounds
Max speed: 321mph (517kmh)
Operational ceiling: 20,600ft (6,280m)
Range: 4,600 miles (7,405km)

This veteran aeroplane dates from the Model 049 Constellation air-liner, which had no time to establish itself in the commercial market before the USAs entry into World War 2, when fifteen were delivered as C-69 military transports. After the war the Constellation achieved a deserved success with the world's airlines, and ten aircraft of the Model L-749 type were completed as long range personnel carriers for the US Air Force. One of these was equipped as a VC-121B with VIP interior, and the remainder as PC-121A standard transports. A stretch of the Constellation resulted in the Model L-1049 Super Constellation with a much increased seating capacity in its 18ft 4in (5.59m) longer fuselage, and the service equivalents of this model included four C-121A VIP transports, thirty-three C-121Cs for the USAF and thirty-two R7V-1s for the Navy. Capacity of the C-121C (and the generally similar R7V-1, some of which became C-121G on transfer to MAC) is one hundred and six passengers, or seventy-two passengers plus forty-seven casualty litters with their

attendants, or a 40,000lb (18,144kg) cargo payload. In addition to the transport variants, there have been numerous radar or ECM picket and AEW versions with Air Force or Navy formations, serving under such designations as RC-121C (for AEW duties; ten built, later redesignated EC-121C); RC-121D (seventy built, some later to EC-121H); C-121J (ex-R7V-1); EC-121K (ex-WV-2); EC-121L (ex-WV-2E); EC-121M (ex-WV-2Q); WC-121N (for weather reconnaissance; ex-WV-3); EC-121P (ex-WV-2); EC-121Q (converted EC-121D); EC-121R (converted EC-121K and P); EC-121S (converted C-121C); and EC-121T (converted EC-121D). The picket versions, distinguished by a large ventral 'guppy' radome and a second fairing, resembling a submarine conning tower, above the fuselage, carry crews of up to thirty-one men. Other variants have included the EC-121D and H (airborne fighter control) and C-121J (airborne communications relay stations). The Indian Air Force (No. 6 Squadron) operates eight Super Constellations for search and rescue, and one as a transport.

Rockwell International Buckeye

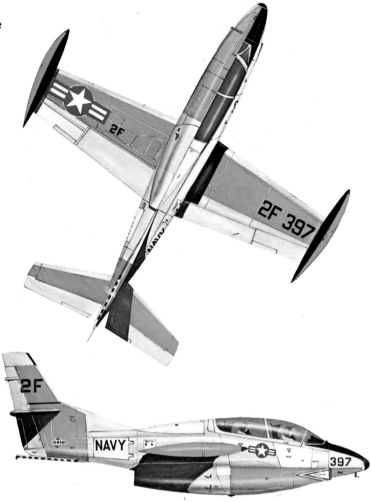

Rockwell International (North American) T-2A
Buckeye of the US Navy (Air Basic Training
Command), *circa* 1963

Span: 37ft 10¼in (11.54m)
Length: 38ft 3½in (11.67m)
Weight: 11,373lb (5,159kg)
Engine: 1×3,400lb (1,540kg) st
   Westinghouse J34-WE-36 turbojet
Max speed: 492mph (792kmh)
Operational ceiling: 42,500ft (12,955m)
Range: 965 miles (1,555km)

The Buckeye was evolved in the late 1950s as a low-cost, multi-stage trainer for the United States Navy, with whom it has been in service since 1959. Its design relied on systems already proven in other North American products, employing a substantially similar wing to the original FJ-1 Fury and a cockpit controls system akin to that used by the piston-engined T-28C trainer. Though a straightforward and unspectacular aeroplane, the Buckeye is nevertheless capable of training naval pilots right through from the *ab initio* flight stage to the full range of manoeuvres required on board the US Navy's aircraft carriers. The T-2A has two underwing attachment points from which 0.50in gun pods, 100lb practice bombs or pods of 2.75in rockets can be suspended for weapons training. The first two prototypes were originally designated XT2J-1, and the first of these (144217) was flown on 31 January 1958. Two hundred and seventeen examples of the single-engined T2J-1 (redesignated T-2A in 1962) were built up to early 1961; on 30 August 1962, one of these was flown with an experimental installation of two smaller 3,000lb (1,361kg) st Pratt & Whitney J60-P-6 engines in place of the single J34. After a second such conversion, ten similar aircraft, designated T-2B, were completed for evaluation by the US Navy; the first of these was delivered to Training Squadron 7 in November 1965, and follow-on contracts for T-2Bs increased the total ordered to ninety-seven. The first production T-2B was flown on 21 May 1965, and deliveries to the USN began in 1966. Following its first flight on 17 April 1968, Rockwell began production of the T-2C, a second twin-engined model, powered by 2,950lb. (1,339kg) st J85-GE-4 engines but otherwise generally similar to the T-2B. One hundred and eighty-three T-2Cs had been ordered by early 1974, and funding for a further twenty-four was requested in the FY 1974 budget. Forty T-2Cs have been ordered by the Greek Air Force. Delivery took place in 1973 of twelve T-2Ds to the Venezuelan Air Force; this model is basically similar to the T-2C but with the carrier landing equipment deleted and some changes in avionics. The T-2A was phased out of US Navy service in early 1973, having been replaced entirely by the B and C models.

Convair F-106 Delta Dart

General Dynamics (Convair) F-106A Delta Dart of the 94th Fighter Interceptor Sqdn, Air Defense Command, USAF, *circa* 1962

Span: 38ft 3½in (11.67m)
Length (including nose probe): 70ft 8¾in (21.56m)
Weight, normal take-off: 35,500lb (16,103kg)
Engine: 17,200/24,500lb (7,802/11,113kg) st Pratt & Whitney J75-P-17 afterburning turbojets
Max speed: 1,525mph (2,455kmh)
Operational ceiling: 57,000ft (17,375m)
Combat radius, standard fuel: 575 miles (925km)
Armament: No guns; 4×Falcon AAMs and 2×Genie rockets internally

Close family resemblence between the F-102 and F-106 is no coincidence, for the F-106 began its development in 1955 as the F-102B. Such were the ultimate differences between the two, however, that a new F designation was allotted. Although retaining the delta-wing and area-ruled fuselage configuration of the subsonic F-102, the F-106s fuselage was entirely redesigned to take the Pratt & Whitney J75, delivering fifty per cent more power than the F-102s J57. To optimise performance at all speeds, the engine intakes were closer to the engine and given variable ducts. The greater power and increased aerodynamic efficiency resulted in the F-106 being almost twice as fast as the F-102. In December 1957 an F-106A set a world absolute speed record of 1,525mph (2,454kmh). It is still one of the most advanced interceptors. Its electronic guidance and fire control equipment, designed to work with the SAGE (Semi-Automatic Ground Environment) defence system, detects its target by radar and launches its four Falcon and/or two Genie missiles entirely automatically. An entire combat mission, between take-off and touchdown, can be flown without the pilot touching a single control. The first to fly, on 26 December 1956, was a production F-106A. The F-106B (first flight 9 April 1958) tandem two-seat combat trainer

has the same combat capability as the A, and is almost as fast. When production ended late in 1960 two hundred and seventy-seven single-seat F-106As and sixty-three F-106Bs had been built. First deliveries were made in July 1959, and by mid-1961 Delta Darts equipped about half the all-weather squadrons of the USAFs Air Defense Command. The F-106A has undergone two major rebuild programmes, giving updated avionics, new digital air data links, improved navigation/identification/ECM/communications systems, new IR sensors, new missiles, the installation of zero-height crew escape systems and provision for underwing drop-tanks and in-flight refuelling capability. In 1970 tests were conducted with an F-106A (58-795) fitted with an improved visibility cockpit hood, optical gun-sight and an M-61A 20mm multi-barrel cannon in a semi-retractable ventral fairing. This gun installation was adopted as a standard fit for in-service aircraft in 1973. In the late 1970s the F-106A/B equipped all but one of Aerospace Defense Command's seven Fighter Interceptor Squadrons, all based in the USA. In 1980 ADC was merged with TAC. Additionally, five ANG squadrons have flown F-106s.

P-3A Orion

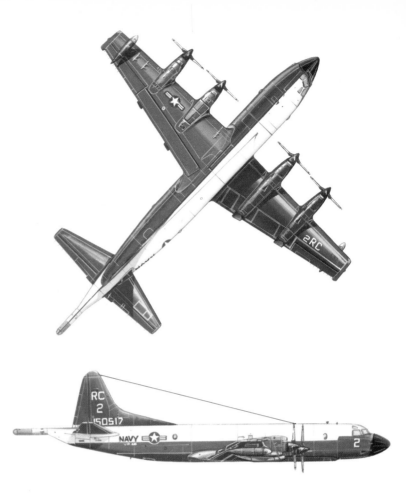

Lockheed P-3A Orion of the US Navy Squadron VP-46, NAS Moffett Field, California, *circa* 1964

Span: 99ft 8in (30.37m)
Length: 116ft 10in (35.61m)
Weight: 134,000lb (60,780kg)
Engines: 4×4,500eph Allison T56-A-10W turboprops
Max speed: 403mph (650kmh)
Operational ceiling: 27,000ft (8,230m)
Range: 1,550 miles (2,495km)

When it became necessary to find a successor to the long-lived Neptune for the maritime patrol squadrons of the US Navy, Lockheed decided to base its entry in the official design competition on its commercial turboprop airliner, the Electra. This entry won the competition and, as the P-3A Orion, entered squadron service in August 1962. As compared with the Electra, the Orion's forward fuselage, which includes the internal weapons bay, is some 7ft (2.13m) shorter; and it has the familiar MAD 'sting' projecting beyond the tail. The wing and tail surfaces are standard Electra components. Inside the Orion's fully-pressurised fuselage are some 2½ tons of electronics equipment, and accommodation for a crew of ten on patrols of up to eighteen hours. The internal ordnance load may be up to 7,252lb (3,290kg), comprising three or four homing torpedoes with nuclear or high explosive warheads, nuclear depth charges, sea mines or other maritime stores. In addition the Orion has ten underwing attachment points for external stores. One of these is normally occupied by a searchlight, but the remaining nine may be utilised for additional mines or torpedoes, rocket pods or Zuni rocket launchers. Initial flight testing was conducted with a modified Electra airframe, first flown on 19 August 1958, followed by a YP3V-1 operational prototype on 25 November 1959. The US Navy initially ordered two basic production models, the P-3A and P-3B. Of these, one hundred and fifty-seven were P-3As, those from the 110th aircraft onwards having more sensitive detection equipment and being known as Deltic P-3As. First flight by a production P-3A was made on 15 April 1961, and the first operational Orion units were VP-8 and VP-44. Four examples of a weather reconnaissance version, the WP-3A, were delivered in 1970. Three P-3As were delivered to the Spanish Air Force in 1973. The P-3B (one hundred and forty-four built) is basically similar to the P-3A except for higher-powered (4,910ehp) Allison T56-A-14 engines, and this version has also been delivered to the air forces of Australia (ten for No. 11 Squadron), New Zealand (five for No. 5 Squadron) and Norway (five for No. 333 Squadron). Electronics reconnaissance versions for the US Navy, distinguished by large radomes above and below the fuselage and by the absence of the MAD tail-boom, are designated EP-3E (ten converted from P-3As and two others from previously-converted EP-3Bs). The third basic version of the Orion was the P-3C, first flown on 18 September 1968. This entered service in the following year and has considerably more advanced computer-based detection and control equipment. More than one hundred P-3Cs had been delivered by early 1974. One of these was delivered as the RP-3D, a specially-equipped aircraft for oceanographic research with Squadron VXN-8. The P-3F, of which the Imperial Iranian Air Force has ordered six, is generally similar to the P-3C except for some equipment changes.

Lockheed U-2

Lockheed WV-2 flown by Lockheed for the US Air Force Flight Dynamics Laboratory, *circa* 1964

Span: 80ft 0in (24.38m)
Length: 49ft 7in (15.11m)
Weight: 15,850lb (6,842kg)
Engine: 1×11,200lb (5,080kg) st Pratt & Whitney J57-P-37A turbojet
Max speed: 495mph (797kmh)
Operational ceiling: 55,000ft (16,775m)
Range: 2,200 miles (3,540km)

There was a story that CIA, officially the initials of the US Central Intelligence Agency, stood also for 'Caught In the Act'; and certainly no aeroplane in history earned the latter description with such world-shaking effect as the U-2 in which Gary Powers was shot down over the Soviet Union on 1 May 1960. Whether or not the U-2 design was acutally sponsored by the CIA, there is no doubt that prior to this time it was working on cloak-and-dagger reconnaissance missions, for all its 'utility' category designation and its official description as a high altitude research aeroplane. The U-2 has served principally with the National Aeronautics and Space Adminstration, and with the 4028th and 4080th Strategic Reconnaissance Squadrons (Weather) of Strategic Air Command in the USA. The U-2 was flown for the first time in August 1955, and before its exposure as a spy-plane had flown from bases as far apart as Alaska, Pakistan, Japan, Nationalist

China, Germany and the United Kingdom; there was evidence as late as 1965 that Chinese Nationalist pilots were still being trained in the USA to fly the U-2. Production of the U-2 comprised forty-eight U-2As, U-2Bs and U-2Cs and five U-2Ds. The U-2A has a J57 jet engine with auxiliary fuel in pinion tanks, and is a single-seater like the U-2B and C, which have the more powerful 17,000lb (7,711kg) st J75 engine. The U-2D is a 2-seat version of the B. Most of the U-2As – about thirty are thought to have been built – were later brought up to U-2B or C standard. The remainder, for their weather reconnaissance role, were redesignated WU-2A. Among the U-2s tasks in more recent years have been the High Altitude Sampling Programme of upper atmosphere research on behalf of the Defense Atomic Support Agency, and the use of two aircraft by NASA in 1971-72 in connection with the launch of ERTS-A, the first Earth Resources Technology Satellite.

Hughes Osage

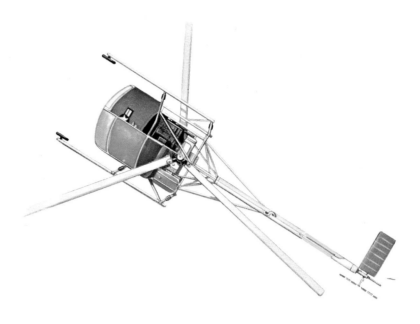

Hughes Model 200 (TH-55A Osage) of the US Army Primary Helicopter School, Fort Wolters, Texas 1963

Main rotor diameter: 25ft 3½in (7.71m)
Length: 21ft 10¾in (6.67m)
Weight: 1,600lb (725kg)
Engine: 1×180hp Lycoming H10-360-A1A
  4-cyl horizontally-opposed type
Max speed: 86mph (138kmh)
Operational ceiling: 11,500ft (3,500m)
Endurance: 3hr 20min

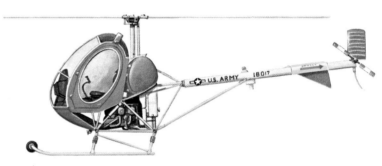

This deceptively slight-looking, ultra-light helicopter has progressively amassed a substantial sales record since the first production machine was delivered in October 1961, and about seventeen hundred examples had been sold by the beginning of 1972. Under its original designation of Model 269 it was initiated as a private venture in September 1955 by the Aircraft Division of the Hughes Tool Company, and N78P, the first of two prototypes, was flown for the first time in October 1956. Powered by a 170hp Lycoming engine, this machine had a triangular girder-type tailboom, a plain skid landing gear, and accommodated two occupants in side-by-side seats. In 1958 five developed Model 269As were ordered for evaluation by the US Army under the designation YHO-2HU, the first of these aircraft bearing the serial number 58-1327. Changes from the prototype included replacement of the openwork tailboom by a simple tubular structure, on which a modified stabiliser was mounted further aft and on the starboard side only; widening of the cabin; and the fitting of ground handling wheels at the forward extremities of the landing skids. In this form the helicopter was granted FAA Type Approval on 9 April 1959, and in July 1960 Hughes decided to place the aircraft in production. The basic 2-seat version was the Model 269A, while a 3-seat model was offered as the 269B. The major customer for the 2-seat variant was the US Army which, after thorough evaluation at Fort Rucker, Alabama, selected it as a standard primary light helicopter trainer with a first contract for twenty machines. Orders for the TH-55A Osage eventually totalled seven hundred and ninety-two for the US Army, and similar aircraft are in service with the Algerian Air Force (eight), Brazilian Navy (nine), Colombian Air Force (six), Ghana Air Force (three), Indian Navy (ten), Japan Air SDF (forty-nine), Nicaraguan Air Force (one) and Swedish Army (two). Undoubtedly an important factor in the selection of the Hughes design for the training role was the simplicity of its controls (it has a clutchless, Vee-belt drive) and of its construction and maintenance. Its slender lines belie its sturdy construction, and general handling qualities are said to be excellent. Several hundred 2- and 3-seat models are in world-wide commercial or private operation. A production and marketing licence is held by Bredanardi in Italy. In 1965 the 2- and 3-seat civil variants were redesignated, respectively, Models 200 and 300, of which the latter remained current in 1972. It is available with standard or deluxe finish, may be fitted with twin floats in addition to the normal wheel/skid gear, and has a QTR (quiet tail rotor) which reduces the overall noise level by some 80 per cent. A stretcher pannier or two baggage carriers can be fitted externally. The Model 300 (as the Hughes 269B) was certificated by the FAA on 30 December 1963. It differs principally from the Model 200 in having a 180hp Lycoming HIO-360-A1A engine and a 3-person bench seat, on which the middle occupant sits slightly back from the other two. Also in production, as the Model 300C (originally Model 269C, first flown in August 1969), is a developed version capable of carrying a 45 per cent greater payload.

Sikorsky Tarhe

Sikorsky CH-54A, pre-series aircraft of the US Army. Data apply to production version

Main rotor diameter: 72ft 0in (21.95m)
Length: 70ft 3in (21.41m)
Weight: 42,000lb (19,050kg)
Engines: 2×4,500shp Pratt & Whitney T73-P-1 turboshafts
Max speed: 127mph (204kmh)
Operational ceiling: 13,000ft (3,962m)
Range: 253 miles (407km)

Sikorsky's first crane helicopter, the S-60, was a research vehicle designed and built from funds shared between the US Navy and the parent company. Work on the design started in May 1958, the S-60 being given the powerplant, rotor and transmission systems of the S-56 helicopter. The 2,100hp Pratt & Whitney R-2800 engines were mounted in outrigged pods into which the main undercarriage wheels could be partially retracted. The S-60, registered N807, first flew on 25 March 1959 and was demonstrated extensively until it was lost during a test flight in April 1961. By this time, however, Sikorsky had already begun to build a prototype of the bigger S-64A, and this machine (N325Y) was flown on 9 May 1962. The S-64A retained the same basic rotor system as the S-60, though employing a 6-blade main rotor. It differed from the smaller machine in having a pair of 4,050shp JFTD12A turboshafts mounted side-by-side on top of the fuselage boom, and had no fin area below the boom. Ground clearance beneath this boom is 9ft 4in (2.84m) and the main wheel track is 19ft 9in (6.02m), hence loads of considerable size can be fitted underneath the S-64A. The landing gear can be lengthened and shortened hydraulically, so that the helicopter can 'crouch' on its load, raise it off the ground and then, if desired, taxi with it to a more suitable take-off point. Two additional prototypes, N305Y and N306Y, were completed for evaluation by the Federal German forces. Re-registered D-9510 and D-9511, they were operated under the aegis of the former Weser Flugzeugbau. After evaluation of the original

prototype at Fort Benning, Georgia, the US Army placed a pre-series order in June 1963 for six S-64As with the military designation CH-54A (originally YCH-54A). Five of these were delivered in 1964-65 and operated with the 478th Aviation Company supporting the US Army's 1st Cavalry Division in Vietnam. Eighteen more CH-54As (Army name Tarhe) were ordered in 1966, and total orders for this version stood at about eighty in mid-1972, later aircraft having uprated -4A engines of 4,620shp each. Loads which can be lifted by the S-64A/CH-54A include trucks or palletised containers holding a field hospital unit, forty-eight casualty litters, sixty-seven troops or 22,890lb (10,382kg) of cargo. One CH-54A in Vietnam has successfully lifted eighty-seven troops, and of three international height records set by the CH-54A in 1965, two were still unbeaten in 1972. Meanwhile the Sikorsky-owned Sp64A and the sixth aircraft of the US Army's original order were used to further the acceptance of the type for the civil market, for such operations as ship-to-shore loading or unloading of cargo vessels or support of oil drilling operations. Two aircraft for the latter role, designated S-64E, were delivered in 1968 to the Rowan Drilling Co of Texas. During 1967, N325Y carried out tests with the 23-seat Budd XB-1 Skylounge pod, designed to speed connection between the airports of Los Angeles and the city centre, and Sikorsky has developed the UMP (Universal Military Pod) for the US Army versions, capable of carrying personnel or of being used as a mobile field surgical unit or air ambulance.

Piasecki Pathfinder

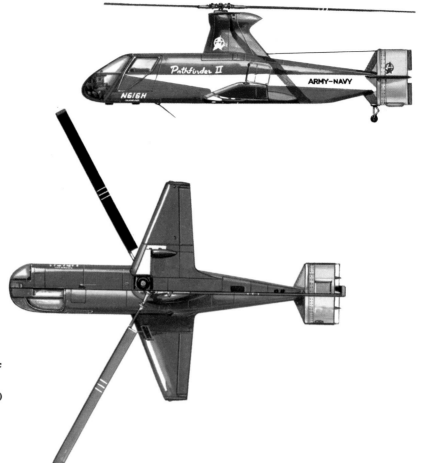

Piasecki 16H-1A Pathfinder II, 1965

Rotor diameter: 44ft 0in (13.41m)
Wing span: 24ft 0in (7.32m)
Length: 37ft 3in (11.35m)
Weight: 8,150lb (3,697kg)
Engine: 1×1,250shp General Electric
**   T58-GE-5 turboshaft**
Max speed: 230mph (370kmh)
Operational ceiling: 18,700ft (5,700m)
Range: 450 miles (725km)

The Piasecki Aircraft Corporation has been engaged since the early 1960s on a series of compound helicopter research designs known by the name Pathfinder. The concept first took material form as the Model 16H-1 Pathfinder prototype (registration N616H). This aircraft was developed as a private venture and flew for the first time on 21 February 1962, undertaking this flight as a 'pure' helicopter without using the 3-blade ducted tail fan. No wings were fitted at that stage, the cabin was unfaired, and the retractable landing gear was fixed in the extended position. Small stub-wings, which could be folded, and a fully-enclosed cabin to accommodate a pilot and four passengers, were added later in the year. Powered by a 550shp UACL PT6B-2 turboshaft engine, the Pathfinder had a 41ft 0in (12.50m) diameter 3-blade rotor, a fuselage length of 25ft 0in (7.62m) and a gross weight of 5,700lb (2,585kg). In all, it amassed a total of 185 flying hours, during which speeds of up to 170mph (273kmh) were attained. Subsequently, Piasecki received a joint US Army/US Navy contract to develop a compound helicopter capable of providing data on flight by such aircraft at speeds of up to 230mph (360kmh). As part of this programme the original aircraft was redesigned to become the Model 16H-1A Pathfinder II, in which form it made its second 'first' flight on 15 November 1965. Modification work had begun in 1964, ground tests were carried out in the summer of 1965, and initial hovering trials were completed by the end of the year. The principal design changes in the Pathfinder II were the enlargement of the fuselage, lengthened to accommodate

eight persons; the installation of a 1,250shp General Electric T58-GE-5 engine; and the adoption of a larger-diameter rotor, a new drive system and a new tail fan. By May 1966 the Pathfinder II had flown some 40 hours, during which it had achieved level speeds of up to 225mph (362kmh), had flown sideways at up to 35mph (55kmh) and backwards at 32mph (52kmh), and had made 20 autorotative flights. For the final phase of the Army/Navy programme, in the summer of 1966, it was refitted with a 1,500shp T58-GE-5 engine, having new design air intakes ahead of the wing leading edges, and received the new Model designation 16H-1C. Since then Piasecki has announced several designs based upon the Pathfinder configuration, although up to 1972 none of these had been built. In 1968 it announced the Model 16H-3 Pathfinder III, a twin-turbine design using the 16H-1A fuselage with two T58-GE-10s and 4-blade rotor and tail fan, for search and rescue, ASW and military utility applications. The 16H-3H Heli-Plane project, for an eight-passenger executive transport with twin PT6 or TPE 331 engines, was superseded in 1969 by the 9/15-seat 16H-3J commercial transport project; this in turn was redesignated 16H-3K in 1971, following the proposal to install more powerful PT6B engines. In 1971 Piasecki was reported to be working on a high-performance development of the original Pathfinder, designated 16H-1H, to seat a pilot and 4 passengers. Intended to be powered by a 986shp Turboméca Astazou XVI engine, it was planned to have a maximum speed of 202mph (325kmh) and a range of 440 miles (708km).

Courier

Helio U-10A Super Courier of the USAF, *circa* 1965

Span: 39ft 0in (11.89m)
Length: 31ft 0in (9.45m)
Weight: 3,400lb (1,542kg)
Engine: 1×295hp Lycoming GO-480-G1 D6 6-cyl horizontally-opposed type
Max speed: 167mph (269kmh)
Operational ceiling: 20,500ft (6,250m)
Range: 660 miles (1,062km)

The Super Courier can trace its ancestry back to the two-seat, 65hp Helioplane, first flown on 8 April 1949 and itself based on the Piper Vagabond. The idea behind the design was to produce a lightplane with particularly good STOL and low-speed handling qualities, and from the original Helioplane evolved by Dr Otto Koppen and Mr Lynn Bollinger were subsequently developed a succession of later models which included the H-391 Courier (first flown 1952), H-392 Strato-Courier (1957) and H-395 Super Courier. The last-named was a 4/5-seat aircraft, and was first flown in 1958. Later that year three Super Couriers were evaluated by the USAF under the designation L-28A. In 1962, when the US adopted a new designation system common to all three services, these became known as U-10As, and an additional quantity was ordered for 'special military duties' with Strategic and Tactical Air Commands. In the following year orders were placed by the US Army (twenty) and the Air National Guard (twenty-four). The standard USAF version is still the U-10A, but later versions are the U-10B and U-10D. Both have greater range than the U-10A; the U-10B, fitted with paratroop doors, has a maximum endurance of more than ten hours, and the U-10D can seat six passengers in addition to the pilot. Super Courier operations in South-east Asia included leaflet-dropping, sky-shouting and other psychological warfare activities, and the dropping of medical supplies and comforts to beleaguered South Vietnamese communities.

General Dynamics Hustler

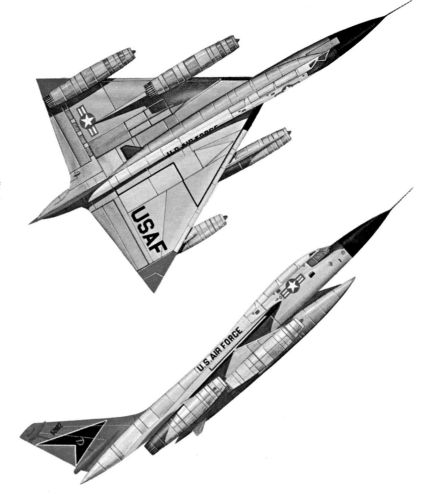

General Dynamics (Convair) B-58A Hustler of the Flight Text Centre, Systems Command, USAF, *circa* 1964

Span: 56ft 10in (17.32m)
Length: 96ft 9in (29.49m)
Weight: 164,500lb (74,616kg)
Engines: 4×10,000/15,600lb
   (4,536/7,076kg) st General Electric
   J79-GE-5B afterburning turbojets
Max speed: 1,385mph (2,230kmh)
Operational ceiling: 60,000ft (18,300m)
Range: 1,200 miles (1,930km)

Although outweighed in sheer numbers by the larger aeroplane by more than seven to one, the Hustler's designed purpose was to form, with the Boeing Stratofortress, the front-line retaliation force of the USAFs Strategic Air Command. The Command received its first B-58A in March 1960, somewhat more than three years after the type began flight testing, and the last of the eighty-six production B-58As built was delivered in October 1962. From these SAC maintained an operations-ready force of about eighty Hustlers, assigned to the 43rd and 305th Bomb Wings based in the USA. The thirty evaluation aircraft included two XB-58 prototypes (first flight 11 November 1956), eleven YB-58A for service test, and one NB-58A engine testbed. Ten of these thirty aircraft were brought up to production B-58A standard in 1961, and eight others were converted to TB-58A combat trainers. The Hustler was the world's first supersonic strategic bomber, and established nearly a score of world speed and pay-load/altitude records. It has an unrefuelled range of some 2,000 miles (3,220km), and over even longer ranges with the use of in-flight refuelling could maintain average speeds in excess of 1,000mph (1,610kmh). A 3-seater, the Hustler had no internal weapons bay, having been designed as a complete weapons system with an under-fuselage 'mission pod' which formed part of the overall area-ruling of the aircraft in its fully-equipped condition. The lower half of the pod contained fuel, which was used first and then jettisoned; the upper half of the pod contained either bombs, camera packs or ECM equipment. As an alternative to the pod, four small-size nuclear weapons could be carried under the centre of the fuselage. The Hustler's internal equipment included a high degree of automated target location and weapon direction systems; a complete ejection capsule for each member of the crew; and a radar-aimed Vulcan multi-barrel 20mm cannon in the tail-cone for rearward defence. All Hustlers were withdrawn from front-line USAF service in 1970.

Grumman Widgeon

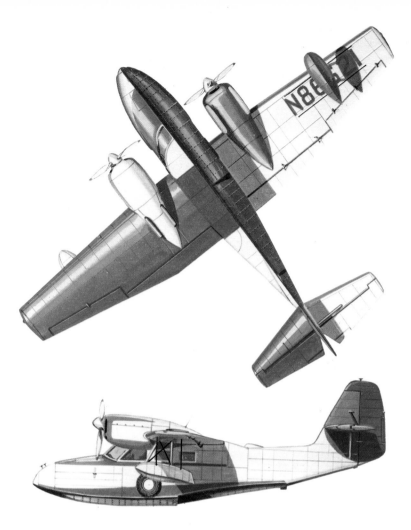

Grumman G-44A Super Widgeon of the US Fish and Wildlife Service, *circa* 1966

Span: 40ft 0in (12.19m)
Length: 31ft 1in (9.47m)
Weight: 5,500lb (2,495kg)
Engines: 2 × 270hp Lycoming GO-480-BID 'flat six'
Max speed: 185mph (298kmh)
Operational ceiling: 18,000ft (5,486m)
Range: 1,000 miles (1,610km)

In many respects a smaller edition of the G-21 Goose, the Grumman G-44 was evolved in the first instance as a 4/5-seat commercial amphibian, the first prototype (NX 28633) making its maiden flight in July 1940. The first order to be placed, however, was that of the US Navy for twenty-five of a 2/3-seat anti-submarine patrol and general utility version, the J4F-1, for service with the US Coast Guard, Performance in the former role was poor, though one sinking of a U-boat, in 1942, was recorded – a creditable result considering that the aircraft was unarmed and could carry only a single 200lb (91kg) depth bomb. During 1942 delivery took place of sixteen OA-14s to the USAAF, by which time also the US Navy had begun to receive the first examples of the J4F-2, which it employed either as a utility transport, accommodating a crew of two and three passengers, or as an instrument trainer. Fifteen J4F-2s were supplied under Lend-Lease to the RAF (which at first named them Gosling I before adopting the name Widgeon)

and were employed primarily as communications aircraft in the West Indies during 1943-45. One hundred and thirty-one J4F-2s were purchased by the US Navy, including those allocated to the RAF. Military production of the Widgeon ended in 1945, but after World War 2 some redesign of the Widgeon's hull was undertaken, the modified aircraft being given the manufacturer's model number G-44A. About fifty were built by Grumman for the civil market; forty similar aircraft, manufactured under licence by the Société de Constructions Aéro-Navales in France as the SCAN30 were later sold to the USA, where they became known as Gannet Super Widgeons after being fitted with 300hp Lycoming R-680 radial engines. McKinnon Enterprises Inc has produced other Super Widgeons (and was still doing so in 1970) by converting existing Widgeons into executive aircraft with a powerplant of two 270hp Lycoming GO-480 'flat-six' engines.

Grumman OV-1 Mohawk

Grumman OV-1B Mohawk of the US Army, 1966

Span: 48ft 0in (14.63m)
Length: 41ft 0in (12.50m)
Weight: 19,230lb (8,722kg)
Engines: 2 × 1,150shp Lycoming T53-L-15
   turboprops
Max speed: 297mph (478kmh)
Operational ceiling: 30,300ft (9,235m)
Range: 1,230 miles (1,980km)

When the first mock-up of the Mohawk (then known as the AO-1) was completed in 1957, the aircraft had a single fin and rudder with a high-mounted tailplane; the change to the present twin unit was one of several improvements made before the first Mohawk (57-6463, one of nine YAO-1AF test aircraft, later redesignated YOV-1A) was flown on 14 April 1959. The Mohawk's main function is to provide observation and reconnaissance cover for the US Army, although it is fully capable of more active participation in land engagements. It can operate in all weathers, and from grass fields and short, unprepared emergency landing strips, thanks to an excellent STOL performance; it has been described as 'very hard to upset aerodynamically'; and the large forward-mounted cabin for the 2-man crew affords a generous field of vision in all directions. There were four basic models. The OV-1A (sixty-four built) has a 42ft 0in (12.80m) wing span and is equipped with standard-type aerial reconnaissance cameras; the OV-1B (one hundred and one built) has a 6ft 0in (1.83m)

greater wing span and carries sideways-looking airborne radar, for terrain mapping, in a long, torpedo-like pod slung beneath the lower starboard side of the fuselage; the OV-1C (one hundred and thirty-three built) is similar to the OV-1A but with infra-red surveillance equipment; and the OV-1D (thirty-seven built), with the extended wings of the OV-1B, is a version capable of rapid interchange from infra-red to SLAR capability, so fulfilling the roles of both the B and C models. The Mohawk entered service in 1962, and production ended in December 1970. For offensive missions, the Mohawk has four underwing attachment points on which napalm or fragmentation bombs, anti-tank weapons or auxiliary fuel tanks, up to a maximum load of 3,740lb (1,696kg), can be carried. The US Army has plans to update a substantial number of B and C model Mohawks to OV-1D standard, and about 16 other OV-1Bs to EV-1E electronic intelligence aircraft. Mohawks are also involved in a number of other Army programmes intended to extend its ECM capability.

Douglas Cargomaster

Douglas C-133B Cargomaster of Military Airlift
Command, USAF, *circa 1966*

Span: 179ft 8in (54.76m)
Length: 157ft 6½in (48.02m)
Weight: 286,000lb (129,725kg)
Engines: 4×7,500ehp Pratt & Whitney
    T34-P-9W turboprops
Max speed: 323mph (520kmh)
Operational ceiling: 29,950ft

The Cargomaster, easily the largest American transport in
service prior to the arrival of the Lockheed Star-Lifter, was
built in comparatively modest numbers to provide a small but
select force of large logistic transport aircraft for the Military
Air Transport Service (now called Military Airlift Command).
The original production order was placed in 1954, and the first
of thirty-five C-133A Cargomasters (54-135) made its maiden
flight on 23 April 1956; deliveries to the US Air Force began in
October 1957. With a huge cylindrical, pressurised fuselage
capable of transporting an Atlas, Thor or Jupiter missile, the
C-133A had an integral loading ramp in the rear fuselage
underside, and side-loading doors in the forward fuselage for
alternative cargo loads. Its 90ft (27.43m) long, 13,000 cu ft (368
cu m) hold could accept 96 per cent of all US Army field force

vehicles or equipment. Production of the Cargomaster came
to an end in April 1961 after the construction of fifteen
C-133Bs, an improved version with uprated engines, a five-ton
greater capacity, and clamshell rear doors which added 3ft
(0.91m) to the usable length of the cargo hold. The first C-133B
(59-522) was flown on 31 October 1959. Capacity of the C-133B
was more than 110,000lb (49,900kg) of freight or 200 fully-
equipped troops; a 4-man crew was usual, although on
especially long hauls a relief crew could also be carried. A
series of accidents resulted in the grounding of the
Cargomaster force in early 1965, but by May all the C-133Bs
and about two-thirds of the C-133As were back in service.
Phasing out of those remaining in service began in 1971.

Bell HueyCobra

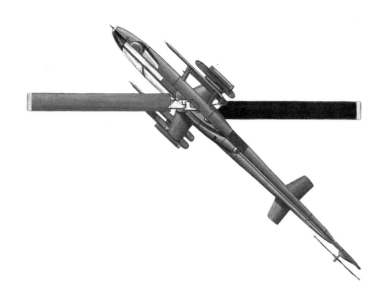

Bell AH-1G HueyCobra of the US Army 1967

Main rotor diameter: 44ft 0in (13.41m)
Length: 44ft 5¼in (13.54m)
Weight: 9,500lb (4,309kg)
Engine: 1 × 1,400shp Lycoming T53-L-13
   turboshaft, derated to 1,100shp
Max speed: 196mph (315kmh)
Operational ceiling: 11,400ft (3,475m)
Range: 230 miles (370km)
Armament: 2 × XM.159 Launchers each
   with nineteen 2.75in FFAR rockets

The Bell Model 209 HueyCobra came into being as a result of a crash programme initiated by the US Army when the campaign in Vietnam revealed the need for a fast, well-armed aircraft to provide escort and fire support for the CH-47A Chinook. Bell had already investigated the potential of an armed support helicopter with the OH-13X Sioux Scout, a tandem-seat derivative of the Model 47 flown in September 1963 with a 260hp Lycoming TVO-435 engine. A development along similar lines of the UH-1 Iroquois was, therefore, the logical follow-on to this approach, and this was proposed and accepted by the US Army in 1965. A prototype of the new aircraft (N209J) was flown for the first time on 7 September 1965, having the same rotor and transmission systems and the same T53-L-13 engine as the UH-1C Iroquois. The entirely new fuselage has a low silhouette and extremely narrow frontal area (3ft 2in = 0.965m at its widest point) which renders the HueyCobra easy to conceal on the ground and a much less easy target in the air than a conventional helicopter. In December 1965, N209J arrived at Edwards Air Force Base for service trials, and two pre-series AH-1Gs were ordered on 4 April 1966. Nine days later came an order for one hundred and ten production aircraft, a total that had risen to eight hundred and thirty-eight by the end of 1968. A further two hundred and forty were added subsequently, and production of these was nearing completion in 1972. Delivery of production Huey-Cobras to the US Army began in June 1967, the type becoming operational in Vietnam in the early autumn. Thirty-eight of the above AH-1Gs were allocated to the US Marine Corps in 1969,

in advance of the delivery of its own order for AH-1J SeaCobras (see below). The AH-1G has also been ordered by the RAAF (eleven) and Spanish Navy (four). On a typical mission the AH-1G can reach its target in about half the time taken by the Iroquois, can remain in the combat zone much longer and can wield twice the fire-power. The first production machines had an Emerson TAT-102A (Tactical Assault Turret) under the nose, in which is mounted a 7.62mm six-barrelled General Electric GAU2B/A Minigun, operated by the co-pilot/gunner from the front seat. Later-production aircraft have an XM-28 armament system incorporating either two Miniguns, two 40mm grenade launchers, or one of each. The stub wings have four attachment points for stores which are fired by the pilot. Initially these points carried XM-159 pods each containing nineteen 2.75in rockets, but other loads may comprise XM-157 pods with seven rockets each, two XM-18 Minigun pods, or an XM-35 20mm gun kit. The airframe is capable of being fitted, alternatively, with a turret capable of firing one M-61 Vulcan multi-barrel 20mm gun, an XM-197 three-barrel 20mm gun, or a three-barrel 30mm gun. The crew seats and cabin sides are armour-protected. A twin-turbine version of the HueyCobra, powered by a 1,250shp UACL T400-CP-400 Turbo Twin Pac engine, is in production for the US Marine Corps as the AH-1J SeaCobra. An initial quantity of forty-nine AH-1Js was ordered in May 1968, and delivery of these began in mid-1970. The AH-1J is dimensionally almost identical to the AH-1G, and carries a substantially similar armament.

Sikorsky HH-3

Sikorsky HH-3E of the USAF Aerospace Rescue and Recovery Service in Southeast Asia camouflage, 1967 (One of two aircraft to make the first non-stop Atlantic crossing by helicopter

Main rotor diameter: 62ft 0in (18.90m)
Length: 57ft 3in (17.45m)
Weight: 22,050lb (10,002kg)
Engines: 2 × 1,500shp General Electric
 T58-GE-5 turboshafts
Max speed: 162mph (261kmh)
Operational ceiling: 11,100ft (3,385m)
Range: 465 miles (748km)

By early 1972 more than seven hundred military and civil examples of the S-61 twin-turbine helicopter had been delivered, and the type has been in service in various roles since 1961. It was ordered to meet a 1957 US Navy requirement for a submarine hunter/killer aircraft, and in prototype form was known as the XHSS-2, making its maiden flight on 11 March 1959. Service trials were conducted in 1960 with seven YHSS-2s, the production HSS-2 (now SH-3A) Sea King being delivered to US Navy Squadrons from September 1961. This model carries dunking sonar submarine search gear and homing torpedoes, and is powered by T58-GE-8B engines; manufacturer's designation is S-61B. Nine SH-3As were converted to RH-3A for mine countermeasures work, and three others are used by the US Air Force for missile site support and drone recovery. Three SH-3As were supplied in 1963 to Japan, where Mitsubishi is completing a further eighty for the Japan Maritime Self-Defence Force, and United Aircraft Corporation in Canada completed all except four of the forty-one CHSS-2s ordered by the Royal Canadian Navy. Eight similar VH-3As, with 12-passenger VIP interiors, serve as special transports with the US Army (two) and Marine Corps (six). A version generally similar to the SH-3A for transport or rescue duties is the S-61A; nine serve with No. 722 Squadron of the Royal Danish Air Force in the air/sea rescue role. Three, designated CH-3B, are operated by the USAF on missile site support and drone recovery; and in 1967 ten

31-seat troop/cargo transport S-61A-4s began to be delivered flown for the first time on 9 September 1961, was essentially the same aircraft minus its fixed base. An enlarged version of the BO103 was proposed as the BO104, but this project was supplanted by the more promising BO105. The first BO105 prototype, powered by a pair of Allison 250-C18 turboshaft engines and using a conventional hinged-rotor installation, encountered ground resonance problems which eventually caused its destruction. The second prototype, which flew for the first time on 16 February 1967, was similarly powered but introduced the 4-blade rigid rotor which is standard on production aircraft. The third prototype (first flight 20 December 1967) was powered by two MAN-Turbo 6022 turboshafts. Two pre-production aircraft followed, one of which had 400shp Allison 250-C20 engines, and a choice of the -C18 or -C20 is available to purchasers of production BO105s. In addition to the pilot the BO105 will accommodate four or five passengers with their baggage; orders for about sixty had been placed by early 1972, by which time about a dozen had been delivered. The BO105 is certificated for operation in the United States, where Boeing holds a manufacturing and marketing licence. The non-articulated rotor, whose foldable blades are reinforced with glassfibre, was developed over several years by Bölkow in association with Sud-Aviation and was initially flight-tested on one of the latter company's Alouette II Astazou helicopters.

Sikorsky Sea Stallion

Sikorsky CH-53A Sea Stallion of the US Marine Corps, 1967

Main rotor diameter: 72ft 3in (22.02m)
Length: 67ft 2in (20.47m)
Weight: 35,000lb (15,875kg)
Engines: 2×2,850shp General Electric
T64-GE-6 turboshafts
Max speed: 195mph (314kmh)
Operational ceiling: 18,550ft (5,654m)
Range: 258 miles (415km)

Currently the largest and heaviest helicopter in the western world, the S-65A is something of a hybrid, its fuselage being, in essence, a scaled-up version of that used on the S-61R, while its rotor and transmission system and certain other dynamic components are inherited from the S-64 Skycrane. The flat-bottomed body is watertight, and has sponsons amidships in which are housed fuel tanks and the main undercarriage members when retracted. The nosewheel is also fully retractable. The S-65A carries a crew of three and can airlift thirty-eight troops and their equipment, twenty-four casualty litters and four medical attendants, or some 8,000lb (3,629kg) of cargo within the fuselage. A let-down rear ramp provides access for such military loads as two jeeps, two Hawk missiles, or a 105mm howitzer and its carriage. A slung load of some 13,000lb (5,897kg) can be lifted on an under-fuselage hook. In August 1962 it was announced that the S-65A had been selected as a new ship-borne heavy assault transport for the US Marine Corps, with the military title CH-53A Sea Stallion. A prototype flew on 14 October 1964, and delivery of the first one hundred and six production CH-53As began in September 1966. Standard powerplant is two T64-GE-6 turboshaft engines, though the 3,080shp T64-GE-1 or 3,435shp T64-GE-16 may be fitted. One CH-53A with

T64-GE-16 engines has been flown at a gross weight of 51,900lb (23,541kg), of which 28,000lb (12,927kg) was payload and fuel. The HH-53B, flown for the first time on 15 March 1967 has 3,080shp T64-GE-3 engines, a rescue hoist, jettisonable auxiliary fuel tanks and a telescopic in-flight refuelling probe. It also has machine gun positions fore and aft. The HH-53B is employed by the Aerospace Rescue and Recovery Service of the US Air Force, and delivery of eight, ordered in September 1966, began in June 1967. It was followed by the improved HH-53C (fifty-eight built), powered by 3,435shp T64-GE-7 engines and equipped for the recovery of Apollo spacecraft. An improved model for the US Marine Corps, designated CH-53D, has 3,695shp T64-GE-412 or 3,925shp T64-GE-413 engines and can carry up to sixty-four troops. For the US Navy, Sikorsky is producing the RH-53D for mine counter-measures duties, and was due to begin delivery of thirty in late 1972. Under development for the USN is the CH-53E, to be powered by three 4,390shp T64-GE-415 turboshafts. Military S-65s have been exported to Austria (two) and Israel (ten), and one hundred and fifty-three are being licence-built for the Federal German armed forces as the CH-53G, under a programme managed by VFW-Fokker.

Kaman Huskie

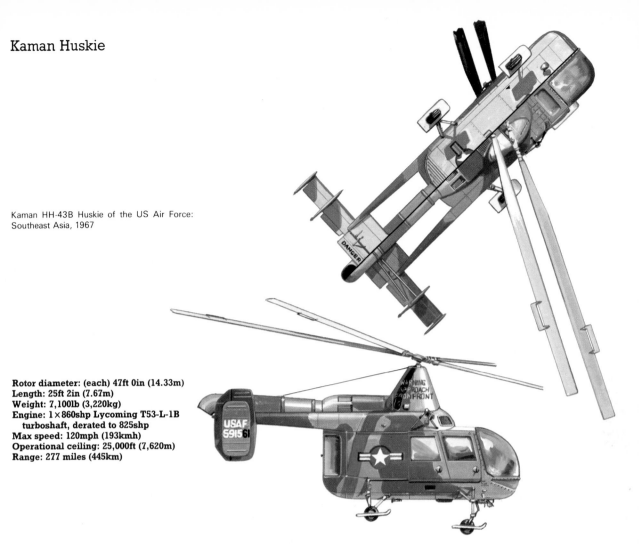

Kaman HH-43B Huskie of the US Air Force: Southeast Asia, 1967

Rotor diameter: (each) 47ft 0in (14.33m)
Length: 25ft 2in (7.67m)
Weight: 7,100lb (3,220kg)
Engine: 1×860shp Lycoming T53-L-1B turboshaft, derated to 825shp
Max speed: 120mph (193kmh)
Operational ceiling: 25,000ft (7,620m)
Range: 277 miles (445km)

As the Kaman Model 600, the Huskie won a US Navy design competition in 1950 and a contract was placed for it 'off the drawing board'. The K-600 was basically an enlarged development of Kaman's earlier HTK-1 and employed a similar system of contrarotating, intermeshing rotors. The new type was required initially for liaison and general duties with the Marine Corps, by whom it was designated HOK-1. The first of two XHOK-1 prototypes flew on 27 September 1956, and delivery of eighty-one HOK-1s to the USMC began in April 1958. Twenty-four examples of the HUK-1, a utility model, were built for the US Navy itself, and eighteen H-43As (first flight 19 September 1958) were completed for the US Air Force. Accommodation in the original HOK-1 provided for a two-man crew plus five passengers or two stretchers and two medical attendants, while the H43As, acquired for local crash and rescue duties at USAF airfields, could carry two fire-fighters and their equipment or four stretchers and a medical attendant. The H-43A, HUK-1 and HOK-1, redesignated HH-43A, UH-43C and OH-43D in 1962, were all powered by variants of the 600hp R-1340 piston engine. The UH-43C and OH-43D were withdrawn from US Navy service in 1965. Following the employment of one HOK-1 as a testbed for the

Lycoming XT53 turboshaft engine, two turbine-powered versions of the Huskie were selected for production. The first of these was the H-43B (later HH-43B) rescue version, first flown on 13 December 1958. Powered by an 825shp Lycoming T53-L-1B engine, and having an enlarged cabin seating up to eight passengers, the HH-43B became the major production version of the Huskie, one hundred and ninety-three being built to meet USAF and MAP orders. Foreign air forces which received HH-43Bs included those of Burma (twelve), Colombia (six), Morocco (four), Pakistan (six) and Thailand (three). In August 1964 the first flight took place of the HH-43F, an outwardly similar version which has a 1,150shp T53-L-11A turboshaft derated to 825shp, giving the Huskie an improved and sustained performance in 'hot and high' localities. Accommodation is rearranged to allow up to eleven passengers to be carried in addition to the pilot, and range is increased to 504 miles (810km). Forty HH-43Fs, including fourteen for the Imperial Iranian forces, were completed before Huskie production came to an end in 1965. In August 1962 Kaman flew the prototype (N10029) of the twin-turbine K-1125 Huskie III, but development of this type was subsequently suspended.

Grumman Hawkeye

Grumman E-2A Hawkeye of US Navy Squadron VAW-III (Detachment C), USS *Kitty Hawk*, circa 1967

Span: 80ft 7in (24.56m)
Length: 56ft 4in (17.17m)
Weight: 49,638lb (22,515kg)
Engines: 2×4,050ehp Allison T56-A-8/8A
    turboprops
Max speed: 315mph (508kmh)
Operational ceiling: 31,700ft (9,660m)
Range: 1,905 miles (3,065km)

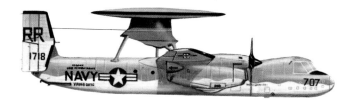

The name of Fennimore Cooper's famous American hero is an apt choice for the Grumman E-2, even though the airborne Hawkeye does not carry a single gun. The E-2 is the lynch-pin of the US Navy's Airborne Tactical Data System, the initial E-2A production model having been delivered in 1964-67 for service with VAW-11 in the Pacific and VAW-12 in the Atlantic. Hawkeyes operate in teams of two or more aircraft, flying at altitudes in the region of 30,000ft (9,145m) to provide long-range early warning of potential threats from hostile surface vessels and fast-flying aircraft. The key to this system is the powerful search radar, carried in the 24ft (7.32m) diameter radome on the Hawkeye's back, which rotates once every ten seconds while the aircraft is in flight. In addition, the substantial fuselage contains detection and digital computers, data link systems and other complex electronics which account for nearly a quarter of the aircraft's total weight. The Hawkeye's radome can be lowered nearly 2ft (0.61m) to facilitate stowage aboard the parent carrier. Three systems operators are carried, together with two pilots, in the pressurised cabin. Originally designated W2F-1, an aerodynamic prototype flew for the first time on 21 October 1960; a fully-equipped prototype followed on 19 April 1961.

The US Navy began to receive the initial production version, the E-2A, in January 1964, and sixty-two of this model were eventually completed, the last being delivered in the spring of 1967. In the same year first details were announced of the E-2B, with enlarged outer fins, improved avionics, provision for in-flight refuelling and other modifications. All operational E-2As were brought up to this standard, beginning in 1969, the first flight by an E-2B taking place on 20 February 1969. This version was serving in 1974 with VAW-113, VAW-116, VAW-125 and VAW-126. A few E-2As have been converted to TE-2A crew trainers. The latest version so far announced is the E-2C, a prototype of which flew for the first time on 20 January 1971. Production began in the following summer, and ten E-2Cs had been delivered by spring 1974. Altogether, twenty-eight E-2Cs are on order, for delivery by the end of 1975; the first unit to receive this version was VAW-123, in November 1973. The E-2C differs from the E-2B primarily in having AN/APS-120, an advanced radar capable of detecting airborne targets in a 'land-clutter' environment. A transport derivative of the Hawkeye, the C-2 Greyhound, is described separately.

Vigilante

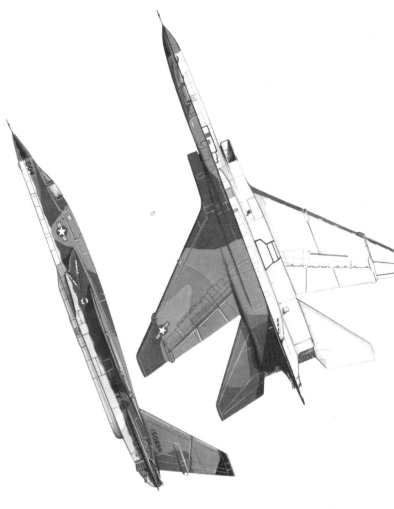

North American RA-5C Vigilante of US Navy Squadron RVAH-13, USS *Kitty Hawk* (CVA-63), Southeast Asia, spring 1966

Span: 53ft 0½in (16.16m)
Length: 75ft 10in (23.11m)
Weight: 80,000lb (36,287kg)
Engines: 2×11,870/17,860lb
  (5,385/8,101kg) st General Electric
  J79-GE-10 afterburning turbojets
Max speed: 1,385mph (2,230kmh)
Operational ceiling: 64,000ft (19,500m)
Range: 3,000 miles (4,830km)

Making its maiden flight in XA3J-1 prototype form (145157) on 31 August 1958, the Vigilante is probably the most advanced carrier-based reconnaissance/strike aircraft in service today in any part of the world. Not long after its entry into US Navy service, with Heavy Attack Squadron VAH-7, in June 1961, the emphasis on the Vigilante's primary role was switched from attack, for which it was originally designed, to that of a Mach 2 reconnaissance aeroplane with a secondary strike capacity. To this end the fifty-five A-5As and six A-5Bs (first flight 29 April 1962) which constituted the first production models were converted to RA-5Cs (the latter before delivery), and a further ninety-one aircraft were built as RA-5Cs. Production ended in November 1970. A unique weapon delivery system was introduced at the outset of the Vigilante's design. This consisted of a tunnel running longitudinally from the central weapons bay, between the two engine tail pipes, and through which the Vigilante's nuclear or high explosive stores could be ejected rearwards. The A-5B (later redesignated YA-5C) incorporated enlarged wing flaps and additional fuel tankage

in a hump behind the second cockpit. These features, together with aerial reconnaissance cameras and side-looking airborne radar in a long ventral pack, also distinguish the RA-5C. The first RA-5C was flown on 30 June 1962, and this model entered service in June 1964 with RVAH-5 aboard the USS *Ranger.* Six or more RA-5Cs were assigned to each 'Forrestal' class carrier, and in 1965 two of the smaller 'Midway' class began modernisation to enable them to operate Vigilantes. The Vigilante is operable over a wide speed range in all weathers, at high or low level, and carries a crew of two. Range may be extended by underwing pylon tanks; in the attack role the four pylons may be used for napalm canisters, 1,000lb or 2,000lb bombs, or air-to-surface missiles. In 1971 North American Rockwell put forward to the USAF a proposal for a Mach 2+ interceptor version of the Vigilante, designated NR-349 and having a third J79-GE-10 engine installed in the weapons bay, but this was not proceeded with.

Cessna A-37

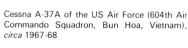

Cessna A-37A of the US Air Force (604th Air Commando Squadron, Bun Hoa, Vietnam), *circa* 1967-68

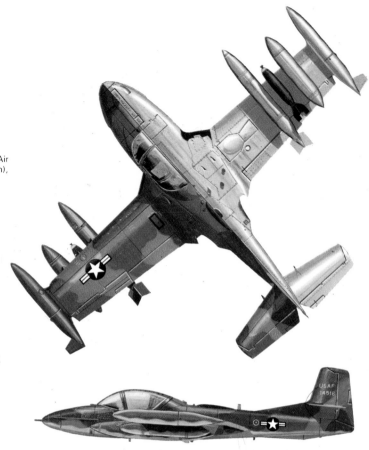

Span: 35ft 10½in (10.93m)
Length: 29ft 3½in (8.93m)
Weight: 12,000lb (5,443kg)
Engines: 2×2,450lb (1,111kg) st General
    Electric J85-GE-17A
Max speed: 478mph (769kmh)
Operational ceiling: 41,765ft (12,730m)
Range: 250 miles

As the US Air Force's first aircraft designed from the outset as a primary and intermediate jet trainer, the Cessna T-37 marked a departure from the practice of years by adopting a side-by-side seating arrangement. The first of three XT-37s flew on 12 October 1954, and these were followed by eleven T-37A evaluation aircraft. This original production model was powered by 920lb (417kg) st Continental J69-T-9 engines (licence version of the French Marboré II), and a further five hundred and twenty-three were completed. With 1,025lb (465kg) st J69-T-25 (Marboré VI) engines and other refinements the aeroplane became known as the T-37B, and the T-37As also were eventually converted to T-37B standard. From 1960, all USAF trainee pilots commenced their tuition on T-37s, but in 1965 it was decided that a few hours on T-41 piston-engined trainers before transition to jets would prove more economical. After this, T-37 pilots would normally graduate to the Northrop T-38A. The T-37B trainer (four hundred and forty-seven built) was also sold to foreign air forces under the Military Assistance Program, as was the T-37C (two hundred and fifty-two built), an armed version with provision for two 250lb (113kg) bombs, two gun or rocket pods or four Sidewinder missiles underwing. Recipients of the T-37 included the West German Luftwaffe (forty-seven

T-37B), the Fôrca Aérea Brasileira (sixty-five T-37C), the Fôrca Aérea Portuguesa (thirty T-37C), the Fuerza Aérea del Perú (fifteen T-37B), and the Cambodian (T-37C), Chilean (T-37B/C), Colombian (ten T-37C), Royal Hellenic (twenty T-37B), Pakistan (twelve T-37B), Royal Thai (eight T-37B) and Turkish (T-37B) air forces. Cessna also produced two prototypes designated YAT-37D, a higher-powered armed attack version for service in Vietnam. The first of these was flown on 22 October 1963, and in 1966 the USAF ordered thirty-nine T-37Bs to be converted to similar standard under the designation A-37A. This version, which became operational in October 1967, has eight underwing stores points for two machine-gun pods, two 2.75in rockets, and four practice bombs; or, in place of the gun pods, two 250lb bombs or four Sidewinder missiles. The A-37B, built from the outset for the same role, has 2,850lb (1,293kg) st J85-GE-17A engines, provision for in-flight refuelling, and a much wider variety of underwing ordnance, up to a maximum load of 5,680lb (2,576kg). The first A-37B was flown in September 1967, and deliveries began in May 1968. Orders for the A-37B totalled four hundred and sixteen by mid-1973, including twenty-four for Peru and others for the USAF and the air forces of Chile (sixteen), Guatemala and South Vietnam.

Thunderchief

Republic F-105D Thunderchief of the US Air Force, Vietnam, *circa* 1967-68

Span: 34ft 11½in (10.65m)
Length: 67ft 0⅛in (20.43m)
Weight: 52,546lb (23,832kg)
Engine: 1×17,200/26,500lb
(7,802/12,030kg) st Pratt & Whitney
J75-P-19W afterburning turbojet
Max speed: 1,388mph (2,235kmh)
Range: 920 miles (1,480km)

Hailed on its appearance as 'the world's most powerful one-man aeroplane', and as 'a re-usable missile', the Thunderchief is indeed large for a single-seat aircraft and can carry a frightening array of internal and external weapons. Last design by the Republic Aviation Corporation before it became a Division of Fairchild Hiller Corporation in mid-1965, the Thunderchief was initiated as a private venture, receiving official support when an evaluation batch of fifteen aircraft was ordered by the USAF in 1954. These were completed as two YF-105As, three RF-105Bs (later redesignated as special-test JF-105Bs) and ten F-105Bs. The YF-105As, the first of which (54-0098) was flown on 22 October 1955, were powered by Pratt & Whitney J57-P-25 engines pending availability of the definitive engine, the more powerful J75. The latter engine was fitted to the first F-105B, which flew on 26 May 1956 and introduced such major design changes as an area-ruled fuselage and swept-forward air intakes. A further sixty-five true production F-105Bs followed, having J75-P-5 engines instead of J75-P-3s. Deliveries, to squadrons of the 4th Tactical Fighter Wing of the USAF, began in May 1958. At that time the F-105B, which could carry 8,000lb (3,630kg) of bombs internally and a further 4,000lb (1,814kg) externally, was the heaviest single-seater ever to enter USAF service. However, only three TAC squadrons were equipped with the F-105B day fighter-bomber, as this was quickly superseded in production by the all-weather F-105D, which became the major service version. A more powerful engine, the 26,500lb (12,030kg) st J75-P-19W, was installed in the F-105D, whose versatility was increased by the ability to carry its entire 12,000lb weapon load externally if required, provision for four Sidewinder air-to-air or Bullpup air-to-surface missiles, and more sophisticated avionics including an air data computer, Doppler navigation system, a toss-bombing computer and NASARR search and ranging radar. As in the F-105B, an M61 Vulcan 20mm multi-barrel cannon is installed in the forward fuselage. The first F-105D was flown on 9 June 1959. It entered production shortly afterwards, and deliveries to Tactical Air Command began in May 1960. Six hundred and ten F-105Ds were built, eventually equipping more than thirty USAF squadrons. In 1970 some thirty F-105Ds were being modified to carry a newly-developed bombing system called T-Stick II; these aircraft are identifiable by a deep 'saddleback' dorsal spine fairing from the cockpit to the fin. An operational trainer version, the F-105F, was ordered in 1962. This has a 2ft 7in (0.79m) longer fuselage, to accommodate a second cockpit in tandem, and fin height and area is increased compared with the F-105D. The first F-105F flew on 11 June 1963, and one hundred and forty-three were completed before production ended in 1964, bringing total manufacture of Thunderchiefs, including prototypes, to eight hundred and thirty-three. By the late 1960s the F-105B model had been withdrawn to units of the Air National Guard, but both the F-105D and F-105F continued to be used extensively in the Vietnam campaigns until 1973, and were subject to various equipment modernisation programmes.

Lockheed StarLifter

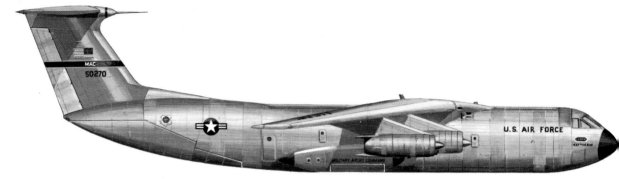

Lockheed C-141A StarLifter of the 437th
Military Air Wing, USAF, *circa* 1967

Span: 159ft 11in (48.74m)
Length: 145ft 0in (44.20m)
Weight: 316,600lb (143,600kg)
Engines: 4×21,000lb (9,525kg) st Pratt &
    Whitney TF33-P-7 turbofans
Max speed: 564mph (908kmh)
Operational ceiling: 41,600ft (12,680m)
Range: 4,080 miles (6,585km)

The first jet aircraft designed from the outset as a military cargo aeroplane, the StarLifter's purpose is to provide fast transportation over global ranges for the USAF Military Airlift Command. It is not the largest-capacity US transport, this distinction now belonging to the later C-5A Galaxy, but it is much faster than earlier transport aircraft. This was graphically demonstrated by a C-141A which transported a 50,000lb (22,680kg) payload over 7,500 miles (12,070km), a feat which it accomplished in 18¼ flying hours; a similar operation would have taken 30½ hours by Hercules or 41¾ hours by Globemaster. An 88,000lb (39,916kg) Minuteman container, one hundred and fifty-four troops, one hundred and twenty-seven paratroops, eighty casualty litters with medical staff, or 94,000lb (42,638kg) cargo load, are all within the StarLifter's capacity; and the aircraft can be unloaded, re-loaded and ready for take-off in less than half an hour. A flight crew of four is carried, together with a relief crew for very long range missions. The C-141A was declared the winner of a USAF design competition in March 1961, and the first of five development aircraft was flown on 17 December 1963. Production C-141As became operational with the 44th and 75th Air Transport Squadrons of Military Airlift Command in 1965, and in August of that year were operating in Vietnam. One hundred and thirty-two C-141As were ordered initially by the US Air Force, a reduction on the original requirement due to procurement of the giant C-5A to follow in the late 1960s; but this was later increased to a total of two hundred and eighty-five, which equipped fourteen MAC squadrons. Production was completed in late 1967.

General Dynamics F-111

General Dynamics F-111A of Tactical Air Command, USAF, *circa* 1967

Span: 63ft 0in (19.20m); swept: 31ft 11½in (9.74m)
Length: 73ft 6in (22.40m)
Weight: 91,500lb (41,504kg)
Engines: 2×12,500/21,000lb (5,670/9,525kg) st Pratt & Whitney afterburning turbofans
Max speed: 1,650mph (2,655kmh) above 36,000ft (11,000m)
Operational ceiling: over 60,000ft (18,300m)
Range on internal fuel: over 3,800 miles (6,100km)
Armament: 1×20mm M61 Vulcan multi-barrel cannon in internal weapon bay
Max bomb load: 1,500lb (680kg) internally instead of M61 gun; 28,000lb (12,700kg) externally

Winner of the US Defence Department's 1961 Tactical Fighter Experimental competition, the 'swing-wing' F-111 had an extremely unhappy development and early service career. A Senate investigating sub-committee, reporting in 1971, found that five major errors of judgement had been made. The cost of acquiring about five hundred F-111s exceeded that estimated for the 1,700 originally required – and that less than one hundred approached the required standard. Originally, eighteen F-111As for the USAF and five F-111Bs, with a shorter nose and extended-span wings, for the USN, were procured for evaluation. However, the naval version was overweight for its carrier-based fleet defence fighter role, and that programme was cancelled in mid-1968 after two additional examples had been completed. Evaluation of the F-111A, flown on 21 December 1964, was followed by one hundred and forty-one production examples, delivery beginning in 1967. Within five days of their first combat sorties in Vietnam, two were lost. A reconnaissance version designated RF-111A flew on 17 December 1967. Two F-111Ks from a cancelled British requirement for fifty were assigned to the USAF as YF-111As for experimental duties. The F-111A, which became subject to high-speed, high-altitude flight restrictions, was superseded by the F-111E with modified air intakes (ninety-four built) and the F-111D with improved avionics and TF30-P-9s (ninety-six built). SAC's requirement for two hundred and ten FB-111A two-seat bombers, was reduced to

seventy-six, delivery beginning in October 1969. The two prototypes were converted F-111As, the first being flown as an FB-111A on 30 July 1967. The FB-111A had Mk IIB avionics, the F-111Bs longer-span wings, TF30-P-7s and a maximum warload of fifty 750lb bombs (two internally, the rest on eight underwing pylons). Delivery of twenty-four similar F-111Cs, with TF30-P-3s and Mk I avionics, began in 1973 to the RAAF for strike duties. Following the F-111E for the USAF were eighty-two F-111F fighter-bombers, combining the F-111Es and As best features with more powerful TF30-P-100s, giving a considerably enhanced performance and capability. As this version has shown, the General Dynamics F-11 is a fully-viable combat aircraft, and its unfortunate career has been more due to mismanagement than to fundamental design defects. It was the first combat aircraft produced with variable-geometry wings, and the first tactical fighter designed to satisfy the joint needs of the USAF and the USN. The wings have 16 degrees of sweep fully-forward, and 72.5 fully-swept. External loads can be carried beneath the fuselage, the fixed portion of the wings, and the outer wings on pylons which pivot, as the wings sweep, to align fore and aft. The important new role of ECM tactical jamming is assigned to the EF-111A, distinguished by its large fin-tip antenna pod and bulged weapons bay. It first flew on 10 March 1977, and the first of forty-two (to be converted by Grumman from F-111Fs) was delivered to the USAF in 1981.

Cessna 0-2

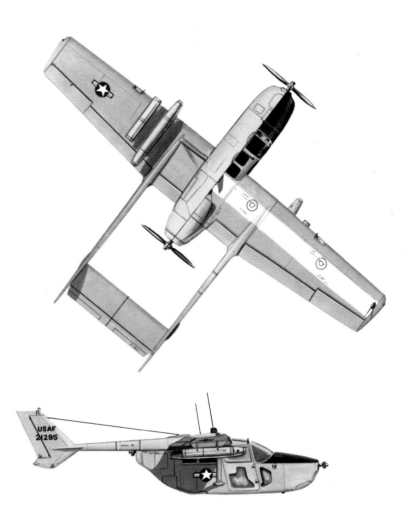

Cessna 0-2A (Forward Air Controller's aircraft) of the USAF, 1968-69

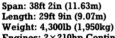

Span: 38ft 2in (11.63m)
Length: 29ft 9in (9.07m)
Weight: 4,300lb (1,950kg)
Engines: 2×210hp Continental 10-360-C
    6-cyl horizontally-opposed type
Max speed: 199mph (320kmh)
Operational ceiling: 18,000ft (5,490m)
Range: 755 miles (1,215km)

Cessna's first CLT (centre-line thrust) aircraft to fly was the Model 336 Skymaster, which made its first flight on 28 February 1961. Between then and January 1965, one hundred and ninety-five Skymasters were built before giving way to the much-improved Model 337 Super Skymaster with restyled rear nacelle, fully-retractable landing gear and considerably superior performance. One of the attractions of the Model 337 (see the *Private Aircraft* volume in this series) is its low operating noise level, and this was no doubt a factor in the USAF decision of 1966 to replace its O-1 Bird Dog FAC (Forward Air Controller) aircraft by the later Cessna type. The initial military version, designated O-2A, seats up to six people, has full dual controls and is fitted with four underwing attachments for gun pods, rocket launchers, photo-flares or other stores. Two hundred and ninety-nine O-2As were ordered by the USAF, and twelve were supplied in 1970 to the

Imperial Iranian Air Force for liaison, observation and training. A psychological warfare version, designated O-2B, is basically similar but carries advanced systems for communications, air-to-ground broadcasting and leaflet dropping. Thirty-one were produced initially for the USAF by converting commercial Model 337s, delivery of these beginning in March 1967; by December 1970 a combined total of five hundred and ten O-2A/O-2Bs had been delivered. 'Off the shelf' commercial Cessna 337s have been supplied in small numbers to the Ecuadorean Air Force and the Venezuelan Navy. Reims Aviation in France, which licence-builds and markets the commercial 337, flew on 26 May 1970 the prototype of a military STOL version known as the FTMA-Milirole, fitted with larger-area flaps; but no production of this version was undertaken.

Grumman Greyhound

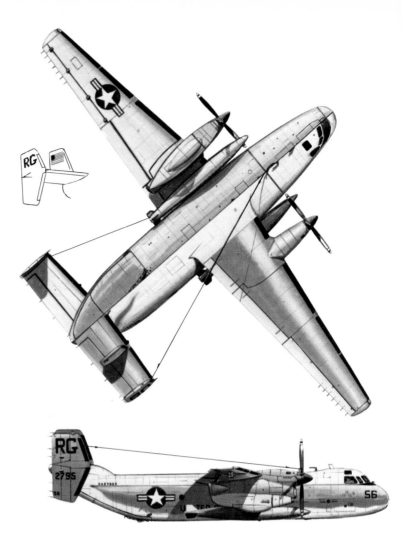

Grumman C-2A Greyhound of the US Navy
Squadron URC-50, *circa* 1968

Span: 80ft 7in (24.56m)
Length: 56ft 8in (17.27m)
Weight: 54,830lb (24,870kg)
Engines: 2×4,050ehp Allison T56-A-8/8A
  turboprops
Max speed: 352mph (567kmh)
Operational ceiling: 28,800ft (8,870m)
Range: 1,650 miles (2,660km)

To meet a US Navy requirement for a COD (Carrier On-board
Delivery) supply transport, Grumman modified its basic E-2
Hawkeye design (which see) in similar fashion to its earlier
adaptation of the S-2 Tracker into the C-1 Trader. The process
consisted basically of mating the wings, powerplant and tail
unit (without dihedral) of the E-2A with a new and enlarged
fuselage, provided with a ramp and loading doors at the rear
and capable of accommodating a variety of palletised or other
cargo, up to a maximum of 10,000lb (4,535kg), twenty

stretchers and four attendants, or up to thirty-nine passengers.
The first of two flying prototypes was flown on 18 November
1964, and delivery of an initial batch of seventeen C-2A
Greyhounds was made during 1966-68, the first operator
(December 1966) being Squadron VRC-50. Delivery of a
further seven C-2As was completed in 1971. The Greyhound
carries a flight crew of two, has similar all-weather capability
to the Hawkeye, and can be catapulted from, and make
arrested landings on, current types of US aircraft carrier.

Rockwell Bronco

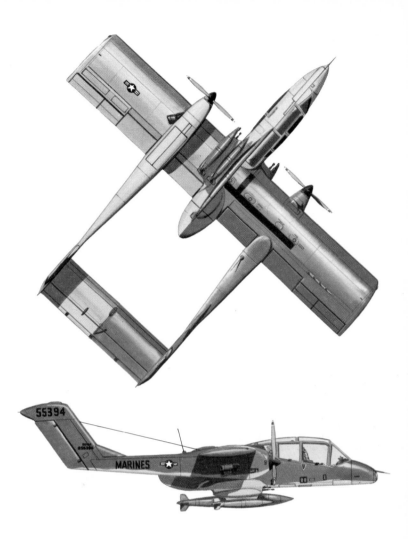

North American OV-10A Bronco of the US Marine Corps, *circa* 1968

Span: 40ft 0in (12.19m)
Length: 41ft 7in (12.67m)
Weight: 9,908lb (4,494kg)
Engines: 2×715ehp Ai Research T76-G-410/411 turboprops
Max speed: 281mph (452kmh)
Range: 228 miles (367km)

Although employed predominantly by the US Air Force, the Bronco was the outcome of a LARA (Light Armed Reconnaissance Aircraft) design competition announced by the US Navy at the end of 1963. From a number of competing designs the North American NA-300 was selected in the following August, and a development contract followed for seven YOV-10A evaluation aircraft. The first of these was flown on 16 July 1965, each of the first four aircraft having a 30ft 0in (9.14m) wing span and 600shp T76-GE-6/8 engines. The seventh YOV-10A was fitted with Pratt & Whitney T74 turboprops, but it was the sixth aircraft which eventually set the standard for the initial production version by having uprated T76 engines, a 10ft 0in (3.05m) increase in wing span, anhedral on the stub wings which provide four of the aircraft's seven external stores stations, and several other detail changes. There were changes also to the original specification, involving the installation of a self-sealing fuel system and armour protection for the two-man crew, with the result that flight testing of the production configuration did not begin until March 1967, some 5 months after the placing of the initial production contracts. The first production OV-10A was flown on 6 August 1967. By April 1969 one hundred and fifty-seven OV-10As had been built for the USAF, ninety-six for the US Marine Corps and eighteen for the US Navy. Production then ended, but was resumed later in the year to fulfil orders for six OV-10Bs and twelve OV-10B(Z)s for the Federal German government and thirty-two OV-10Cs for the

Royal Thai Air Force. The first OV-10B was flown on 3 April 1970. The OV-10B(Z), which flew for the first time on 3 September 1970, was purchased for target-towing duties. It differs in having a dorsally-mounted pod containing a 2,950lb (1,338kg) st General Electric J85-GE-4 turbojet engine to boost performance. Plans for the remaining eleven to be fitted in Germany with this installation had not been implemented up to 1974. The first OV-10C was flown on 9 December 1970. Deliveries of the OV-10A to the USAF and USMC began in February 1968, the first units to become operational with Broncos being the 19th Tactical Air Support Squadron (August 1968) and VMO-2 (July 1968) respectively, both in Vietnam. In combat, the Bronco has proved itself an able and versatile performer, pleasant to fly, easy to manoeuvre and capable of withstanding considerable battle damage. As already indicated, the OV-10A has two stub-wings sprouting from the lower fuselage; these have four built-in 0.30in machine-guns, and four attachment points for a total of up to 2,400lb (1,088kg) of externally-mounted weapons. A fifth stores point on the fuselage centre-line can carry a 1,200lb (544kg) load, and provision exists for a 500lb (227kg) capacity station under each wing so long as a maximum weapons load of 3,600lb (1,632kg) is not exceeded. The stub-wings and armament capability are omitted from the OV-10B, though an auxiliary fuel tank can be carried on the centre-line station; the OV-10C is basically similar to the OV-10A but does not have the provision for underwing stores.

Hercules

Lockheed C-130E Hercules of the 778th Tactical Airlift Squadron, 464th Tactical Airlift Wing, USAF, Southeast Asia, 1968.

Span: 132ft 7in (40.41m)
Length: 97ft 9in (29.78m)
Weight: 155,000lb (70,310kg)
Engines: 4 × 4,050ehp Allison T56-A-7 turboprops
Max speed: 368mph (592kmh)
Operational ceiling: 23,000ft (7.010m)
Range: 4,700 miles (7,560km)

Since it first entered service in December 1956, Lockheed's versatile and ubiquitous C-130 transport has far exceeded the twelve labours of its Grecian namesake. This middle-sized tactical haulier, which, say its pilots, is 'built like a truck and handles like a Cadillac', has been built in more than forty variants, serves with as many countries, and fulfils a range of duties far beyond those of its original specification. More than thirteen hundred Hercules had been ordered by the end of 1974, with production continuing. Within the same basic airframe, the payload and performance of the Hercules have increase steadily since the first of the two YC-130 prototypes (53-3396) made its maiden flight on 23 August 1954. Initial production included two hundred and sixteen C-130As (first flight 7 April 1955), fifteen RC-130As for aerial survey and two hundred and thirty C-130Bs with higher-powered engines and extra fuel. Included in these figures were one AC-130A gunship, two GC-130A drone carriers, eleven JC-130As, a number of conversions to RC-130S for aerial survey duties, twelve ski-fitted C-130Ds (converted for As for USAF Polar supply duties), one NC-130B, five WC-130Bs, seven C-130Fs (converted from Bs for the US Navy), forty-six KC-130F assault transports/ refuelling tankers for the US Marine Corps, four Navy LC-130F/Rs on skis, for Polar supply, and twelve search and rescue HC-130Gs, also converted from Bs. The major production version, for the US forces and for export, has been the C-130E, of which the first example was flown on 25 August 1961. This is essentially an extended-range version, with larger underwing fuel tanks; it entered service in April 1962, and five hundred and nine were built. Apart from those for the US forces, Hercules have been ordered by the air arms of Abu Dhabi (two C-130H), Argentina (three C-130E and five C-130H), Australia (twelve C-130A and twelve C-130E), Belgium (twelve C-130H), Brazil (eleven C-130E and five C-130H), Canada (twenty-four C-130E and five C-130H, designated CC-130), Chile (two C-130H), Colombia (three C-130B), Denmark (three C-130H), Greece (four C-130H), Indonesia (ten C-130B), Iran (twenty-eight C-130E and thirty-two C-130H), Israel (twelve C-130E and four C-130H),Italy (fourteen C-130H), Libya (eight C-130H), Malaysia (six C-130H), Morocco (six C-130H), New Zealand (five C-130H), Nigeria (six C-130H), Norway (six C-130H), Pakistan (nine C-130B including four ex-Iran), Peru (four C-130E), Saudi Arabia (twelve C-130E, ten C-130H and four KC-130H), South Africa (seven C-130B), Spain (four C-130H and three KC-130H), Sweden (two C-130E and two C-130H), Turkey (eight C-130E), Venezuela (six C-130H), South Vietnam (thirty-two C-130A) and Zaïre (three C-130H). Commercial Model L-100 Hercules are operated on behalf of their governments by the Gabon (one), Kuwait (two) and Philippine (four) Air Forces. The C-130H has more powerful engines than the C-130E, which it superseded as the basic production model, but is otherwise generally similar. Accommodation is for a crew of four and up to ninety-two troops, sixty-four paratroops, seventy-four stretchers and two attendants, or a maximum freight payload of 45,000lb (20,410kg).

Grumman A-6 Intruder

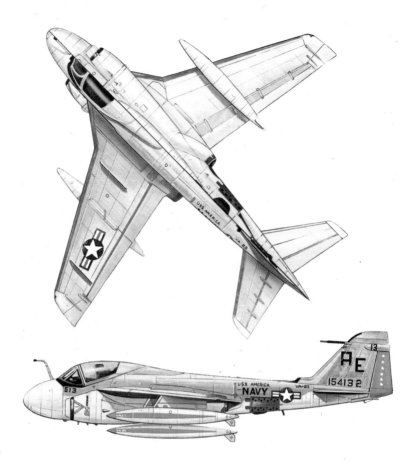

Grumman A-6A Intruder of VA-85, US Navy, USS *America,* south-west Pacific area, *circa* 1968

Span: 53ft 0in (16.15m)
Length: 54ft 7in (16.64m)
Weight: 60,626lb (27,500kg)
Engines: 2 × 9,300lb (4,218kg) st Pratt & Whitney J52-P-8A turbojets
Max speed: 685mph (1,102kmh) at sea level
Operational ceiling: 41,660ft (12,700m)
Typical combat range: 1,920 miles (3,090km)
Armament: None
Max bomb load: 15,000lb (6,804kg) externally

Chosen in late 1957 from eleven designs, the first of eight two-seat A-6A (originally A2F-1) development aircraft flew on 19 April 1960 with downward-tilting engine tailpipes to give 30 degree thrust deflection to aid take-off; subsequent aircraft have fixed pipes with 7 degree deflection. Replacing Skyraiders on USN attack carriers, it entered service in February 1963, and by mid-1965 was flying in the Vietnam conflict, being well suited to operations in this territory. The Intruder looks deceptively slight for the loads it carries, but is slightly larger than the Buccaneer, fulfilling a similar role with the RN and RAF. For carrier stowage, the A-6s upward-folding wings reduce span to 25ft 4in (7.72m). The four stores stations carry loads include thirty 500lb bombs, four pods each containing four 5in Zuni rockets, Bullpup air-to-surface missiles, auxilliary fuel tanks, or nuclear weapons. There is a semi-recessed weapons bay in the fuselage. The initial USN version, the A-6A, was fitted with DIANE (Digital Integrated Attack Navigation Equipment). When A-6A production ended in December 1969, four hundred and eighty-two A-6As had been built. Subsequent versions included the EA-6A, A-6B, EA-6B, A-6C, KA-6D and A-6E. The USMCs EA-6A (twenty-one

built, plus six converted from A-6As) is an attack escort using ECM to protect strike aircraft, and has a limited strike ability. The A-6B was an A-6A conversion with improved avionics, permitting carriage of anti-radar missiles; the first of nineteen flew in 1963. The prototype EA-6B Prowler flew on 25 May 1968. An updated EA-6A with a 3ft 4in (1.02m) longer nose and a four-man crew, one hundred and two will be ordered. EA models have a large radome on top of the fin. The A-6C, an A-6A conversion, had a ventral turret containing FLIR (forward-looking infra-red) sensors to detect 'difficult' targets, especially at night; twelve A-6As were modified to A-6C standard. The KA-6D is an A-6A variant, fifty-four of which were converted from A-6As; it first flew on 23 May 1966 and is in use as a carrier-borne 'buddy' refuelling tanker. The A-6E (over 300 ordered) which flew on 27 February 1970 and entered service in 1972, is a further avionics update of the A-6A, with improved weapon delivery. First flown on 22 March 1974, the A-6E TRAM (target recognition attack multi-sensor), carries a ventral fuselage package containing infra-red and laser equipment in addition to standard A-6E avionics.

Vought A7 Corsair

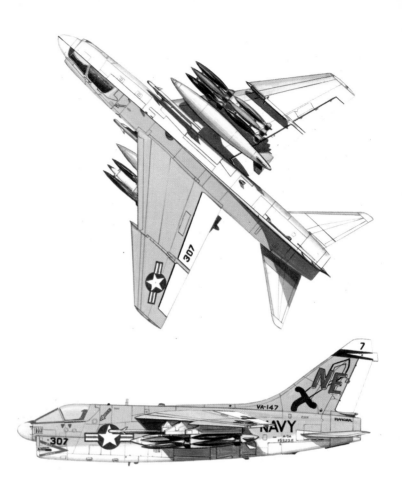

Vought A-7A Corsair II of the US Navy (Squadron VA-147, USS *Ranger)*, Vietnam 1968

Span: 38ft 8¾in (11.80m)
Length: 46ft 9in (14.25m)
Weight: 38,000lb (17,237kg)
Engine: 1×11,350lb (5,150kg) st Pratt & Whitney TF30-P-6 turbofan
Max speed: 578mph (930kmh)
Range: 810 miles (1,305km)

The Corsair II (in fact the third Vought aeroplane to bear the name), visibly declaring its descent from the F-8 Crusader, was the winner of four competing designs to meet a US Navy requirement, outlined in 1963, for an attack aircraft to succeed the McDonnell Douglas Skyhawk in the late 1960s. In the event the Skyhawk has continued to flourish, but this has not prevented the Corsair II from being manufactured in substantial numbers, both for the USN and the US Air Force. The Corsair lacks the Crusader's variable-incidence wing, and has a non-afterburning engine, since only a subsonic performance was required: but it has a greater range than the Skyhawk and can carry up to 15,000lb (6,804kg) of externally-mounted rockets, bombs and missiles on six underwing pylons and two stations on the fuselage sides. The early models also had a built-in 20mm gun armament in the front of the fuselage. The first of seven evaluation A-7s was flown on 27 September 1965, and four of these were delivered to the US Naval Air Test Center at Patuxent River in September 1966, as A-7As. Ling-Temco-Vought subsequently built one hundred and ninety-nine of the A-7A version (TF30-P-6 engine), deliveries of which were completed in the spring of 1968. The first operational A-7A unit was Squadron VA-147, which commissioned in February 1967 and went into action (from the USS *Ranger)* in the Vietnam theatre in the following December. The A-7B was a developed version, with uprated TF30-P-8 engine giving 12,200lb (5,534kg) thrust; one hundred and ninety-six were built, the first one flying on 6 February 1968 and the last being delivered in April 1969. The TF30-P-8

also powered the first two examples of the A-7D, the first of which flew on 6 April 1968, but the three hundred and eighty-seven production A-7Ds ordered up to 1974 are fitted with 14,250lb (6,465kg) st TF41-A-1 turbofans, a version of the Rolls-Royce Spey built by Allison Motors. The first TF41-powered A-7D was flown on 26 September 1968, and deliveries began three months later. These are employed in the fighter/strike role by the USAFs Tactical Air Command, whose first formation to equip with the A-7D was the 54th Tactical Fighter Wing. The two 20mm cannon of the original models are replaced in the A-7D by a single Vulcan M-61A1 multi-barrel 20mm cannon, installed in the port side of the lower front fuselage. In July 1969 deliveries began to the US Navy of the A-7E, which is essentially similar to the A-7D and has more advanced avionics than earlier USN models. This version entered operational service in 1970 with VA-146 and VA-147 (USS *America)*. By early 1974, A-7E orders for the US Navy totalled four hundred and eighty-eight aircraft, of which the first sixty-seven have TF30-P-8 turbo-jet engines (and are thereby designated A-7C to avoid confusion) and the remainder have 15,000lb (6,804kg) st TF41-A-2 turbofans. A further sixty have been ordered by Greece. Projected versions of the Corsair II have included the unbuilt KA-7F refuelling tanker; the A-7G, similar to the A-7D but with an uprated Spey engine, put forward as a potential Hunter replacement for the Swiss Air Force; and the tandem two-seat YA-7H, first flown on 29 August 1972. This is a private-venture prototype operational trainer.

Martin B-57

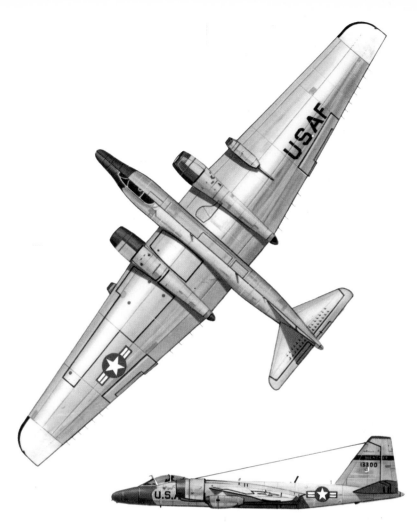

General Dynamics (Martin) RB-57F of the 58th Weather Reconnaissance Squadron, USAF, during 'Exercise Coldcat', Singapore, early 1969

Span: 122ft 5in (37.32m)
Length: 69ft 0in (21.03m)
Weight: 63,000lb (28,576kg)
Engines: 2 × 16,500lb (7,484kg) st Pratt & Whitney TF33-P-11A turbofans and 2 × 2,900lb (1,315kg) st Pratt & Whitney J60-P-9 auxiliary turbojets
Max speed: 411mph (661kmh)
Operational ceiling: 60,800ft (18,500m)
Range: 1,475 miles (2,374km)

The innovations and elongations introduced by Martin and other US engineers on the willing Canberra airframe during the past 20 years make it difficult to recognise, in some of the final models, any connection at all with William Petter's original design. After building eight B-57As and sixty-seven RB-57As virtually to the Canberra B.2 pattern (except for a change of power-plant), Martin introduced the first US modifications on its main production versions, the B-57B, of which two hundred and two were built. This intruder bomber had a new, two-man, tandem-seat cockpit, pylons for underwing stores, eight 0.50in guns in the wing leading edges and a Martin-designed rotating bomb door on which the aeroplane's 6,000lb (2,722kg) internal load was carried. B-57Bs were supplied to the Chinese Nationalist, Pakistan (twenty-one) and Vietnamese Air Forces, and a number were recalled from the Air National Guard for active bomber duties in the mid-1960s. Thirty-eight B-57Cs were basically the same aeroplane fitted with dual controls; one B-57C was supplied to Pakistan. Martin then built twenty RB-57Ds, in both single- and two-seat forms, which had 11,000lb (4,990kg) st J57-P-37A engines and a 106ft (32.31m) wing span as compared with the

original 64ft (19.51m). This model was intended for photographic and electronics reconnaissance duties, and two were supplied to the Chinese Nationalist Air Force; the rest served with Air Defense Command and the Pacific Air Force. The B-57E designation covered sixty-eight examples of a target-towing adaptation of the B-57B. In June 1964 General Dynamics (Convair) delivered to the 58th Weather Reconnaissance Squadron the first of twenty-one RB-57Fs, a further B-57B or RB-57D conversion with an enormous 122ft 5in (37.32m) span wing, revised vertical tail surfaces, turbofan main engines and two optional auxiliary turbojets in underwing pods. These aircraft, since redesignated WB-57F, were for strategic as well as weather reconnaissance, and for air sampling at extreme altitudes. Further-modified versions of the B-57B, used in Southeast Asia, included the EB-57B for electronic counter-measures and sixteen examples of the Westinghouse/Martin B-57G, which has a much-modified nose section with radar and sensor fairings, laser rangefinder, and infra-red and low light level TV detection gear for night interdiction. The B-57G was also a B-57B conversion.

Boeing B-52 Stratofortress

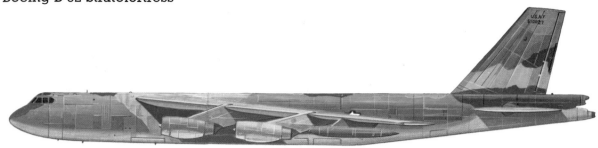

Boeing B-52G Stratofortress of the 93rd BW,
USAF, 1968

Span: 185ft 0in (56.39m)
Length: 157ft 7in (48.03m)
Weight: 480,000lb (217,720kg)
Engines: 8 × 13,750lb (6,237kg) st Pratt &
    Whitney J57-P-43WB turbojets
Max speed: 630mph (1,014kmh) at 40,000ft
    (12,200m)
Operational ceiling: 55,000ft (16,750m)
Range: 8,000 miles (12,875km)
Armament: 4 × 0.50in machine-guns
Max bomb load: 42,000lb (19,050kg),
    including 2 × Quail decoy missiles,
    internally; 9,000lb (4,082kg), including
    2 × Hound Dog ASMs, externally.
    Currently carries 8 × SRAM ASMs
    internally; 12 × SRAM ASMs and
    nuclear free-fall bombs externally

Boeing's giant B-52 seems almost certain to be the last of the big 'heavies', such have been the changes in global strategy since it entered USAF service in June 1955. Certainly using an inter-continental bomber to drop propaganda leaflets over North Vietnam was the antithesis of cost-effectiveness, and far from the B-52s designed role. The XB-52 prototype flew on 2 October 1952, followed by one YB-52, three B-52As and fifty B-52B and RB-52B, initial production models. SAC had in 1974 about four hundred and fifty B-52s, approximately a third being the tall-finned B-52C, D, E and F (respective production totals thirty-five, one hundred and seventy, one hundred and eighty-nine), differing in power, electronics and equipment; their maximum internal bomb load is 60,000lb (27,216kg). The remainder were B-52Gs or Hs; the former has a marked performance increase and a cropped vertical tail, and was the first model to carry the Hound Dog stand-off missile. The G's internal load included two Quail decoy missiles and 20,000lb (9,072kg) of bombs and has a tail turret with four remotely-controlled 0.50in machine-guns. Decoy rockets could be carried under wing. The first B-52G flew on 26 October 1958 and first deliveries to SAC were made the following February; one hundred and ninety-three were built. The final version, the B-52H (first flight 6 March 1961); one hundred and two built up to June 1962) is similar to the G except for 16,000lb (7,257kg) st Pratt & Whitney TF33-P-1 turbofans, further increasing range and performance, and a multi-barrel cannon in the tail. The B-52H has flown more than 12,500 miles (20,117km) unrefuelled. All serving B-52s have been modernised and strengthened for low-level penetration missions. A modernisation programme on ninety-six G and H models enables carriage of up to twenty Short-Range Attack Missiles. Some two-hundred G and H models have Hughes FLIR (forward-looking infra-red) sensors in twin under-nose fairings and EVS (Electro-optical Viewing System) night vision equipment installed. In 1975-77 eighty B-52Ds were rebuilt to extend their lives.

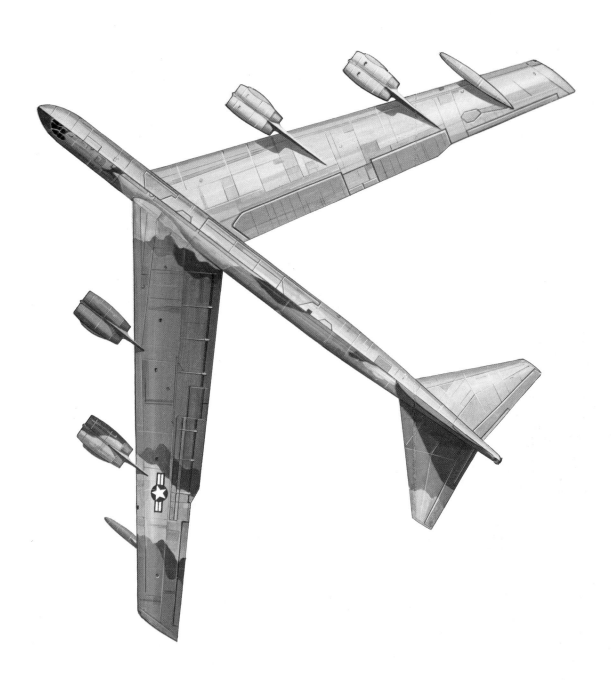

Beechcraft U-21

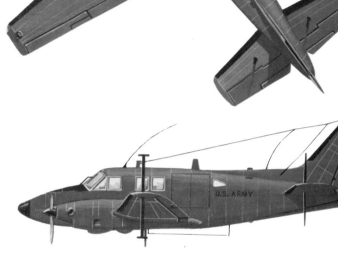

Beechcraft RU-21D of the US Army, Southeast Asia 1970

Span: 45ft 10½in (13.98m)
Length: 35ft 6in (10.82m)
Weight: 9,650lb (4,377kg)
Engines: 2×550shp United Aircraft of
   Canada PT6A-20 turboprops
Max speed: 245mph (395kmh)
Operational ceiling: 25,500ft (7,775m)
Range: 1,167 miles (1,878km)

First of the post-war Beech 'twins' adopted by the US armed forces was the Twin-Bonanza, four of which were acquired by the US Army as YL-23s for evaluation in 1952. Subsequent contracts covered fifty-five L-23As, forty L-23Bs, eighty-five L-23Ds and six L-23Es, to which the name Seminole was applied. Most of the A and B models were later brought up to D standard, and in 1962 the L-23D and L-23E were redesignated U-8D and U-8E respectively. The U-8F (originally L-23F) was a developed version with a larger fuselage, and was based on the Model 65 Queen Air; three pre-series and sixty-eight production examples were completed for the US Army, and others were supplied to the Japan Maritime Self-Defence Force (twenty-nine) and the air forces of Uruguay and Venezuela (six). On 22 June 1961 Beech flew the prototype of a new and improved Queen Air, the Model 65-80, with 380hp IGSO-540-A1A engines and a sweptback fin and rudder; this in turn was superseded by the Model 65-A80, with a 5ft 0in (1.52m) increase in wing span, enlarged nose section and higher gross weight. From the remodelled Queen Air was developed the military U-21, principally to provide the US Army with a new light transport and utility aircraft for use in Southeast Asia. A prototype was evaluated in 1963, and deliveries of the production U-21A (corresponding to the commercial Model 65-A90-1) began in May 1967. One hundred and twenty-four were ordered, followed by three U-21Bs and two U-21Cs; these all have 550shp PT6A-20 engines. Standard utility transport version is the U-21A, accommodating a crew of two and up to ten passengers or three stretchers. The RU-21A and electronics reconnaissance RU-21D are 'special-purpose' models. With 620shp PT6A-29 engines and a gross weight of 10,900lb (4,944kg) the aircraft is known as the RU-21B (=Model 65-A90-2) and RU-21C (= Model 65-A90-3); the RU-21E is an electronics reconnaissance version of the Model 65-A90-4, of which sixteen were ordered in 1970; the U-21F, of which five were ordered in 1971 together with seventeen RU-21Fs, corresponds to the pressurised King Air A100. Three Super King Air 200s for the US Army, for electronics reconnaissance, are designated RU-21J. Standard King Air C90s have been ordered by the USAF (one VC-6B), JMSDF (one) and Spanish Air Ministry (six); and King Air A100s by the Royal Moroccan Air Force (six) and Spanish Air Ministry (two).

Seasprite

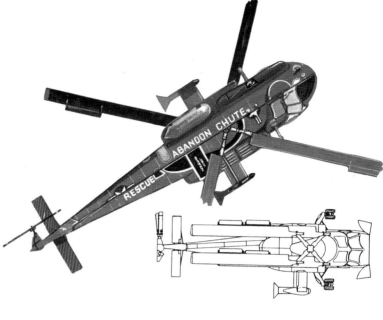

Kaman SH-2D Seasprite of the US Navy late 1971

Main rotor diameter: 44ft 0in (13.41m)
Length: 40ft 6in
Weight: 12,500lb (5,670kg)
Engines: 2 × 1,350shp General Electric
  T58-GE-8F turboshafts
Max speed: 168mph (270kmh)
Operational ceiling: 22,500ft (6,858m)
Range: 445 miles

Winner of a 1956 US Navy competition for a fast, long range all-weather utility helicopter, the Kaman Model K-20 Seasprite entered production in 1961, initial models consisting of eighty-eight UH-2As (originally HU2K-1) and one hundred and two UH-2Bs. These were preceded by four prototypes, the first of which (147202) was flown for the first time on 2 July 1959, powered by a 1,025shp T58-GE-6 turboshaft engine. Power-plant of the UH-2A and B is a single 1,250shp T58-GE-8. These Seasprites replaced earlier piston-engined helicopters for a range of duties that included reconnaissance, supply, carrier 'plane guard', communications, ship-to-shore transport and casualty evacuation, although the principal role was that of search and rescue. Flown by a crew of two, the Seasprite can accommodate up to eleven passengers or four stretchers in the cabin, and has a watertight body for landings at sea. In flight, the wheeled undercarriage is fully retractable, emphasising the aircraft's unusually clean lines. The UH-2A had more comprehensive electronics and navigational equipment than the UH-2B and was able to operate in all weathers. First UH-2A deliveries were made to the US Navy's squadron HU-2 in December 1962, and the type first went to sea aboard USS *Independence* in June 1963. The UH-2B followed suit, with Detachment 46 of HU-4 in USS *Albany,* two months later, and both types have been employed extensively in the Pacific and Southeast Asia. In March 1965 Kaman completed the first of two UH-2B conversions in which two T58-GE-8Bs were installed, in pods on either side of the rotor pylon, to give the Seasprite a more sustained

performance and twin-engined reliability. Starting in 1967, existing UH-2As and -2Bs were converted to similar configuration, with slightly more tail area and minor alterations to the cockpit and rotor pylon; they were then re-designated UH-2C. About sixty such conversions had been delivered by the end of 1970. The UH-2C and all subsequent models now have twin 1,350shp T58-GE-8F engines. A small batch of UH-2s was acquired by the US Army, which named the aircraft Tomahawk. One of these (14-9785), with a 1,500shp T58-GE-10 engine, was evaluated in an armed ground support role, and another (14-7978) was evaluated in the mid-1960s as a high-speed compound helicopter, with a 2,500lb (1,134kg) st YJ85 turbojet pod on the starboard side of the cabin and later with small fixed wings to off-load the main rotor. This aircraft was flown at 216mph (348kmh) before the stub wings were fitted. Neither of these achieved production status, but six examples were delivered to the US Navy, for operation in Southeast Asia, of an armed and armoured version known as the HH-2C. Operable at an overload take-off weight of 12,800lb (5,806kg), these have an improved main rotor assembly, a 4-blade tail rotor and twin-wheel main landing gear units. They are employed for search and rescue operations in combat areas and are armed with a chin-mounted Minigun turret and waist-mounted machine-guns. The HH-2D, of which fifty were delivered to the USN from February 1970, is a similar conversion from earlier single-engined models, having the structural improvements of the HH-2C but lacking the guns and armour protection.

Galaxy

Lockheed C-5A Galaxy prototype in the insignia
of Military Airlift Command USAF, 1969. *Data
apply to production version*

Span: 222ft 8½in (67.88m)
Length: 247ft 10in (75.54m)
Weight: 769,000lb (348,810kg)
Engines: 4×41,000lb (18,600kg) st
    General Electric TF39-GE-1
Max speed: 518mph (834kmh)
Operational ceiling: 34,000ft (10,360m)
Range: 3,749 miles (6,033km)

Currently the world's largest military transport aircraft, and
exceeded in size and gross weight only by later models of the
commercial Boeing 747, the Galaxy came into being as the
result of the CX-4 requirement issued by the USAFs Military
Air Transport Service (now Military Airlift Command) in 1963
for a large logistics transport aircraft. This and other
requirements were subsequently combined in a revised
requirement, CX-HLS (Cargo Experimental-Heavy Logistics
System), for which Boeing, Douglas and Lockheed were
invited in 1964 to develop their initial designs further. At the
same time, General Electric and Pratt & Whitney were invited
to develop an appropriate powerplant for the aircraft. By the
end of 1965 the choice had been made of a
Lockheed/General Electric association to proceed to the
hardware stage with what was then known offically as the
C-5A Galaxy. Eight test and evaluation aircraft were built,
construction beginning in August 1966 and being followed by
the flight of the first Galaxy (66-8303) on 30 June 1968. All eight
aircraft were assigned to the flight test programme, which
extended into mid-1971. Some eighteen months before this,
however, the first of eighty-one production C-5As had been
delivered to the USAF, on 17 December 1969. The USAF has
four operational Galaxy squadrons, and the first two of these,
based at Charleston AFB, South Carolina, and Travis AFB,
California, were already carrying out regular operations to
and from Southeast Asia and Europe by mid-1971. The third
squadron was also based at Travis AFB, and the fourth at
Dover AFB, Delaware. An important factor in the CX-HLS
specification was that the Galaxy should, despite its greater
size, be capable of operating from the same 8,000ft (2,440m)
runways as the C-141 StarLifter, and of landing on semi-
prepared runways of no more than 4,000ft (1,220m) in combat
areas. To distribute runway load, the Galaxy has a 28-wheel
landing gear, consisting of a 4-wheel nose unit and four
6-wheel main bogies. It carries a normal crew of five, with a
rest area at the front of the upper deck for up to fifteen people,
including a relief crew. The interior is divided into forward
and rear upper compartments and a single lower deck, total
volume of all three compartments being 42,825 cu ft (1,212.7
cu m). The C-5A is intended primarily as a freighter, in which
role typical loads may include two M-60 tanks or sixteen 15cwt
lorries; or one M-60, two Iroquois helicopters, five M-113
personnel carriers, one M-59 2½ ton truck and an M-151 5cwt
truck; or ten Pershing missiles with their towing and
launching vehicles; or thirty-six standard load pallets.
Straight-in cargo loading can be accomplished via the
upward-hinged nose and the rear-fuselage ramp/door,
simultaneously if necessary. If required as a personnel
transport, the C-5A can carry seventy-five troops on the rear
upper deck and two hundred and seventy on the lower deck.
In early 1975 the Imperial Iranian Air Force was expected to
order ten Galaxies.

North American F-100 Super Sabre

North American F-100D Super Sabre of the
308th Tactical FS, 31st Tactical TW, USAF,
Vietnam, 1969-70

Span: 38ft 9¾in (11.82m)
Length (excluding probe): 49ft 4in
  (15.04m)
Weight, normal take-off: 34,050lb
  (15,445kg)
Engine: 11,700/16,950lb (5,307/7,688kg) st
  Pratt & Whitney J57-P-21A
  afterburning turboject
Max speed: 910mph (1,464kmh) at
  35,000ft (10,670m)
Operational ceiling: 36,000ft (11,000m)
Radius on internal fuel: 534 miles
  (860km)
Armament: 4×20mm M39E cannon
Max bomb load: 6×1,000lb bombs, or
  2×Sidewinder or Bullpup AAMs or
  rocket pods

The Super Sabre, whose YF-100A prototype (the first of two) flew on 25 May 1953 after four years design work, deserves its niche in aviation history as the first fully supersonic warplane to enter quantity production. It began life under the company designation Sabre 45, the figure indicating the degree of wing sweepback, but subsequent development rendered it a completely new design. First production model was the F-100A day fighter (two hundred and three built) with 9,700lb (4,400kg) st J57-P-7 or -39 engines, four 20mm M-39E cannon and six stores attachment points. The F-100A, first flown on 29 October 1953, entered USAF service in September 1954; eighty, brought up to F-100D standard, were supplied to the Chinese Nationalist Air Force. The F-100C, first flown on 17 January 1955, was a fighter-bomber version with a 7,500lb (3,402kg) external load on eight strong-points and able to refuel in flight. Production totalled four hundred and seventy-six, of which two hundred and sixty were later released to the Turkish Air Force; they latterly served with the ANG. A number of design refinements, including a taller fin, appeared in the F-100D (first flight 24 January 1956), which

entered production in 1956. In addition to the standard quarter of 20mm cannon, the F-100D could carry four Sidewinders and, for attack missions, two Bullpup missiles and/or a wide variety of conventional weapons up to a maximum of 7,500lb (3,402kg). The F-100D was the major production version, 1,274 being built, and was used extensively by the USAF in Vietnam in 1966-71, where the F-100 flew more sorties than had the North American P-51 in World War 2, by day and night. Others were supplied under MAP terms to the French and Danish air forces. Final version of the Super Sabre, which brought total production to 2,292 before completion in October 1959, was the 2-seat F-100F, which flew for the first time on 7 March 1957 following the flight of a TF-100C prototype on 6 August 1956: three hundred and thirty-nine F-100Fs were built. With two 20mm cannon and a 6,000lb weapons load, this model could perform either tactical attack roles or combat training duties and served in Vietnam in ground attack, fighter, electronic warfare and forward air control roles. The Danish and Turkish air forces, as well as the USAF, received quantities of the F-100F.

Blackhawk

Sikorsky S-67 Blackhawk prototype, 1972

Main rotor diameter: 62ft 0in (18.90m)
Wing span: 27ft 4in (8.33m)
Length: 64ft 9in (19.74m)
Weight: 24,400lb (11,067kg)
Engines: 2 × 1,500shp General Electric
   T58-GE-5 turboshafts
Max speed: 203mph (327kmh)
Service ceiling: 17,000ft (5,180m)
Range: 1,122 miles (1,805km)

Originating under the Sikorsky project designation AH-3, the S-67 Blackhawk was designed in 1969 as a 'tank killer' gunship helicopter, and a company-funded prototype (N671SA) flew for the first time on 20 August 1970. Incorporated in the design are proven dynamic components based on those of the S-61R, and a number of features of Sikorsky's earlier S-66 design, which was evolved for the US Army's AAFSS (Advanced Aerial Fire Support System) competition of 1965. Added to these, in an airframe having the typical low drag, low frontal area profile demanded of the contemporary gunship helicopter, are a number of other features which are new to this class of aeroplane. They include an all-moving tailplane, which is set in a vertical attitude for hovering and can be used in the conventional position during horizontal flight to trim the fuselage independently of the main rotor – a useful factor in aligning a gunship to concentrate fire upon a target. The Blackhawk has five-blade main and tail rotors, the former having swept-back blade tips. Much of the work of the anti-torque tail rotor can be undertaken by the cambered vertical fin, and indeed the S-67 can be flown and landed safely even if the tail rotor is shot away. The landing gear consists of twin retractable pairs of main wheels and a tailwheel, the S-67 being unusual in that it touches down on the tailwheel first. The outer stub-wings, which are detachable, have (for the first time in a helicopter) speed brakes on both upper and lower surfaces. These improve several aspects of performance,

including manoeuvrability, diving angle and time on target. The wings have four attachment points for external weapons, and can carry 16 TOW, Swingfire, HOT or similar missiles, thirty-two 5in Zuni rockets or eight launchers containing a total of one hundred and fifty-two 2.75in folding-fin rockets. Beneath the fuselage (and, optionally, the nose) can be fitted turrets for 7.62mm Miniguns, 20 and 30mm cannon or a 40mm grenade launcher. The Blackhawk carries a two-man crew for the anti-tank role, and a fuselage compartment permits the transport of six fully-armed troops. In unarmed configuration this compartment can be enlarged to seat up to fifteen troops. Alternative applications for the Blackhawk include long range rescue, with two 300 US gallon (1,136 litre) underwing drop-tanks; anti-submarine warfare; or as a flying crane, carrying up to 7,000lb (3,175kg) of externally-slung cargo with the wings removed. Up to autumn 1972 no further examples of the S-67 had flown. The prototype set a helicopter world speed record on 14 December 1970, beating it five days later with a new record of 220.885mph (355.485kmh). Although larger than other contemporary gunship designs, the Blackhawk is highly manoeuvrable, and can be rolled and perform split-S turns without difficulty. In the late summer of 1972 the Blackhawk, Bell KingCobra and Lockheed Cheyenne (which see) took part in a US Army fly-off competition, from which the Cheyenne was eliminated.

KingCobra

Bell Model 309 KingCobra, second prototype, 1972

Main rotor diameter: 48ft 0in (14.63m)
Wing span: 13ft 0in (3.96m)
Length: 49ft 0in (14.93m)
Weight: 14,000lb (6,350kg)
Engine: 1 × 2,050shp Lycoming T55-L-7C
   turboshaft
Max speed: 230mph (370kmh)
Hovering ceiling: 4,000ft (1,220m)

The KingCobra, as its name suggests, is basically a further development of the HueyCobra/SeaCobra family of helicopter gunships already in wide-scale service with the US Army and Marine Corps. It is, in effect, a slightly stretched version of the latter's AH-1J SeaCobra, having a 4ft 7in (1.40m) longer fuselage and a 4ft 0in (1.22m) greater diameter main rotor. Wider-chord blades are fitted to both the main and tail rotors, and the former have double-swept tips to reduce the noise level and improve their high-speed performance. Two prototypes of the KingCobra have been built. The first of these (N309J) was flown on 10 September 1971, and first details of the aircraft were announced later the same month. The

KingCobra was developed primarily with existing AH-1 customers in mind; hence the first prototype satisfies the USMCs preference for a twin-engined configuration in having an 1,800shp UACL T400-CP-400 Turbo Twin Pac power-plant, while the second prototype (first flown in January 1972) has a single 2,050shp Lycoming T55-L7C turboshaft engine. Other modifications, compared with the SeaCobra, include an increase in wing span from 10ft 4in (3.15m) to 13ft 0in (3.96m), permitting increases in internal fuel load and external stores-carrying capability; strengthened airframe and landing gear, to absorb the greater engine power; and the addition of a ventral fin to improve directional stability and control. The

KingCobra has four underwing stores points, on which a typical load would be eight Hughes TOW missiles and two pods each containing nineteen 2.75in folding-fin rockets. The 'chin' turret can mount a multi-barrel 30mm or 20mm gun, and modifications to the nose area include the installation of FLIR (forward-looking infra-red) sensors, a laser rangefinder, low light level television and an enlarged ammunition bay. Due to its lighter weight and smaller weapons load than the Blackhawk, Bell claims that the KingCobra can be produced at much lower cost than either of its original competitors, since existing 'Cobra production assemblies can be utilised with minimal modification. With the Sikorsky Blackhawk (which see), the KingCobra took part in an initial US Army flight test competition in 1972, but its future remained undecided at the time of closing for press.

Cheyenne

Lockheed AH-56A Cheyenne prototype in US
Army finish, 1972

Main rotor diameter: 51ft 3in (15.62m)
Wing span: 26ft 8½in (8.14m)
Length: 54ft 8in (16.66m)
Weight: 18,300lb (8,301kg)
Engine: 1×3,925shp General Electric
**   T64-GE-16 turboshaft**
Max speed: 244mph (393kmh)
Operational ceiling: 20,000ft (6,100m)
Range: 1,225 miles

Lockheed began its study of modern rotorcraft techniques in 1958, a comparatively late entry into this field of aircraft design. The rigid-rotor principle, as used in the Cheyenne, has only been achieved in practical form in comparatively recent times. Lockheed first tested the basic soundness of its rigid-rotor concept in the CL-475 prototype (N6940C) in late 1959, and from this designed the larger two-seat CL-595, three of which were built. One of these, designated XH-51N, was delivered to NASA for wind tunnel tests; the other two, designated XH-51A (serial numbers 151262 and '63), were evaluated by the US Army and Navy. First XH-51A to fly was 151262, which made its maiden flight on 2 November 1962, powered by a 500shp Pratt & Whitney T74 turboshaft engine. Later, one was converted into a compound helicopter, with a 2,600lb (1,180kg) st J60-P-2 turbojet on the port side of the fuselage and a pair of stub wings to off-load the rotor during forward flight. In May 1965 this aeroplane flew faster than any previous rotorcraft, achieving a level speed of 272mph (438kmh). The AH-56 Cheyenne is also a turbine-powered compound helicopter using a rigid-rotor system for lift and a pusher propeller at the rear for forward propulsion. During forward flight nearly 90 per cent of the Cheyenne's engine power is diverted to the tail propeller. More than a dozen US manufacturers competed with Lockheed for the original AAFSS (Advanced Aerial Fire Support System) contract, from which a choice between projects from Lockheed and Sikorsky was resolved in March 1966, when Lockheed received a contract for ten development aircraft. The first of these, for dynamic tests, was rolled out in May 1967, the first flying prototype (66-1127) took to the air on 21 September 1967, and two more development aircraft were delivered later. The remaining six were 'frozen' in a partially-completed condition. In January 1968 the US Army took up an option to buy three hundred and seventy-five Cheyennes, which were scheduled to enter service in the early 1970s as armed escorts for larger support helicopters and as ground attack aircraft. This contract was, however, cancelled in spring 1969, although development of the Cheyenne continued. In 1972 it was involved in a fly-off competition, for a new Army requirement, with the Sikorsky Blackhawk and Bell KingCobra (which see). The Cheyenne was eliminated as a result of this competition, and its future remained undecided at the time of closing for press, although Lockheed is to continue developing the advanced rigid-rotor control system. The crew are seated in tandem, the co-pilot/gunner occupying the front seat and controlling the nose turret, which mounts either a 7.62mm Minigun or a 40mm grenade launcher, and can be traversed through 180 degrees. A 30mm cannon with a full 360-degree field of fire is mounted in a barbette below the rear fuselage. Two strong-points beneath each wing are stressed to take Hughes TOW (Tube-launched, Optically-tracked, Wire-guided) anti-tank missiles or pods of 2.75in (70mm) rockets. Computer sighting is installed for weapon firing.

Lockheed Viking

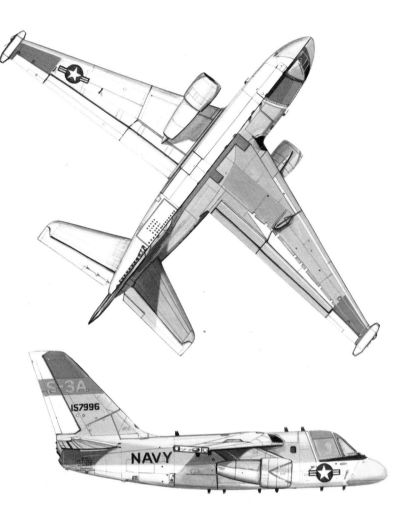

Lockheed S-3A Viking, fifth development aircraft for the US Navy, summer 1973

Span: 68ft 8in (20.93m)
Length: 53ft 4in (16.26m)
Weight: 42,500lb (19,277kg)
Engines: 2 × 9,275lb (4,207kg) st General
   Electric TF-34-GE-2 turbofans
Max speed: 403mph (649kmh)
Operational ceiling: 35,000ft (10,670m)
Range: 2,303 miles (3,705km)

Five of America's major aircraft manufacturers submitted proposals in April 1968 to meet the US Navy's requirement for a replacement for the venerable Grumman S-2 Tracker in the carrier-borne ASW role. In the following August the choice was reduced to the competing designs of General Dynamics (Convair) and Lockheed, and the latter company (in partnership with LTV Aerospace) was finally selected by Naval Air Systems Command to develop the new aircraft. The initial contract called for the completion of six development aircraft (later increased to eight), and up to the end of 1974 US Navy firm orders for the S-3A totalled one hundred and forty-six production examples, of the currently-planned procurement of one hundred and eighty-seven. A full-sized mock-up of the S-3A was completed in 1970, and the first of the development aircraft (157992) was rolled out in November 1971 and flew for the first time on 21 January 1972, nearly two months ahead of schedule; deliveries to the USN for BIS

(Bureau Investigation and Survey) testing began in October 1973, followed by the first deliveries of squadron aircraft (to VS-41 for training) in February 1974. The initial S-3A version of the Viking carries a crew of four, each on a zero-zero ejection seat; its ASW equipment includes an on-board computer and data processer, and the latest and most sensitive MAD gear, acoustic and non-acoustic sensors, ECM gear and radar. A divided weapons bay in the centre fuselage can accommodate four bombs, mines, depth charges or torpedoes, and there is a triple ejector rack beneath each wing for carrying mines, cluster bombs, rocket pods, flare launchers or auxiliary fuel tanks. There is a considerable stretch potential in the Viking's design which will allow for an increase of the gross weight up to at least 50,000lb (22,680kg) and of the initial electronics by some 50 per cent. Later versions are foreseen to fulfil such roles as flight refuelling tanker, utility transport, ASW command and control or ECM patrol and monitoring.

Tiger II

Northrop F-5E Tiger II, tenth production aircraft for the USAF, as displayed at the Paris Air Show, May/June 1973

Span: 27ft 11⅛in (8.53m)
Length: 48ft 3¾in (14.73m)
Weight: 24,080lb (10,922kg)
Engines: 2×3,500/5,000lb (1,588/2,268kg)
st General Electric J85-GE-21
afterburning turbojets
Max speed: 1,058mph (1,703kmh)
Operational ceiling: 54,000ft (16,460m)
Range: 875 miles (1,408km)

Four years of indecision and apparent indifference followed the maiden flight, on 30 July 1959, of Northrop's N-156F Freedom Fighter, a compact, nimble and versatile design aimed at the smaller air forces of the world which needed up-to-date but none-too-expensive equipment. Northrop built, as a private venture, three prototypes of the N-156C (as it was originally known), in parallel with the N-156T two-seat trainer version which became the T-38A Talon. The third prototype, representing an improved model and designated N-156F, flew for the first time in May 1963, by which time the US Defense Department had selected the type, in single-seat F-5A and two-seat F-5B forms, for delivery under its Military Assistance Program to several NATO and SEATO air forces. The first production F-5A was flown in October 1963, and the first foreign delivery, a squadron of thirteen, was made to the Imperial Iranian Air Force in February 1965. Iran eventually received one hundred and four F-5As, thirteen RF-5As and twenty-two F-5Bs, of which some have in recent years been returned to the US for allocation to South Vietnam; some have also reportedly been transferred to Pakistan. Subsequent recipients have included the air forces of Nationalist China, Ethiopia, Greece, Libya, Morocco, Norway, South Korea, the Philippines, Thailand and Turkey. Orders from Northrop production had totalled six hundred and twenty-one F-5As (including reconnaissance RF-5As) and one hundred and thirty-four F-5Bs by the beginning of 1974. In addition, CASA of Spain assembled thirty-six SF-5As and thirty-four SF-5Bs for the Ejército del Aire; Canadair built one hundred and fifteen

of an improved model (eighty-nine CF-5As and twenty-six CF-5Ds) for the Canadian Armed Forces, and seventy-five NF-5As and thirty NF-5Bs for the Royal Netherlands Air Force. The F-5A and F-5B have broadly similar performances, the F-5B dispensing with the single-seater's two 20mm. Colt-Browning M-39 guns and carrying a second crew member. Both models have provision for up to 6,200lb (2,812kg) of stores on five external stations, and a Sidewinder air-to-air missile at each wingtip. In response to the Defense Department's IFA (International Fighter Aircraft) programme for an F-5 successor for MAP countries, Northrop re-engined an F-5B with two 5,000lb (2,268kg) st YJ85-GE-21 turbojets and modified the airframe for improved performance, fuel load and operational versatility. This prototype, designated YF-5B-21, flew for the first time on 28 March 1969, and in November 1970 this version (now redesignated F-5E) was selected in preference to variously-modified developments of the Lockheed F-104, McDonnell Douglas F-4 and Vought F-8 to fulfil the MAP requirement. Major airframe differences in the F-5E include a wider fuselage; increased-area wings, extended forward in a wing/body airflow strake at the roots and having full-span leading-edge flaps; and an improved fire control system. Airfield performance is improved (there is a runway arrester hook and provision for JATO), and so is manoeuvrability. The F-5E is intended primarily for the air superiority role, with two nose-mounted M-39 20mm cannon and a Sidewinder at each wingtip.

Grumman F-14 Tomcat

Grumman F-14A Tomcat of VF-1, US Navy, US
Naval Air Station Miramar, California, 1973

Span: 64ft 1½in (19.54m); wings swept:
  38ft 2½in (11.65m)
Length: 61ft 11⁹/₁₀in (18.89m)
Weight: 74,348lb (33,724kg)
Engines: 2×20,900lb (9,480kg) st Pratt &
  Whitney TF30-P-412A afterburning
  turbofans
Max speed: over 1,450mph (2,333kmh)
  above 36,000ft (11,000m)
Operational ceiling: above 50,000ft
  (15,240m)
Typical combat radius: 450 miles (724km)
Armament: 1×20mm M61A1 Vulcan six-
  barrel cannon; 4×Phoenix or Sparrow
  AAMs under fuselage; and/or
  4×Sidewinders or 2×Phoenix or
  Sparrows under wings
Max bomb load: 14,500lb (6,577kg) of
  bombs and/or missiles, ECM pods etc.

The Tomcat, developed in place of the cancelled F-111B for the USN, was declared winner over four other competitors in a Navy design programme in January 1969 and is a two-seat, multi-purpose carrier-based fighter. The first of twelve development aircraft flew on 21 December 1970, but crashed on the landing approach after its second test flight nine days later. A second F-14 flew on 24 May 1971. The USN has planned procurement of five hundred and twenty-one F-14As; about four hundred were in service by 1981. Pre-revolutionary Iran received eighty. Avionics and other features are based on those already developed by Grumman for the F-111B, and landing gear on that of the A-6 Intruder. The F-14A has a fixed armament of one M61-A1 Vulcan 20mm multi-barrel cannon, with six hundred and seventy-five rounds, in the port side of the lower front fuselage. There are recessed stations under the fuselage, and pylons beneath the fixed portion of the wings, on which can be carried six Phoenix and two Sidewinder, or four Sparrow and four Sidewinder, air-to-air missiles; or drop tanks. The F-14As computer-controlled radar and weapon systems can engage up to six aircraft at one time, and can detect targets at 185km (115 miles), although,

ironically, most sightings are visual. The Tomcat can also be operated in the attack role, carrying bombs or bomb-and-missile combinations up to a maximum external load of 14,500lb (6,577kg). The F-14A is unique among variable-geometry ('swing-wing') aircraft in having, in addition to variable-sweep wings, small movable foreplane surfaces housed inside the leading-edge roots of the fixed portions of the wings. Fulfilling a similar function to the 'moustaches' of the Dassault Milan, these can be extended forward into the airstream as the main wings swing backward, controlling changed in the centre-of-pressure position. The wings themselves have 20 degrees of sweep when fully forward and 68 degrees when fully back. The first operational USN Tomcat unit was VF-1; with VF-2, this squadron flew the first operational F-14A sorties, from the USS *Enterprise,* in March 1974. A carrier wing normally comprises two F-14 squadrons. By 1980 sixteen USN squadrons operated the F-14; when not at sea they are shore-based at NAS Miramar, California, and NAS Norfolk, Virginia. Engine problems in service required modifications to the TF30 turbofans.

McDonnell Douglas F-15 Eagle

McDonnel F-15A Eagle, development aircraft, 1973

Span: 42ft 9¾in (13.05m)
Length: 63ft 9in (19.43m)
Weight: 56,000lb (25,401kg)
Engines: 2×25,000lb (11,340kg) st
(approx) Pratt & Whitney F100-PW-100
afterburning turbojets
Max speed: over 1,650mph (2,655kmh)
above 36,000ft (11,000m)
Operational ceiling: above 66,900ft
(20,390m)
Range with FAST packs: more than 3,450
miles (5,560km)
Armament: 4×Sidewinder and
4×Sparrow AAMs and 1×20mm
M61A1 six-barrel cannon
Max bomb load: 16,000lb (7,257kg)
externally

McDonnell Douglas's F-15 design was declared the winner of a USAF competition over proposals from Fairchild Hiller and North American Rockwell, in December 1969 for a new air superiority fighter to counter the ascendancy of Soviet fighters in this category, particularly the MiG-25. The Eagle is a single-seat, twin-turbofan all-weather fighter, armed with a built-in rapid-firing gun (initially the 20mm M61-A1, with 1,000 rounds) and four Sparrow and four Sidewinder AAMs. It has a secondary attack capability and a radar capable of detecting low-flying targets, but the basic roles are air-to-air interception, fighter sweep, escort and combat air patrol. Particular emphasis has been placed on the dog-fighting aspects of manoeuvrability and acceleration – an area in which the gap between US and the latest Soviet fighters had widened appreciably. Initial funding covered the production of twenty development aircraft (including two two-seaters, and the first of these (71-0280) flew on 27 July 1972, followed by the first two-seat TF-15 on 7 July 1973, which has a similar combat capability, encompassing reconnaissance and attack roles, and was thus redesignated F-15B. The first Eagles were delivered to USAF TAC in November 1974. The USAF plans an eventual purchase of seven hundred and forty-nine; about two thirds of these had been delivered by 1981. Those delivered since mid-1979 are F-15Cs (single-seat) and F-15Ds (two-seat) with extra internal fuel, plus provision for FAST (Fuel And Sensor Tactical) Packs – pallets for fuel and reconnaissance/ECM gear, which fit flush against the intake trunks. Five weapons stations on the standard F-15 permit carriage of up to 16,000lb of ordnance; additional weapons can be attached to the FAST packs. The Strike Eagle two-seat attack version has advanced nav/attack radar, Pave Tack night/all-weather targeting pods, with infra-red tracking and laser-spot designation, and up to 24,000lb of weapons. USAF Eagles were serving in 1981 with the 1st, 33rd and 49th TFW, and two training wings, in the USA; the 36th TFW and 32nd TFS in Europe, and part of the 18th TFW in Okinawa. Foreign customers include Israel (twenty-five), Japan (one hundred) and Saudi Arabia (sixty). Ironically, the light-weight, 'low-cost', highly maneouvrable, Mark 2 General Dynamics F-16 air superiority fighter was developed to counter the F-15As sophistication. The F-15 and F-16 provide the basis of TAC through the 1980s, but the F-15 will be most numerous.

Lockheed SR-71

Lockheed SR-71A of the 9th Strategic Reconnaissance Wing, USAF, Beale AFB (California), as displayed at SBAC's Farnborough International Air Show, September 1974

Span: 55ft 7in (16.95m)
Length: 107ft 5in (32.74m)
Weight: approx 170,000lb
Engines: 2×approx. 23,000/32,500lb
(10,430/14,740 kg) st Pratt & Whitney
J58 (JT11D-20B) afterburning by-pass
turbojets
Max speed: approx. 2,300mph (3,700kmh)
Operational ceiling: over 80,000ft
(24,400m)
Range: approx. 2,980 miles (4,800km)

The SR-71, with its impressive and unorthodox appearance, began to be conceived in 1959, under the Lockheed designation A-11, not long before the Powers affair exploded the 'research aircraft' myth of the same company's U-2, and may be assumed to have been evolved originally for a similar purpose – with the important difference that it is built to perform its duties at Mach 3.5. The original three A-11s (60-6934/5/6, the first of which flew for the first time on 26 April 1962) were converted during 1964 as YF-12A prototypes, for evaluation under the US Defense Department's IMI (Improved Manned Intercepter) programme; two of these were responsible in 1965 for several world-class performance records, including the first over-2,000mph absolute speed record, which was still unbeaten by the beginning of 1975. In addition to its high altitude capability, the YF-12A was designed to carry four Hughes Falcon interception missiles in each of the fairings flanking the long forward fuselage. A fourth aircraft (60-6937) was designated YF-12C, and acted as prototype for the SR-71A strategic reconnaissance version, which has a longer and somewhat cleaner fuselage without the ventral fins of the YF-12A. Both versions are two-seaters, the accommodation being in tandem under individual cockpit hoods. The first of about twenty-one initial production SR-71As (61-7950) flew for the first time on 22 December 1964, and about a dozen more may have been built subsequently. Strategic Air Command, which began to receive the SR-71A in January 1966, has stated that the 'Blackbird' has repeatedly exceeded the YF-12A speed record since entering service, and can cross the USA coast to coast in under an hour. The first and, to date, only SR-71A unit is the 9th (formerly 4200th) Strategic Reconnaissance Wing at Beale AFB, California. One SR-71B pilot trainer, with reinstated ventral fins and a raised rear cockpit, was also delivered at the beginning of 1966. This aircraft was subsequently destroyed in a crash, but was replaced by an SR-71A, suitably converted and redesignated SR-71C.